BODY/POLITICS

WOMEN AND THE
DISCOURSES OF
SCIENCE

BODY/POLITICS

WOMEN AND THE
DISCOURSES OF
SCIENCE

edited by
Mary Jacobus,
Evelyn Fox Keller,
Sally Shuttleworth

ROUTLEDGE · New York & London

Published in 1990 by

Routledge
An imprint of Routledge, Chapman and Hall, Inc.
29 West 35 Street
New York, NY 10001

Published in Great Britain by

Routledge
11 New Fetter Lane
London EC4P 4EE

Library of Congress Cataloging in Publication Data

Body politics.
   Includes index.
   1. Women—Physiology—Philosophy.   2. Feminism.
3. Science in literature.   4. Science—History.
I. Jacobus, Mary.   II. Keller, Evelyn Fox, 1936–
III. Shuttleworth, Sally, 1952–
QP31.5.B63   1989   305.42   89-10124
ISBN 0-415-90130-8
     0-415-90131-6 (pb)

British Library Cataloguing in Publication Data

Body politics : women, literature, and the discourse of
   science.
   1. Women. Body. Psychosocial aspects
I. Jacobus, Mary   II. Keller, Evelyn Fox, 1936–   III.
Shutterworth, Sally
305.4

ISBN 0-415-90130-8
     0-415-90131-6 (pb)

Contents

Acknowledgments

This collection is based on papers originally given at a conference on "Women, Science, and the Body: Discourses and Representations" co-organized by the editors at the Society for the Humanities, Cornell University, in 1987, in conjunction with the Cornell Women's Studies Program. The editors would like to thank the Director of the Society for the Humanities, Jonathan Culler, for funding the conference and for his assistance in preparing the manuscript. Thanks also to the staff of the Society for the Humanities and, in particular, to Laura Brewer and Tamar Katz for helping to prepare the papers for publication.

Introduction

Increasingly in the modern world, scientific discourses have come to articulate the authoritative social theories of the feminine body. The essays in *Body Politics: Women and the Discourses of Science* focus on the intersection of literary, social, and scientific discourses concerning the feminine body in order to reveal their explicit material effects. Drawing together work by scholars in the fields of philosophy, history of science, sociobiology, literary theory, semiotics, film, political science, and anthropology, the collection emphasizes the political urgency of the relationship between science and the feminine body. The issues raised within the confines of each essay range historically from the beginnings of the nineteenth century to those in yesterday's newspaper; but each has contemporary social and political relevance. Three themes are in one way or another brought to prominence throughout—sexuality, reproduction, and war. All constitute primary physical concerns in all cultures; here, they are located in the specific, evolving discourses that have historically defined our understanding of the feminine body while, at the same time, they are linked to the concerns of our own particular, western, cultural and technological present. Without attempting to be comprehensive, the collection indicates some of the directions in which a feminist analysis of scientific discourses as varied as psychoanalysis, medicine, anthropology, and primatology might lead. It leads us, for example, to an analysis of what nineteenth-century advertising can tell us about the relation between myths of "female circulation" and industrial capitalism, of what twentieth-century slimming aids may tell us about the cost for women, in bodily terms, of our so-called consumer society. Primatology, similarly, may be viewed as the soap opera of contemporary sociobiological narratives of sexual evolution which, in turn, enact the dramas of twentieth-century economic competition. Debates over

1

surrogacy may reactivate long-standing debates within theology about the status of the subject or about the relation between sexuality and reproduction; fantasies surrounding the production of the atomic bomb may replicate the marginalization of women already inscribed in the material practices of science.

Body Politics: Women and the Discourses of Science suggests the ways in which changing material technologies—alongside and in interaction with changing discursive technologies—at once reflect and (re)construct our understanding of the contours of the feminine body. Throughout the collection, individual essays concentrate on the interconnection between theories of production and theories of reproduction—on the relation between the fictions, discourses, and representations involved in scientific ideology and the practice or material effects of science in our society, particularly as they affect women. Notions about the individual body and the body politic permeate theories which construct the ideological reality within which the subject comes to be gendered, inhabiting a body whose biological and sexual manifestations are coded in specific ways at specific times. Twentieth-century advances in artificial fertilization and the "crisis" in childbirth management, the discovery of DNA and the construction of the atomic bomb, the social and sexual divisions of labor intimately connected with prostitution and with the invention and cure of "female" maladies in the nineteenth century, the role played by advertising in disciplining the modern feminine body, or the discrepancy between scientific and popular versions of modern menstruation, the shaping effects on primatology of twentieth-century attitudes towards the female orgasm—these historically and culturally specific instances, along with the legal, medical, ethical, social, and methodological debates surrounding them, remind us that many of the crucial focuses for scientific contestation have involved or invoked the feminine body. It goes without saying that the body, whether masculine or feminine, is imbricated in the matrices of power at all levels, and not just, or even primarily, on the level of theory; but the feminine body, as the prime site of sexual and/or racial difference in a white, masculine, western political and sexual economy, is peculiarly the battlefield on which quite other struggles than women's own have been waged. It is for this reason that attempts to reclaim the feminine body—whether under the aegis of "choice" or by way of constructivist accounts—have played such an important part in the liberatory as well as liberal discourse of contemporary feminism.

Women as the Material of Science

The last two centuries have witnessed an increasing literalization of one of the dominant metaphors which guided the development of early modern science. For Bacon, the pursuit of scientific knowledge was figured rhetorically as the domination of the female body of nature, illuminated by the light of masculine science. With the professionalization of science, and the development of ever more sophisticated technologies of control, the metaphorical base of this epistemological quest has become explicit material practice. The full weight of the power and authority enjoyed by science in our culture has been brought to bear on the female body. From the beginnings of the medicalization of childbirth in the nineteenth century, we are now faced in the 1980s with a situation in which all aspects of reproduction have come under the command of science. Viewed as medical events, pregnancy and childbirth can be monitored and controlled by the latest technology, while in the laboratory, women's role in reproduction is increasingly open to question; IVF and the burgeoning of genetic engineering offer to fulfill, with undreamt of specificity, earlier visions of science as the virile domination of the female body of nature.

But it is not only in the reproductive sphere that science impacts on the feminine body; nor are the points of contact solely those of material control. As the epistemological rhetoric of early modern science suggests, ideologies of gender often operate most forcibly outside the explicit arena of reproductive politics, or the social interaction of the sexes. The essays in this collection explore the intersection of ideological and material scientific practice on the terrain of the feminine body—tracing, for example, the connections between contradictions in economic ideology and scientific representations of sexuality, or the role played by gender ideology in that ultimate sanctum of masculinist science, weapons research. Ideologies of gender enter into the most unlikely realms of scientific inquiry, informing and shaping the perception of scientists and even the direction of experimentation (not to mention public reaction). But we also find, conversely, that scientific representations of the feminine body are themselves a constitutive part of wider social discourses that are informed and shaped in their turn by economic, class, and racial ideologies. By teasing out some of these connections, the essays in this book suggest how the fluid, symbolic reservoir of cultural associations focused on the feminine body operate in scientific discourses to produce historically specific material effects.

In contemporary feminist theory, no issue is more vexed than that of determining the relations between the feminine body as a figure in discourse and as material presence or biological entity. The debates surrounding this question in recent years have been the most highly charged, but also perhaps the most fruitful. Current thought covers the spectrum from biological essentialism to full-blown linguistic constructivism. While some schools of feminism focus centrally on biological difference and on the female reproductive role, others insist on the socially constructed nature of sexual difference. Yet to speak of a spectrum of thought, as if positions shaded into one another along a linear continuum, is perhaps misleading; it fails to do justice to the shifting complexity of contemporary theory, where unexpected alliances have been forged and continually disrupt this horizontal axis. In Kristeva's work, for instance, we find an emphasis on, indeed, a celebration of, the maternal, yoked to an uncompromising insistence on the role of language in constructing subjectivity. As the contributions to this volume all reveal, it *is* possible to highlight the maternal function without acceding to biological essentialism, and to focus on the feminine body as a figure in discourse without disregarding material effects (or the material practices of which this figure is itself an effect). Despite their different theoretical allegiances, the editors and contributors to this volume attempt to address the specificity of the feminine body without lapsing into either an ahistorical essentialism or an insufficiently material consideration of the multiple ways in which the feminine body has been constructed.

Amidst the complexities of current feminist debate, one thing emerges clearly: we cannot speak of the feminine body as if it were an invariant presence throughout history. There is no fixed, experiential base which provides continuity across the centuries; our perceptions and interpretations of the body are mediated through language and surrounding culture. Hence, they are always subject to historical change, shifting in accordance with the differing ways in which the body is articulated and located within the intersecting and competing discourses of each era. While intuition might privilege our sense of direct experiential access to this most tangible of material entities, the body, cultural analysis tells another story. Martin's study of women's responses to menstruation in contemporary Baltimore, or Bordo's analysis of anorexia, both suggest that perceptions of one's own body—whether of shape or function—are culturally controlled. Nor is it possible to draw a line between the production of gender identity as a social construct, and the immutable facts of biological differentiation, since the scientific articulation of sexual difference is itself subject to all the multiple determining pressures of social ideology.

The more distant the historical period, the easier it becomes to identify these pressures and the ways in which they have framed scientific discourse; the Victorian medical and social discussions of the female body examined by Shuttleworth and Poovey, for example, offer themselves readily to ideological dissection, revealing the economic and gender assumptions at stake. As we come closer to our own time, when science wields unprecedented cultural authority, and massive material investments guarantee its truths, demystification grows more difficult. Professionals close ranks, and the increasingly technical formulations of scientific and medical research set many disciplines outside the range of easy scrutiny by those who are not themselves within the field. Scientific discourses focused on the female body, however, prove a luminous exception to this rule. The dominant tropes of failed production and violent dissolution which figure in the depictions of menstruation in the contemporary medical textbooks examined by Martin reveal, as clearly as nineteenth-century accounts, the unselfconscious operation of economic and gender ideology. Within the field of sociobiology, too, Haraway explores the debate which rages around that ever-problematic topic—feminine sexual pleasure—to reveal not only how gender assumptions have historically structured primate research, but also how the forms of feminist challenge are themselves framed by the logic of late-capitalist economics.

Scientific formulations of sexual differences shift in accordance with changes in the economic organization of society—but also, as many of these essays emphasize, in response to technological developments. With the coming of the industrial revolution and our entry into the machine age, the Victorians were forced to address the interface between the human and the machine in terms very different to those employed by Descartes. Political economists of the era extolled the virtues of the machine which seemed to offer a corrective to the inefficiency and indiscipline of human labor, endowing machinery with the agency and productive powers previously assigned only to human life. Within this framework, woman, as reproductive vehicle, came increasingly under scrutiny as the forces of production and reproduction were drawn into ideological alignment. Historical studies of the interplay between Victorian constructions of the forces of production and reproduction such as those by Poovey and Shuttleworth lay the foundation for essays which explore contemporary manifestations of this alignment—an alignment which, as Martin, Treichler, Haraway and Keller all point out, continues to dominate, albeit in rather different forms, the economic and biological rhetoric of the 1980s.

The questions raised by technological developments in the nineteenth century gave rise to the genre of science fiction in which new visions of subjective, biological, and sexual identity are put into play. Doane's analysis of the interface between the maternal body and the machine in contemporary science fiction films points to the ways in which developments in reproductive technology now figure semiotically in popular cultural projections as devastating threats both to stable identity and to our symbolic signifying systems. In recent years, imaginative projections of transformed reproductive processes scarcely seem to keep pace with the speed of research. While human reproduction through cloning may still be a long way off, advances in artificial reproduction have already provoked heated public debate. Technological developments and the practice of surrogacy have forced into the open, and into battle, the differing cultural meanings and assumptions focused on the feminine body. The papal encyclicals on artificial reproduction, and the legal and journalistic pronouncement on the Baby M case, as Jacobus argues, serve to expose notions of unitary subjecthood encoded in both theology and language by opening a gap between feminine desire and reproduction. Even at the level of everyday reproduction in our society, the entry of technology into the normal processes of childbirth has fundamentally shifted our understanding of birth itself. As Treichler's analysis of the changing meanings of the verb "deliver" reveals, technological and professional dominance is now enshrined within language; the role of the mother has been written out of a birth process which is now projected as an interaction between doctor and fetus.

In exploring the relations between discourse and scientific practice, and their ideological and material impact on both the feminine body and feminine subjectivity, the essays in this collection illuminate and comment on one another across their historical, disciplinary, and theoretical divides. While responsive to the ways in which scientific ideologies of the feminine body shift in line with economic and political changes, the essays also reveal the historical persistence of these symbolic formations, showing how they are subtly retained, revived, or recast in different eras. The symbolic field of gender ideology possesses a momentum of its own which is neither entirely congruent with, nor a simple reflection of, other social forces. This very sinuousness provides the foundations of its power. As a (seemingly) unchanging and autonomous reservoir of images, it helps to naturalize the specific scientific constructions of femininity in each era, while also permitting the social and cultural displacement of more obviously intractable ideological issues onto the realm of gender. Thus problems in the ideological organizations of laissez-faire economics may be symbolically resolved by being recast in terms of gender, while, conversely, dangers of technological prowess are represented, in science fiction, in tropes of male anxieties about female sexuality, or, in nuclear discourse, in tropes of appropriated female procreativity. By attempting to demystify the operations of sexual ideology within science while historicizing its changing material manifestations and practices, the essays in this collection attest to the persistence and power of the discourses of science to define the feminine body as the object of knowledge par excellence—as subjected rather than subject, and hence as the site of crucial feminist struggle in the realm of both politics and theory.

Woman as the Subject of Science

It is a truism that whereas nature, the body that scientific knowledge takes as its object, is traditionally constructed as feminine, the subject of science, i.e. the scientist, has usually been seen as masculine. The fantasies that attend such gendering of the production and reproduction of knowledge are at once sexualized and territorial (we speak not only of "penetrating" or "unveiling" nature's mysteries but of "opening up new horizons" or "pushing back the frontiers of knowledge"). In other words, hierarchies involving both gender and power—power over, and power to profit economically, in some cases, as Treichler suggests in her account of the medicalization of childbirth—are intimately associated with the ideology and practice of science; we should not be surprised therefore to find the project of managing the female body providing fertile ground for scientific theories which, as Shuttleworth argues, may have as much to do with Victorian theories about political economy as with menstruation. Rhetoric surrounding the feminine body and its functioning or malfunctioning intersects with, and in some cases serves as a displacement of, contradictions in society at large; it requires, therefore, an analysis of the ways in which discourses themselves vie for power. However we look at it, the field of nature turns out to have been colonized already; language has always been there before us.

But language is of itself a means to power as well as a reflection of power relations. If we believe that representations and discourses are a part of the ideologically shaped reality we inhabit, then exploring the power of discourses and representations to construct that reality is one way to understand and hence to subvert the workings of ideology in us and through us. For women, whether viewed as objects rather than subjects of knowledge or defined as the meeting point of nature and culture, scientific discourse has been especially crucial in constructing reality as something they can embody but not know. Associated alternately with nature and with the unconscious, with matter and with mystery, the feminine body functions as the imaginary site where meaning (or life) is generated; yet, in this scheme, women can never be meaning makers in their own right. Hence the compensatory emphasis in feminist theory on the desiring and speaking feminine subject. Feminist analyses of language or knowledge—language which shapes or contests the practice of giving birth in our culture, anthropological modes of inquiry which privilege the visual rather than the oral, narratives which implicate liberal feminism in evolutionary accounts of sexual origins—assume that the ways in which inquiries are conducted will shape a perceived field of knowledge just as they are shaped by the society which gives rise to them. Martin, for instance, uses the language of women to speak an alternative to the knowledge that science claims about menstruation, in turn enabling her to extend a feminist critique of the practice of postmodern anthropology. Haraway uncovers an entire wave of emerging feminist consciousness in the narratives generated by women primatologists. By undertaking such analyses, however, feminists suggest that while meanings, disciplines, and methodologies may be powerful, they are not all-powerful; the very act of politicizing these fictions reminds us that science itself is a practice that can change or be changed. A feminist "body politics" addresses this possibility of change, contesting the inevitability or naturalness of supposedly "scientific" definitions of women's bodies by showing how the discourses and narratives of science not only construct but depend on the very institution of gender which scientists claim to discover or observe.

Not surprisingly, scientific accounts of gender have tended to focus on certain centrally perceived aspects of the feminine body: its reproductive capacities (or failures), its disciplining (or indiscipline), and above all its difference from the masculine body that provides humanist science with its implicit ideal. Often, sexual difference has served to erase other differences—

class and race, for instance.Yet scientific accounts of feminine sexuality, even as they emphasize difference, frequently attempt to assimilate femininity to masculinity, making women a subcategory of men, or feminine desire a reflection of masculinity. French feminist theory has described the politics of scientific inquiry as a specular politics—its tendency to look rather than listen, to identify women with lack (of the phallus) rather than with the symbolic power of language vested in the father, or even, theologically speaking, God the Father. Feminist critiques of psychoanalysis have analyzed the particular complicity of psychoanalytic ways of knowing with this specular economy and its implicit masculine authority, even as they draw on the insights of contemporary psychoanalytic theory to construct other models of knowledge—knowledge, for instance, provided by the unconscious that speaks in language, or, for that matter, in the symptoms of the hysterical body. This is not to suggest that a feminist body politics is a politics of hysteria, or to suggest that the truth of feminist resistance may be found in the nineteenth-century madhouse. Rather, it is to suggest that we should both politicize and historicize the very representations which produce the feminine body as hysterical (or maternal, or fat) at different times and in different places. Poovey, for instance, examines the dominant (masculine) terms of the nineteenth-century representation of prostitution in order to find within it a contradictory space of sexual desire for women themselves; Jacobus explores post-Enlightenment narratives of reproduction in which female sexuality, despite being subsumed under the sign of maternity, returns to fracture fictional, psychoanalytic, theological, and biomedical accounts with the unaccountability of feminine desire.

The twentieth century brings both new demands and new techniques for the containment of feminine desire and female procreativity, even as it discovers new uses for the images these provide. As Doane argues, contemporary science fiction films tend to articulate old fantasies about the relations between women and machines; yet these fantasies of artificial femininity in turn permit a reworking of connections between representation and the maternal. A new body is envisaged by science, with major implications for the traditional humanist subject; this new body also has its counterpart in social representations of, and control over, female eating. For Bordo, contemporary eating disorders can be viewed as an aspect of the regulation of the female body; a semiotic analysis of the cultural representation of slenderness reveals the contradictions on which a consumer society is predicated even as traditionally gendered divisions of labor break down. Here feminist analyses of the functioning of technology in film and the technology of power in contemporary advertising offer an account of the modern (or future) Eve tamed by the very revisions in the traditional representation of women which she seems to initiate. Methodologically dissimilar, psychoanalytic film criticism on one hand, and a Foucauldian approach to the cultural production of meaning on the other, suggest some of the ways in which the feminine body is produced, reproduced, and forcibly reduced in popular contemporary representations, mutating in response to the demands of scientific, political, and economic culture.

The history of sociobiology inscribes a different version of the capacity of scientific discourse to respond to changing economic and political pressures, and its concurrent power to shape our understanding of the female body. Pointing out that sociobiologists have told stories of evolutionary biology structures around the tropes of survival and competitive reproduction, Haraway argues that the narratives generated by feminist primatologists have been culturally marked by the anxieties and exclusions of twentieth-century capitalism. The quest for evidence of primate orgasms provides a map for the politics of sexual pleasure in a world where gender means antagonistic difference. The professional histories of scientists, male or female, provide still other narratives of how the sex war was waged or won in the conceptual arena of primatology. A different kind of sex war surfaces in high scientific discourse, where the dilemmas and challenges of sexual difference become a metaphoric resource for representations not of women, but of life and death. If female inferiority has provided the central trope for the science of life, so too, as Fox Keller reminds us, has its inverted imagery permeated the science of death. Today, as molecular biology has vanquished the secret of life, and nuclear physics the secret of death, a convergence of these different rhetorics conspires to obscure the threat of nuclear annihilation from all of us. Language veils the threat of a thousand suns, inviting us to look, even as it makes us look away.

The discourses of science, so far from transparent or objective, are animated by narratives. Especially peopled by feminine bodies, they are viewed in ways at once conservative and regressive (the universal maternal), technological (the reproductive machine), and biologically impelled (the pleasure-seeking primate). If nineteenth-century discourses cast the feminine body as the malfunctioning organism that embodies society's ills, twentieth-century discourses make the feminine body the site of its contradictory desires and social theories, including those of feminism itself. The science that produced the bomb, with its unimaginable scale of destruction, also contests the place and manner of women's childbirth in the interests of infant survival. The humanist subject who seeks knowledge is put in question by the very terms of a scientific inquiry which has imagined both the unconscious and the cyborg, bisexuality and reproduction without sexual difference—DNA and the atom bomb. What is the lasting appeal of such imaginings? Of such creations? The politics of the (feminine) body, as we know it, are the politics of a social body either denied or disciplined, ideologically encoded or fantastically constructed (any or all at once). Thanks to the scientific discourses which produce it, the feminine body is familiar to us as the site of gestation, generation, illness, menstruation, anorexia, and above all as the site of sexual (as well as racial) difference, with anatomy providing the bedrock of sexuality. But however imagined, the feminine body, thus defined, allows some things to appear settled even as it unsettles: that there is a body always available to be inscribed; that sexual difference exists as an inalienable essence; that even if class is uncertain, the genders will retain their fixed (hierarchical) relations. To analyze the work performed by the languages and representations of science, in both traditional and popular forms, is to begin to unravel the ways in which gender functions to sustain what we think we know—and hence, to begin to unthink it, to imagine other ways of thinking of the social and political body, together, and altogether.

One thing is certain. Body politics will be with us as long as "pro-life" or "pro-choice" remain codes for the imbricated set of legal, social, ethical, political, biological, medical, sexual, and feminist issues focused on female reproduction. When the inaugural action of a new President of the United States is to speak with representatives of the "right-to-life" movement, we know that possession of the feminine body as a site of reproduction is perceived as a matter of national contestation on a par with the global struggle among superpowers, competing economies, and cultures. *Body Politics: Women and the Discourses of Science* suggests why this is so—attempting to wrest the feminine body away from the competing discourses that simultaneously inscribe and appropriate it as the sign of other struggles than women's own, relocating it in the alternative discourses of a liberatory, feminist body politics.

1

In Parenthesis:
Immaculate Conceptions and
Feminine Desire

Mary Jacobus

A parenthesis, according to the OED, is both "an explanatory or qualifying word, clause, or sentence inserted into a passage with which it has not necessarily any grammatical connexion" and a rhetorical figure—"a passage introduced into a context with which it has no connexion, a digression;" a figure defined by Puttenham as a "figure of tolerable disorder." The gap between feminine desire and conception, and between conception and maternal desire, constitutes just such a disordering figure. What it disorders is our sense of a unified, coherent subject; it confronts us instead with the irreducibility of a body that is only metonymically linked to desire. The disordering figure—the intrusion of biology into the psychic realm—applies ultimately to sexuality itself, viewed as a threshold between the psychic and the somatic. An earlier age than ours tended to believe that feminine pleasure and conception went together; but as Thomas Laqueur has argued persuasively, a divorce was effected at the end of the century of Enlightenment, when medical science could no longer link the two.[1] I want to argue that this divorce has a specifically disordering effect on conceptions of the feminine subject; and that attempts to remarry feminine pleasure or desire on one hand, and conception on the other, are motivated not only by the wish to reappropriate femininity under the aspect of maternity, but also by a fundamentally theological imperative to maintain the integrity of the contemporary subject.

I'll be discussing three "scenes" or narratives of reproduction that bear on the distinction between feminine desire and conception. My first is a story by Heinrich von Kleist, "The Marquise of O—"(1808) in which Kleist reads the pregnant body as a sign of unconscious feminine desire despite his portrayal of sexuality as a disordering figure; my second narrative involves Freud's difficulty in accounting for feminine sexuality at all in *Three Essays on the*

11

Theory of Sexuality (1905) and his final reliance on a teleology derived from masculine sexuality; my third instance is the contemporary debate about surrogate motherhood, read in the light of Pope John Paul II's recent statements on artificial fertilization and reproduction and Julia Kristeva's analysis of the cult of the Virgin Mary. My aim in linking these three representations of femininity—one literary, one psychoanalytic, and one theological—is to suggest not only the traditional difficulty in specifying feminine desire without appropriating it to maternity (and hence, ultimately, to paternity) but also the problems that arise even when science, in the guise of contemporary biomedical technology, seems finally to have succeeded in freeing feminine pleasure from reproduction. Politically, women have everything to gain from this separation—the right to pleasure without conception, the right to bodily self-determination (AID [artificial insemination by donor] or abortion), the right, even, to surrogacy itself. But this is not to refuse the implications of sexual difference as they manifest themselves in the reproductive process—in the asymmetry between male fertilization and female pregnancy. To take the example of surrogacy, to treat the sperm donor and the surrogate mother as if they were comparable is to reproduce, not equality, but a traditional, deeply engrained inequality in the position of women vis à vis reproduction, discourse, and even the law, as the notorious Baby M case reveals. For all their unconventional routes to motherhood, I will argue, the Marquise of O—, the Virgin Mary, and Mary Beth Whitehead (the biological mother of Baby M) figure in a discourse of maternity that is bound to reproduce the Law of the Father.

Oedipal Romance and "The Marquise of O—"

The main action of Kleist's story "The Marquise of O—" takes place literally "in parenthesis," while the marquise herself is unconscious. A young widow, "a lady of unblemished reputation and the mother of several well-brought-up children"[2] is surprised by a rabble of Russian soldiers who have stormed the citadel commanded by her father. Just as they are about to gang-rape her, she is rescued by a gallant Russian officer, a count, who seems to her like "an angel sent from heaven" (p. 69), addresses her in French, and leads her to safety. Kleist's narrative continues: "Stricken speechless by her ordeal, she now collapsed in a dead faint. Then—[the dash marks a missing parenthesis] the officer instructed the marquise's frightened servants, who presently arrived, to send for a doctor; he assured them that she would soon recover, replaced his hat and returned to the fighting" (p. 70). The would-be gang-rapists are identified and summarily shot. But before the widow or her family can express their gratitude to the Russian count, he is mis-reported killed in action; his (supposedly) last words are: "Giulietta! This bullet avenges you!" (p. 73); Giulietta is the marquise's name.

Kleist's narrative begins some months later, when the marquise inserts an advertisement in the newspapers to the effect "that she had, without knowledge of the cause, come to find herself in a certain situation; that she would like the father of the child she was expecting to disclose his identity to her; and that she was resolved, out of consideration for her family, to marry him" (p. 68). Kleist's source for the young widow's situation is an anecdote from Montaigne's essay "Of drunkenness" about a French village woman (also a widow) who finds herself unaccountably pregnant. She announces her willingness to marry the father, whereupon a young farmhand of hers comes forward, declaring

> that he had found her, one holiday when she had taken her wine very freely, so fast asleep by her fireplace, and in so indecent a posture, that he had been able to enjoy her without waking her.[3]

Kleist turns Montaigne's bucolic anecdote into a story of inexplicable passion overlaid by refined sentiment and high familial drama. But the bottom line is the same—a woman's unwitting conception of a child as a result of acquaintance rape. Moreover, in Kleist's story the rape takes place in the space of a narrative absence, not outside nature, but outside consciousness. Like a parenthesis, the sexual act resulting in conception is without grammatical or logical connection to its context. Who has lost control here, we might ask— the widow, the Russian count, or Kleist himself? What is the status of a sexual encounter that not only takes place while one party is unconscious and the other in a state of sexual transport, but which must be banished from the story itself?

"The worst condition of man," writes Montaigne, "is when he loses knowledge and control of himself."[4] Drunkenness in Montaigne's essay is an instance of the will overcome by passion. Yet drinking in Montaigne's essay is also placed on the side of pleasure and desire, connected both with the dizzy exploits of war and with the poet's imaginative frenzy—with a form of madness defined as "any transport, however laudable, that transcends our own judgment and reason; inasmuch as wisdom is an orderly management of our soul."[5] By implication at least, the type of madness is not so much drunkenness as sexuality—sexuality defined as a figure for disorder of the soul. Montaigne asks (in Horace's words) "if wine can storm the very fort of wisdom"?[6] In Kleist's story the storming of a fortress leads to the storming of a woman; clearly the exploits of war and the transports of sexual desire are adjacent. Kleist has the count make amends for "the one ignoble action he had committed in his life" (p. 77) by returning unexpectedly to press his suit on the marquise and her astonished family—without, however, confessing his crime ("All were agreed that . . . he seemed to be accustomed to taking ladies' hearts, like fortresses, by storm," p. 79). Although reluctant at first, the young widow (as yet unaware of her pregnancy) finally consents to an engagement; but before the marriage can take place, the count leaves on official business. To her consternation, the marquise's pregnancy meanwhile becomes evident; her father points a gun at her, and she leaves his house for her country estate, taking her children with her. This is how things stand when the count returns to claim the marquise as his wife, undeterred by the news of a pregnancy which he alone has suspected all along. The newspaper advertisement with which the story opens leaves him no option but to reveal himself to her and her family as her repentant rapist—whereupon she furiously refuses to marry him.

Montaigne's "Of drunkenness" goes some way toward explaining how the gallant Russian count might have rescued the marquise from gang-rape only to ravish her himself. Kleist, in fact, tells us more about what motivates the Russian count than about the nature of the marquise's desire for him; indeed, coherent motivation is precisely what she lacks (she has a body instead). We gain access to the count's unconscious processes through the vision of a swan which haunts him during the delirium of his supposedly fatal wound; he remembers

> an occasion on which he had once thrown some mud at this swan, whereupon it had silently dived under the surface and re-emerged, washed clean by the water; that she had always seemed to be swimming about on a fiery surface . . . but that he had not been able to lure her towards him. (p. 82)

We hardly need Freud's observations on "A Special Type of Choice of Object made by Men" (1910) to recognize that the Russian count is in the grip of a fantasy which compels him at once to idealize, to debase, and to rescue the woman he loves: "These various meanings of rescuing in dreams and phantasies can be recognized particularly clearly when they are found in connection with water," writes Freud. "A man rescuing a woman from the water in a dream means that he makes her a mother, which . . . amounts to making her his own mother."[7] So much for the count. But what about the marquise's fantasy—*her* unconscious desire? Critics usually come up with the rapist's apology: she must have wanted it anyway.[8] Is it rather the marquise's body that plays the part of the feminine unconscious in Kleist's story? And if she has a body instead of an unconscious, then the marquise is not a desiring subject in the same sense as the count; the only desiring subject in the story becomes a masculine one.

From the marquise's ambivalence and agitation at the count's tumultuous wooing, we might suspect no more than we do from the Russian officer's flushed face after rescuing the marquise. In her case, however, the body "knows" what is excluded both from her consciousness and from Kleist's narrative. What it knows is glossed by the well-known Freudian formula: child=penis. Before the count's whirlwind courtship, the marquise and her mother have exchanged some frank women's talk. The marquise is suffering from mysterious spells of nausea, giddiness, and fainting fits. She tells her mother: " 'If any woman were to tell me that she had felt just as I did a moment ago when I picked up this teacup, I should say to myself that she must be with child' " (p. 74). Her mother jokes that "she would no doubt be giving birth to the god of Fantasy." The marquise replies (also jokingly) that "at any rate Morpheus, or one of his attendant dreams, must be the father" (p. 74). Soon after this, the Russian count returns from the dead to initiate his whirlwind courtship, "his face a little pale, but looking as beautiful as a young god" (p. 74). If this makes him Morpheus, the marquise is indeed about to give birth to "the god of Fantasy"—the fantasy he has engendered in her. The Russian count dreams of making her a mother (in Freudian terms). By the same token, does the marquise dream of making him a (that is her) father, the father of her fantasy? In the last resort, the count's function in Kleist's narrative is to give her meaning as a woman—filling her empty O with his child. But what she signifies is *his* (i.e., masculine) desire. The fulfillment of this desire rounds off the story with its domestication of sexuality-as-reproduction, or happy ending.

In Kleist's narrative, the progress of the marquise's pregnancy amounts to a discourse of the maternal body—the site where the feminine unconscious speaks. After the count has won her consent to the marriage and departed on his official mission, the marquise begins to notice "an incomprehensible change in her figure" (p. 85). She calls in a doctor and "jestingly told him what condition she believed herself to be in" (p. 86). When he confirms her diagnosis she is outraged, threatening to report him to her father. As he leaves in a huff, she pleads: " 'But, Doctor, how is what you say possible?' " The doctor replies that "she would presumably not expect him to explain the facts of life to her" (p. 86). Yet this seems to be the case; after the doctor's visit the marquise tells her mother that although her conscience is clear, she must now consult a midwife: " 'A midwife!' exclaimed the commandant's wife indignantly, 'a clear conscience and a midwife!' And speech failed her" (p. 88)—just as words had failed Kleist at the crucial moment that engenders his story. Either the marquise has invented "a fable about the overturning of the whole order of nature" (p. 89), or (as the midwife puts it) "young widows who found themselves in her ladyship's position always believed themselves to have been living on desert islands" (p. 90; here the marquise faints for the second time). "With a faltering voice" the marquise then asks the midwife "what the ways of nature were, and whether such a thing as an unwitting conception was possible." Not in her case, replies the midwife; "with the exception of the Blessed Virgin, it had never yet happened to any woman on earth" (p. 91).

An attentive reader of Kleist's story knows by this stage that the marquise conceived her child not outside the realm of nature, but in the parenthetical moment that is excluded both from her consciousness and from Kleist's story. In Kleist's own discourse, it seems that feminine sexuality, however mediated, can never fully submit to textuality. The woman's body—the hollow, open "O—" signified by the marquise's name—remains the site of something at once undecidable and contradictory, in excess of narrative.[9] Just as desire interrupts consciousness as a wordless rift—as madness rather than reason— so conception gives rise to the absurd nonsense that the marquise must talk to herself, her mother, her doctor, and her midwife. Kleist could have specified exactly what took place between the marquise and her rescuer if he wished. Why then his reticence—miming the marquise's double consciousness (that she is pregnant, but that her pregnancy is either a joke or a miracle)? I want to suggest not simply that Kleist saw in Montaigne's bucolic anecdote the potential for a highly wrought Romantic drama of feminine denial and si- lenced desire. Rather, I want to suggest that feminine sexuality in Kleist's story can only be recuperated for narrative under the aegis of an Oedipal conception familiar to modern readers from the writings of Freud.

The unwritten story in "The Marquise of O—" is not so much rape as a difficulty (analagous to Freud's) in accounting for feminine sexuality at all. Kleist solves the problem, as Freud was to do a century later, by subordinating femininity to the Law of the Father. When the count presents himself in answer to the marquise's newspaper advertisement, the marquise—in her father's words, "hysterical"—no longer sees him as an angel, but as a devil. We might take the commandant's adjective seriously for a moment. Hysteria, for Freud, means body language, the conversion of unconscious sexual desire into physical symptoms, of which hysterical pregnancy is one. Remember Dora's hysterical pregnancy exactly nine months after delivering her slap of rejection to Herr K.—a hysterical pregnancy which Freud interprets as the wish that things had gone otherwise, and ultimately as displaced desire for the father. What is the marquise's "hysterical" predicament in Kleist's story? Like Dora's rejection of Herr K., her refusal of the count when he reveals himself as the father of her child could be read as masking unacknowledged desire for a (the) father. The subtext of Kleist's story would thus equate feminine desire and Oedipal desire, making this the informing ideological narrative that is placed in parenthesis from the start.

I want to turn for support to a scene depicting the reunion of the marquise and her father, surely among the most extravagant in the entire story. When the marquise places her advertisement in the newspaper, her mother decides that the time has come for reconciliation. Convincing herself of the marquise's innocence by a ruse, she brings her back to the paternal home. A tearful scene ensues between father and daughter; the commandant's wife leaves them alone together, and when we next see them, the marquise "with her head thrown back and her eyes tightly shut, was lying quietly in her father's arms, while the latter, with tears glistening in his wide-open eyes, sat in the armchair, pressing long, ardent, avid kisses on to her mouth, just like a lover!" (p. 107). Here the father acts the part of the desire-drunk count (perhaps the marquise has fainted again). In an obvious sense, this later scene stands in for the passionate sexual encounter which Kleist had consigned to the parenthesis at the start of his story. But the model of feminine desire that we glimpse here is unmistakably Oedipal—the wish, not to be, but to have the child of her father which (in the Freudian narrative) impels the little girl into the Oedipus complex, into heterosexuality, and finally, *faute de mieux,* into maternity. It's not just that Kleist must transform feminine desire into maternal desire in order to meet the conditions of representability. Rather, the height of representable passion turns out to be an Oedipal encounter between father and (fantastically pregnant) daughter. Kleist's story seems to suggest that every unconscious desire will yield at the moment of its conception, not simply the masculine desire to turn a woman into a mother, but the feminine desire all too readily subsumed under the sign of the daughter's unconscious desire for a child by the father. In Kleist's story, the disordering figure of sexual transport is not only channeled toward reproduction, but ultimately ordered by the Law of the Father.

Instincts and Their Vicissitudes; or, the Romance of the Penis

Freud's difficulty in conceptualizing feminine desire as other than Oedipal, and maternal desire as other than desire for the penis scarcely needs elaborating.[10] I want now to recapitulate the story that he himself calls "Instincts and Their Vicissitudes" (the title of his 1915 essay) and that he tells at greater length in the earlier, much revised *Three Essays on the Theory of Sexuality.* This is a story not unlike Kleist's "Marquise of O—" in suggesting, contradictorily, the perverse and disordered quality of sexuality—its objectlessness and its severence from reproductive aim—while superimposing on this original aberrancy a teleology whereby the sexual instinct is always in quest of normative biological reproduction. Freud argues that the sexual instinct at first wanders eccentrically from the paths laid down by the organism; but in the end, it aims purposively at the continuance of the species by way of heterosexual intercourse. That purposiveness might be called "the romance of the penis"; like all romantic quests, its parentheses and digressions are finally ordered by a telos or end which organizes Freudian theory into a coherent narrative about the relation between sexual desire and reproduction.

For Freud, instinct (*"Trieb"*), biologically considered, lies "on the frontier between the mental and the somatic" (*SE* 14:121–2); instinct itself, however, is already a psychical representation.[11] As far as mental life is concerned, nothing is really outside the realm of (psycho-sexual) representation. Yet the problem of biology remains—surfacing for women in the contentious region of penis envy, the bottom line or bedrock of femininity which for Freud himself finally constituted "a biological fact."[12] For men, biology surfaces in the special case of sexual reproduction. The story told by *Three Essays on the Theory of Sexuality* reveals with particular clarity the difficulty of talking about sexual instincts (i.e., psychical representations) without falling back into talking about the body, and the masculine body at that. To some recent commentators, however, *Three Essays* also contains the story that can't be told by Freud himself—a story about what defeats (phallic) representation, challenges teleology, and puts the subject itself in question.

In *The Freudian Body,* Leo Bersani describes sexual excitement in terms that recall Kleist, as a state when "the organization of the self is momentarily disturbed by sensations of affective processes somehow 'beyond' those compatible with psychic organization."[13] Desire, in Bersani's words, involves "what nearly shatters us, and the shattering experience is, it would seem, *without any specific content*—which may be our only way of saying that the experience cannot be said, that it belongs to the nonlinguistic biology of human life." Psychoanalysis becomes for Bersani "the unprecedented attempt to psychologize that biology [and] to coerce it into discourse."[14] Sexual desire paradoxically unsettles our sense of what it is to be desiring subjects, shattering both consciousness and discourse: psychoanalysis attempts a linguistic recuperation of biology, forcing the body to speak even in parenthesis (the parenthesis that Kleist consigns to narrative silence). We could read "The Marquise of O—" in this light, as an unprecedented attempt to psychologize "the nonlinguistic biology of human life" and coerce it into discourse—an attempt, however, that stumbles into banality precisely where Freud himself does, on the frontier between psychic shattering and the body, the threshold of the unconscious and of biology.

The first of Freud's *Three Essays on the Theory of Sexuality,* "The Sexual Aberrations," is a radical onslaught on sexuality designed to "loosen the bond that exists in our thoughts between instinct and object" (*SE* 7:148). Not only is the sexual instinct independent of an object, but its aim, too, swerves from "the union of the genitals in the act known as copulation" (*SE* 7:149) into paths of perversion or deferral which constitute a veritable map of body surfaces, space, and orifices—skin, mouth, anus, even eye. Typically, the so-called perversions either extend erotogenicity beyond the anatomical regions of the body specifically designed for sexual reproduction, or linger on the intermediary stages without pressing on toward the goal of sexual intercourse (an apt definition of sexuality itself).[15] When in his second essay Freud turns to "Infantile Sexuality," we find that the model for adult sexuality is infantile thumb sucking, an activity detached from the original somatic function it imitates. While thumb sucking "attaches itself to"—props itself upon (*"entsteht in Anlehnung an"*)—a vital somatic function (feeding), it is no longer linked to the taking of nourishment, but rather to fantasy. Infant autoeroticism is propped on the mother; adult sexuality is propped on childhood autoeroticism and polymorphous perversity. Lacan's account of sexual desire—in excess of any possible satisfaction, wandering metonymically from one object to another—develops the implications of what is most radical in Freud's *Three Essays*.

In the last of his three essays, however, Freud attempts finally to account for the normative channeling of sexuality into reproduction. It is at this point that teleology reenters his story as the romance of the penis. What he calls "The Transformations of Puberty" consist less in rediscovering a lost sexual object than in finding a new heterosexual object and replacing sexual aimlessness with a sexual purpose. But what might such a purpose be *for women?* By this point in *Three Essays,* Freud has had to fall back on a self-admittedly unsatisfactory (and certainly outdated) masculine sexual economy which he quaintly calls "the discharge of the sexual products," one in which "the sexual instinct is now subordinated to the reproductive function" (*SE* 7:207). But as Freud himself is forced to acknowledge, an economy of sexual products leaves out of account (among others) children, castrati, and above all, women; how can the theory be made to fit a nonmasculine genital apparatus? Freud never answers this question. Instead, his account swerves toward a version of "end-pleasure" as opposed to "fore-pleasure" (his terms) resolutely focused on a teleology of the penis. "The finding of an object" means that, "in a man, the penis, which has now become capable of erection, presses forward insistently towards the new sexual aim—penetration into a cavity in the body which excites his genital zone" (*SE* 7:222); just so, presumably, the Russian count pressed forward insistently to penetrate the hollow O figured by the marquise's body. Women, by contrast, are left in Freud's account with the problem of (reproductively nonfunctional) clitoral pleasure, or else with the tendency to vaginal frigidity which Freud notoriously viewed as "intimately related to the essence of femininity" (*SE* 7:221).

Since the only function of the clitoris, according to Freud, is that of "pine shavings . . . kindled in order to set a log of harder wood on fire" (*SE* 7:221), feminine pleasure thus remains forever on the side of what Freud calls "fore-pleasure" rather than "end-pleasure"—or, if you like, on the side of a perverse rather than purposive sexuality. In an earlier passage, Freud has seen the "average uncultivated woman" as tending naturally toward the condition of the prostitute, which is that of infantile sexuality, i.e., polymorphous perversity.[16] Feminine sexuality thus comes to occupy an anomalous and contradictory position in Freud's thinking in *Three Essays*. Either feminine sexual pleasure (i.e., clitoral pleasure) is repressed out of existence altogether as the high price of conforming to phallic needs, or it is permanently consigned to the realm of the perverse and the aimless—that infantile and polymorphous perversity that Freud associates especially with the prostitute. In short, it remains unaccountable because it can never be fully subsumed into a telos of the penis, thereby undoing the happy ending of Freud's romance, while forever threatening to disjoin sexuality from reproduction.

Where does this leave women vis à vis not just sexual pleasure, but maternal desire? The answer will be cast in entirely Oedipal terms, when Freud returns a quarter of a century later to the mystery of femininity, accounting for the question of both feminine and maternal desire in terms of the unconscious wish to possess the father's penis. It is this instinct—this "psychical representation"—that forms the feminine subplot to the masculine romance of the penis. A teleology of feminine sexuality is finally achieved in Freud's writing by way of archeology; maternal desire becomes the overlay of infantile penis envy. "In this way," Freud concludes, "the ancient masculine wish for the possession of a penis is still faintly visible through the femininity now achieved" (*SE* 22:128). Freud's drastic solution (penis envy) not only tries to account for what is specific and problematic in the girl's passage through the Oedipus complex as he has defined it; his solution also provides a retrospective explanation for what is otherwise unaccountable in "the transformations of puberty"—namely, the connection for women (as opposed to men) between sexuality and reproduction. Yet, for all his later attempt to marry maternal desire to an Oedipal construction of femininity, Freud's radical perception about the perverse errancy of feminine desire continues to undermine the foundations of his story, much as the parenthetical moment of radical disorder in Kleist's story undermines the Romantic reproductive telos of "The Marquise of O—". Reading Freud and Kleist together, we can glimpse in the parentheses of a masculine economy the possibility of a feminine desire so radically disjoined from reproduction as to create a rift in both subjectivity and narrative. The parenthetical figure of femininity makes nonsense of their stories.

Kristeva and the Holy Family

My third scene for the disjunction between feminine pleasure and procreation involves the one represented by science itself, in the form of the contemporary application of biomedical technology to human reproduction. The theological issues involved in the formation of what sociologists have termed "the artificial family"[17]—the practice of AID, IVF (*in vitro* fertilization), and surrogacy—are not in themselves new, since they abut on earlier debates about artificial birth control. The same definitions of the individual (the subject) and of marriage (sexuality) which have traditionally underpinned the opposition of the Catholic Church to contraception and abortion now underpin its opposition to artificial reproduction. I want, however, to suggest that the theological debate about artificial reproduction and fertilization also bears on the relation of subjectivity to language, and that these may also be evident in the drama played out in the American courts during recent years about what has come to seem (and not only for feminists) the most problematic way to form an artificial family—namely, surrogate motherhood.

Ironically, the first artificial family was the Holy Family. The Virgin Mary herself constitutes the most famous (not to say miraculous) instance of the surrogacy arrangement, in the New Testament at least. Even Catholics would have to concede that God himself set a precedent for third-party intervention between husband and wife. Historians of the cult of the Virgin Mary have pointed out that the Virgin Birth was from the outset a vexed question, even for Christians, and sometimes had to be defended against scurrilous stories, some of them along the lines of Montaigne's bucolic anecdote. The most ingenious of the myths about the origin of Christ (Origen's, in fact) was that he was conceived through the ear by means of the *logos* at the Annunciation— a case of apostrophic conception ("Hail Mary . . ."); when you think about it, this theory is no odder than the more familiar view that an androgynous Holy Spirit disguised as a dove descended on the Virgin Mary. Reproductively speaking, the Virgin's role becomes that of sublime incubator for the Word; or else, as theories of reproduction changed, provider of the material or bodily element necessary for the Incarnation.[18] In time, it also became standard Catholic doctrine to deny not only any loss of virginity on Mary's part but also any taint of original sin attending her own birth, in an immaculate *mise en abyme*. The dogma of the Immaculate Conception finally became official in the middle of the nineteenth century, when Pope Pius IX settled the question for good.[19] The age that gave birth to modern feminism and to psychoanalysis also officially consecrated femininity under the sign of a sacred Mother—firmly subordinated, however, to God the Father.

In "Stabat Mater," her essay on the cult of the Virgin Mary, Julia Kristeva argues that the twentieth-century decline in religion has left women without an available discourse of maternity. She asks: What can the (now attentuated) cult of the Virgin Mary tell us about the social and psychic function of the fantasy of motherhood? The distinctively Kristevan aspect of her inquiry is the claim that this fantasy has a specific function in relation to language. Kristeva defines the "maternal" as "an identity catastrophe that causes the Name to topple over into the unnameable that one imagines as femininity, non-language or body."[20] In Marian iconography, milk and tears become "the metaphors of non-speech, of a 'semiotics' that linguistic communication does not account for."[21] Kristeva glimpses in the Virgin Mother "the tremendous territory hither and yon of the parenthesis of language"—something extralinguistic and heterogenous that tends to "re-establish what is non-verbal . . . a signifying disposition that is closer to the so-called primary processes" or to the unconscious—in other words, a return of the (pre-Oedipal) repressed within the symbolic which corresponds to the Kristevan "semiotic."[22] This is a form of prelinguistic signification mapped on the body itself, in the pre-Oedipal realm where the mother's care for the infant's body installs borders and separations. The mother in Kristevan discourse therefore has a status not unlike that of Freud's "instinct"; she is a psychic representation posited on the frontier between the mental and the somatic, "a strange fold that changes culture into nature, the speaking [subject] into biology." As such, she poses a dangerous threat to the notion of subjectivity itself. The cult of the Virgin Mary finally illustrates Kristeva's underlying thesis that "belief in the mother is rooted in fear, fascinated with a weakness—the weakness of language."[23] Religion, she argues, attempts to overcome this fear by recuperating heterogeneity, via the maternal, for the symbolic system known as the Word—a move that Kristeva is swift to detect since it resembles, parodically, her own.

Given its doctrine on marriage, the family, and the rights of the unborn, the Catholic Church was bound to come out strongly against all forms of artificial reproduction.[24] Pope Paul VI in *Humanae Vitae* (1968) rejected any attempt "which would pretend to separate, in generation, the biological activity in the personal relation of the married couple." Or, as Pope Pius XII had already written in a prophetic moment:

> To reduce the shared life of a married couple and the act of married love to a mere organic activity for transmitting semen would be like turning the domestic home, the sanctuary of the family, into a biological laboratory.[25]

(Or like turning the uterus into a petri dish.) Pope John Paul II's recent "Instruction on Respect for Human Life in its Origins and on the Dignity of Procreation—Replies to Certain Questions of the Day" (1987) simply applies to the current debate formulations derived from these earlier papal statements on contraception and abortion. What is not immediately obvious, however, is why the papal "Instruction" should also involve considerations that are in the last resort linguistic. I want to argue that the Catholic stance on artificial reproduction reflects the same fear that, in Kristeva's analysis, gives rise to the cult of the Virgin Mother. The document states in its introduction that the Church's intervention in the field of artificial reproduction is inspired by love for both man and Christ "as she [sic] contemplates the mystery of the Incarnate Word" (note the traditional gendering of the church).[26] In a text from which the maternal body is otherwise conspicuously absent, we should not be surprised to find the womb or "maternal receptacle" (Kristeva's phrase) functioning here as "a permanent lining"—a necessary complement or supplement—to theological contemplation of the Incarnate Word.

By way of establishing first principles, the papal "Instruction" sets out the relation of what it calls "Anthropology" to "Procedures in the Biomedical

Field"—anthropology here defined as "a proper idea of the nature of the human person in his [sic] bodily dimension," which proves to be that of a " 'unified totality' " (the phrase is Pope John Paul's own), or a nature "at the same time corporal and spiritual."[27] Any intervention on the human body therefore involves what the papal "Instruction" glosses as "the person himself in his concrete reality." The Pope's argument about artificial reproduction is underwritten by the Church's mission to safeguard this notion of personhood, indivisibly corporal and spiritual. To admit the possibility of intervention at the level of conception is to threaten—to shatter or disorder—a theory of the subject founded on a traditional unity-in-duality (body and soul as two-in-one). God alone has the right to undo the subject, thus conceived; the same argument applies to abortion. But notice how the body has been reappropriated. With Kristeva in mind, we might suspect that papal insistence on the importance of the corporal has the function of recuperating heterogeneity (the Kristevan semiotic, or maternal lining) for the Word in the face of an anxiety about its symbolic poverty. It is the mother—the Virgin Mary—who makes the Word "Incarnate."

The language of "Instruction on Respect for Human Life" becomes most charged with respect to marital relations. AID, we are told, does not "conform to the dignity of the couple and to the truth of marriage" because "it objectively deprives conjugal fruitfulness of its unity and integrity," bringing about "a rupture between genetic parenthood, gestational parenthood, and responsibility for upbringing" which "threatens the unity and stability of the family." Surrogacy is the type of such separation, since it "sets up, to the detriment of families, a division between the physical, psychological and moral elements which constitute those families."[28] For the parents, the family is constituted by conjugal fidelity; for the child, it is constituted by continuity between biological and social parenting.[29] Given this definition, it's not surprising that the papal document should have most to say about its ban on "homologous" artificial fertilization (in which both sperm and egg come from the marriage partners themselves, rather than from a third party), even though it seems to contradict neither principle. The argument turns on the connection between procreation and "the conjugal act" (here we are back with Pope Paul VI's 1968 encyclical, *Humanae Vitae*).[30] "The meanings of the conjugal act" (the signifier of marriage) and "the goods of marriage" (the signified) can never be arbitrarily disjoined. Like its view of the subject, the Catholic concept of sexuality depends on that of bodily unity-in-duality, "inseparably corporal and spiritual." What the document calls " 'the language of the body' " (quoting from Pope John Paul himself), must involve both "spousal meanings" and "parental" ones, sexuality inseparably joined to procreation in a shatterproof subject rather than a petri dish.[31]

In effect, the papal "Instruction" produces a regulated system of signification in which the "goods" of marriage must have only unitary, unambiguous "meanings," and "the language of the body" refers to a specifically theological view of the speaking and desiring subject. Thus "fertilization achieved outside the body of the couple [i.e., of the woman's body] remains by this very fact deprived of the meanings and the values which are expressed in the language of the body and in the union of human persons."[32] This amounts to saying that artificial reproduction is meaningless—or, alternatively, that meaning can only be unitary and self-identical. Arguably, then, the underlying threat posed by AID, IVF, and surrogacy is precisely their threat to the Word, since they destabilize imbricated notions of the subject and of language which sustain the entire theological edifice. If goods and meanings are not self-identical— if bodies and words can drift apart, or personal identity ceases to be unified by divine cement, or signifiers and signifieds turn out to have arbitrary rather than natural or God-given relations—then not only does language become an artificial system, but God himself becomes mere (phallo)logocentrism. The papal "Instruction" can finally be read as an attempt to hold the line, not just on artificial reproduction, but on the subject, and not just on the subject, but on language, too, lest they fragment to reveal the disjoined relation between sexuality and reproduction—between the subject and the body—which is the radical insight of Freud's *Three Essays,* or the arbitrary relation between "goods" and "meanings" which is the radical insight of poststructuralist theories of language since Saussure.

Papal views about the organic and spiritual unity of both subjects and signs that sustain the ban on artificial reproduction are unlikely to cut much ice either with poststructuralists or with contemporary feminists of whatever persuasion. But on one issue, that of surrogacy, American feminists at least have been deeply divided. Whatever their view of commercial surrogacy, they are understandably reluctant to claim that a mother's biological tie to her baby differs from that of a father. It smacks of essentialism, not to say biologism. But (it might well be argued), the surrogate mother gives up not just an egg, but a baby—nine months' worth of gestation, and all that it entails, both physical and psychic. Defenders of commercialized surrogacy rejoin sharply (with Judge Sorkow in the "Baby M" case) that women have as much right to sell their wombs as men have to sell their sperm. What we see here, however, is not equality with men, but rather a surfacing of the patriarchal thinking that reduces the role of the biological mother to mere provider of a nurturing uterus. As Dr. Lee Salk put it in his role as national spokesperson for paternal rights, "The role of parent was achieved by a surrogate uterus and not a surrogate mother;"[33] this is what you might call the synecdochic view of surrogacy (part for whole or the equation of uterine function and maternity) with which feminist historians of the relations between women and the body are all too familiar.[34] Despite the fact that on some level such arguments resonate with feminist views that motherhood is artificially constructed or "reproduced" rather than biologically constituted, still, they illustrate once more the socially controlling function that Kristeva ascribes to the cult of the Virgin Mary—its apparent empowering of women, but only at the price of ultimate containment. Although superficially liberated from the confines of the patriarchal family and conjugal fidelity by "the virginal maternal" (Kristeva's phrase), the surrogate mother is finally subsumed under the Law of (God) the Father, or Dr. Salk, on paternal rights.[35]

In other words, the commissioning father in a surrogacy agreement occupies the traditional position of God, and Mary Beth Whitehead was caught up in a battle that was equally obscure to her and to the legal experts on either side of the case—one, moreover, that she was bound to lose, at least initially, given the privileging of the Father in any system of representation that inscribes paternal, Oedipal, or divine desire as primary. By shifting the emphasis from the contractual to the custodial—by treating a disputed surrogacy agreement like any other custody squabble—the judge concerned in the Baby M case may have hoped to off-load one set of highly prejudicial concerns connected with biology; but in the process others entered in, of which the most obvious were social and economic. Less obvious, however, but equally pervasive is the ideological subtext that traditionally privileges the father as property holder, as meaning maker, and as desiring subject. It's no accident, in other words, that hot on the heels of the revelation that Mary Beth Whitehead was once a high-school dropout, a welfare mother, and a go-go dancer came testimony to the effect that she was defective as a subject—that she suffered, as the experts say, from a variety of so-called personality disorders: narcissism, impulsiveness, lack of contact with reality, overinvolvement with her children, failure to keep appointments for psychological counseling, and above all, inability to tell the truth, or a duplicitous relation to language; the Sterns' lawyer in the Baby M case is on record as having set out to prove her "a liar". The implication is that anyone who agreed to surrogacy in the first place had ceded her claims to full personhood (in the papal sense), becoming, as Mary Beth Whitehead herself vividly complained, a mere uterus on legs, and a liar into the bargain.

The only immaculate conception—the only good surrogate uterus—is the one that does away with feminine desire altogether; in any event, the woman loses out. Either she goes quietly and gets her fee plus the everlasting gratitude and forgetfulness of the commissioning couple (the Assumption), or, if she changes her mind, she seems doomed to be the loser in a custody case by virtue of lacking paternal authority. As Kristeva puts it, more abstractly, "Christianity does associate women with the symbolic community, but only provided they keep their *virginity*. Failing that, they can atone for their carnal *jouissance* with their martyrdom.[36] Arguably, any feminine subject who permits herself to be identified primarily in terms of a maternal function has put herself in the same position as either the Virgin Mary or Mary Beth Whitehead. And yet, a refusal to acknowledge that one constituent of women's social and economic oppression, as well as of feminine specificity, comprises the intimately intertwined physical, psychic, and social meanings which we know as "maternity" risks ignoring the real noncomparability of the reproductive process for men and for women. The distinction between femininity and maternity may be crucial for a feminist politics of the body, but recognition of the biological disparity between paternity and maternity is surely equally crucial for any nondiscriminatory social and legal inscription of sexual difference. Even as they refuse the traditional equation of femininity and motherhood, women may be compelled to make at least some claims under the sign of maternity, whether for themselves or on behalf of others, in order to protect themselves in the workplace, under the law, and—as I've tried to argue by way of my three narratives of "Immaculate" conception—in the face of the subtle but powerful workings of paternalist sexual ideologies and the symbolic systems that sustain them.

Notes

[A postscript: The original judgment that stripped Mary Beth Whitehead of her parental rights so that Baby M could be legally adopted by the commissioning "mother" has since been overturned. Mary Beth Whitehead now has parental rights; she does not, however, have Baby M—an outcome that reminds us that in an era famous for proclaiming the sanctity of the family, some families are holier than others.][37]

1. "Near the end of the century of Enlightenment, medical science and those who relied upon it ceased to regard the female orgasm as relevant to generation. Conception, it was held, could take place secretly, with no telltale shivers or signs of arousal"; Thomas Laqueur, "Orgasm, Generation, and the Politics of Reproductive Biology," *Representations* 14 (1986), 1.

2. Heinrich von Kleist, *The Marquise of O—and Other Stories,* trans. David Luke and Nigel Reeves (Harmondsworth: Penguin, 1978), 68. Subsequent page references in the text are to this edition.

3. Donald M. Frame, trans., *The Complete Works of Montaigne* (Stanford: Stanford University Press, 1948), 246.

4. ibid., 245.

5. ibid., 251.

6. ibid., 249.

7. See James Strachey, ed., *The Standard Edition of the Complete Psychological Works of Sigmund Freud,* 24 vols. (London: The Hogarth Press, 1953–74), 11:174. (Subsequent references to Freud's works in the text are to this edition, cited as *SE*.)

8. See, for instance, James M. McGlathery, *Desire's Sway: The Plays and Stories of Heinrich von Kleist* (Detroit: Wayne State University Press, 1983), 81–84 and n.

9. See Mary Poovey, " 'Scenes of an Indelicate Character': The Medical 'Treatment' of Victorian Women," *Representations* 14 (1986):152, where the debate provoked by chloroform is seen giving rise to a discourse whereby the feminine body is silenced: "But the very silence that authorizes these different medical practices also produces at the site of the reproductive body an undecidability that is dangerous to the medical profession and its controlling operations. The silence of the female body actually produces an excess of meanings, and the contradictions that emerge within this excess undermine the authority that medical men both claim and need."

Poovey cites a number of cases where women, while unconscious under the influence of chloroform, shocked medical practitioners with their manifest eroticism—one woman, for instance, reenacting in childbirth "those preliminaries which had led her to the state in which [her medical attendants] now beheld her." (Ibid., 142, 161 n.)

10. See, for instance, "Femininity," *New Introductory Lectures on Psycho-Analysis* (1933), *SE* 22:112–35.

11. See also an addition to the 1915 edition of *Three Essays on the Theory of Sexuality*, where Freud refers to instinct as "the psychical representative of an endosomatic, continuously flowing source of stimulation. . . . The concept of instinct is thus one of those lying on the frontier between the mental and the physical (*SE* 7:168). Elsewhere, however, Freud distinguishes between instinct and its psychical representative; see *SE* 14:112–13. For another discussion of Freud's concept of *"Trieb,"* see also Jean Laplanche, *Life and Death in Psychoanalysis,* trans. Jeffrey Mehlman (Baltimore and London: Johns Hopkins University Press, 1976), 8–14.

12. See "Analysis Terminable and Interminable" (1937), *SE* 23:252.

13. Leo Bersani, *The Freudian Body: Psychoanalysis and Art* (New York: Columbia University Press, 1986), 38.

14. ibid., 39–40.

15. See *SE* 7:150.

16. "In this respect children behave in the same kind of way as an average uncultivated woman in whom the same polymorphously perverse disposition persists. Under ordinary conditions she may remain normal sexually, but if she is led on by a clever seducer she will find every sort of perversion to her taste, and will retain them as part of her own sexual activities. Prostitutes exploit the same polymorphous, that is, infantile, disposition for the purposes of their profession" (*SE* 7:191).

17. See, for instance, R. Snowden and G. D. Mitchell, *The Artificial Family: A Consideration of Artificial Insemination by Donor* (London: George Allen & Unwin, 1981); see also R. Snowden, G. D. Mitchell and E. M. Snowden, *Artificial Reproduction: A Social Investigation* (London: George Allen & Unwin, 1983) for a study of the social implications of artificial reproduction.

18. See Marina Warner, *Alone of All Her Sex: The Myth and the Cult of the Virgin Mary* (New York: Alfred A. Knopf, Inc., 1976), 34–49.

19. See ibid., 236–37. See also Edward Dennis O'Connor, C.S.C., ed., *The Dogma of the Immaculate Conception: History and Significance* (Notre Dame, Indiana: University of Notre Dame Press, 1958).

20. Toril Moi, ed., *The Kristeva Reader* (New York: Columbia University Press, 1986), 162.

21. ibid., 174.

22. ibid., 174–75.

23. ibid., 175.

24. A comic side to the debate is provided by unofficially sanctioned techniques for circumventing the outright ban on artificial fertilization such as the use of a perforated condom; for instance, the technique known as GIFT—"Gamete Intra-Fallopian Transfer"—involves extracting an egg, placing it near sperm cells in a catheter, and then inserting both into the uterus: "Some Catholics have judged the technique acceptable provided that masturbation is not involved in collection of the sperm. A perforated condom is used during intercourse, with the sperm retrieved from the condom afterward." See marginal discussion and comment by Cardinal Joseph Ratzinger and Father Bartholomew Kiely, "Instruction on Respect for Human Life in Its Origin and on the Dignity of Procreation," *Origins: NC documentary service:* 16:40 (March 19, 1987), 699–700.

25. See Peter Singer and Deane Wells, *Making Babies: The New Science and Ethics of Conception* (New York: Charles Scribner's Sons, 1985), 38. Similarly, the Archbishop of Canterbury's 1945 commission into the practice of AID had recommended that it should be a criminal offense, presumably on the grounds of its implications for marriage; see Snowden and Mitchell, *The Artificial Family*, 15.

26. "Instruction on Respect for Human Life in Its Origin and on the Dignity of Procreation," *Origins* 16:40 (March 19, 1987), 699; subsequent quotations are from this text.

27. Ibid., 16:40. 700; the quotation is from apostolic exhortation *Familiaris Consortio* (1982).

28. *Origins*, 16:40. 705.

29. One surprising implication of the papal "Instruction" is that it should by rights ban adoption too in the interests of consistency, surely an irony in the light of the advocacy of adoption by right-to-lifers as an alternative to abortion.

30. *Origins*. 16:40. 705; Pope Paul VI, Encyclical Letter *Humanae Vitae* (1968).

31. *Origins*, 16:40. 706; General Audience on January 16, 1980: *Insegnamenti di Giovanni Paolo II*.

32. *Origins*, 16:40. 706.

33. Gannett News Service, *Ithaca Journal*, 11 February 1987.

34. See, for instance, Ann Oakley, *The Captured Womb: A History of the Medical Care of Pregnant Women* (Oxford: Basil Blackwell, 1984).

35. See ibid., p. 142: "[monotheism] represents the paternal function: patrilinear descent with transmission of the name of the father. . . . is caught in the grip of an abstract symbolic authority which refuses to recognise the growth of the child in the mother's body."

36. *The Kristeva Reader*, 145–46.

37. For an excellent discussion of the issues involved in surrogacy and its bearing on the concept of motherhood, see Juliette Zipper and Selma Sevenhuijsen, "Surrogacy: Feminist Notions of Motherhood Reconsidered," in *Reproductive Technologies: Gender, Motherhood and Medicine*, Michelle Stanworth, ed. (Cambridge: Polity Press, 1987), 118–38.

2

Speaking of the Body:
Mid-Victorian Constructions of
Female Desire

Mary Poovey

One of the most pressing theoretical issues facing feminists today is conceptualizing the complex relationship between "real" women—women as historical agents—and woman—the historically specific representation of the female
that mediates the relationship of women and men to every individual, concrete
woman. This is an important theoretical issue partly because the slippage
between women and woman in various theoretical formulations has been a
source of increasingly acrimonious disagreement among feminists.[1] Lacking
a map of the relation between the two has confounded our attempts to read
texts written by women without either reproducing the ideological system
that subsumes women into woman or simply fantasizing an alternative position within that system despite not really knowing why that position might
exist.[2] Another way to formulate the problem we face is this: Many of us
believe that historical women have been excluded from, or have only gradually
and imperfectly achieved influence upon, the dominant terms of representation; yet all of us encounter representations "signed by women."[3] How can
we account for what seems to be an impossibility? How can we read what so
patently exists? To address these questions in practical terms, we need to be
able to theorize both how women have been able to enter discourses from
which they have been initially excluded so as to begin to represent themselves,
and how to read texts that mark the passage of women from objects of
another's discourse to women as subjects of their own. I won't be able to
discuss all of the facets of this vexing problem here, but I can at least open
the discussion. By analyzing two texts in relation to each other, I want to
offer an example of some of the ways in which representations of woman as
object enabled—and set limits to—women's contributions to their own self-
representation.

My specific subject in this essay is the representation of prostitution in Britain in the 1840s. I have chosen this subject because female sexuality has historically proved to be the most problematic locus of representational issues for women: it has simultaneously promised the most intimate access any historical woman has to her femaleness and consistently eluded anything like a woman-centered definition because female sexuality has occupied a critical place in men's contests for power and therefore in women's social oppression.[4] I focus on prostitution rather than other sexual issues such as intercourse, contraception, or childbirth because, whereas these topics were discussed almost exclusively in medical discourse throughout much of the nineteenth century, the "epidemic" of syphilis transformed prostitution into a social problem of such magnitude that by the 1840s this kind of female sexual behavior was being discussed in forms as various as newspapers, highbrow quarterlies, novels, and "scientific" treatises on venereal disease and sanitation. I have chosen this period because it constitutes a moment of crisis for this discussion—just after the formulation of prostitution as the "Great Social Evil" intensified fears about venereal disease[5] but just before feminists like Josephine Butler entered the public debate, thereby altering the terms in which the issue was addressed. I will argue here that, as she was conceptualized in the 1840s, the prostitute epitomized a contradictory representation of woman that was critical to the consolidation of bourgeois power. Middle-class attempts to solve the problem of prostitution, I will suggest, were actually attempts symbolically to manage—and displace—other social problems without disrupting either the position of the middle class or the conceptualization of sexual relations upon which this class based its claim to moral and social superiority. In the course of addressing larger, more intractable social issues, then, reformers necessarily reproduced the terms in which sexuality—both male and female—could be conceptualized. This is the key to the second part of my argument. Because prostitution *did* raise the issue of female sexuality in a form in which it could not be marginalized, these discussions paradoxically provided the discursive conditions of possibility for women's conceptualizing their own sexuality, and therefore the opening that would eventually enable women to help change the way in which female sexual desire was represented and understood.

Prostitution initially attracted widespread attention in Britain in the 1840s as part of the growing middle-class conviction that the relationship between poverty, immorality, and disease was amenable to intervention and "cure." The first British analysts of prostitution were either doctors or laymen influenced by Evangelicalism or journalists interested in mapping the previously undifferentiated mass of the laboring and indigent poor. Some of the most influential Evangelical contributions to the literature were Dr. Michael Ryan's

Prostitution in London (1839), Ralph Wardlaw's *Lecture on Female Prostitution* (1842), and James Beard Talbot's *The Miseries of Prostitution* (1844). The most important "sociological" study of prostitutes was that section of Henry Mayhew's *Morning Chronicle* series entitled "The Metropolitan Poor." Mayhew's reports were originally published between October 19, 1849, and December 12, 1850; the relevant section of the four-volume collection published in 1861 was entitled "Those That Will Not Work" and dealt not only with prostitutes but also with thieves, swindlers, and beggars.[6] All these works were explicitly or implicitly indebted to a French study of prostitution published in 1836: A. J. B. Paret-Duchatelet's *De la prostitution dans la ville de Paris*. Like Duchatelet's meticulously researched study, the British treatments of the "mighty evil" all aspired to social-scientific objectivity— even though their appeals to statistics were either supplemented by, or abandoned to, the moralistic assumptions that limited commentators' statistical "evidence" in the first place. These assumptions implicitly, and often explicitly, endorsed middle-class values such as monogamy, self-discipline, and cleanliness—so much so that modern analysts like Judith Walkowitz have suggested that what we now call social science originated in a middle-class desire to implement "applied Christianity" within the class whose disciplined labor was instrumental to the consolidation of bourgeois power.[7]

The extent to which discussions about prostitution constituted discussions about class can be seen from two related concerns that repeatedly appear in these texts: the fear that inadequate housing for the urban poor and factory workers leads to "immorality"; and the fear that disease, both venereal and otherwise, is exacerbated, if not caused, by working-class overcrowding and inadequate sanitation. What interests me here is not just that anxieties about class were showing up in bourgeois reformers' discussions of prostitution, urban housing, and sanitation, but the fact that the terms in which many of these commentators conceptualized the prostitute symbolically "solved" the class issues they alluded to but did not foreground. To suggest how and why this was true, I want to examine in some detail a review essay that summarized the conclusions of the decade's major contributions to this subject. Published in 1850 in the *Westminster Review*, W. R. Greg's treatment of "the great social vice of Prostitution" takes to its logical conclusion the image of the prostitute that his predecessors had developed during the 1840s.[8]

Greg's explicit design in his essay on prostitution was to convince "those who have hitherto thought of prostitutes only with disgust and contempt, to exchange these sentiments for the more just and more Christian feelings of grief, compassion, and desire to soothe and save" (p. 249). Greg argues that such a public change of heart is necessary because seeing the prostitute as a victim will transfer responsibility to its proper object and thereby form a basis for social reform. At the heart of Greg's plea for sympathy is his representation of "the horrors which constitute the daily life of the women of the world."

No woman would voluntarily choose such a life, Greg explains; no matter what "the unknowing world" imagines, no prostitute enjoys "licentious pleasures." Middle-class society, Greg proclaims,

> the unknowing world—is apt to fancy [the prostitute] revelling in the *enjoyment* of licentious pleasures . . . wallowing in mire because she loves it. Alas! there is no truth in *this* conception. . . . Passing over all the agonies of grief and terror she must have endured before she reached her present degradation; the vain struggles to retrieve the first false, fatal step; the feeling of her inevitable future pressing her down with all the hopeless weight of destiny; the dreams of a happy past that haunt her in the night-watches, and keep her ever trembling on the verge of madness;—passing over all this, what is her position when she has reached the last step of her downward progress, and has become a common prostitute? . . . Insufficiently fed, insufficiently clad, she is driven out alike by necessity and by the dread of solitude, to wander through the streets by night, for the chance of earning a meal by the most loathsome labour that imagination can picture. . . . For, be it remembered, desire has, by this time, long ceased . . . repetition has changed pleasure into absolute repugnance; and those miserable women ply their wretched trade with a loathing and abhorrence which only perpetual semi-intoxication can deaden or endure. The curses, the blows, the nameless brutalities they have to submit to from their ruffianly associates of the brothel and saloon, are as nothing to the hideous punishment inherent in the daily practice of their sin. Their evidence, and the evidence of all who have come in contact with them, is unanimous on this point—that gin alone enables them to live or act; that without its constant stimulus and stupefaction, they would long since have died from mere physical exhaustion, or gone mad from mental horrors. (p. 240)

Greg explicitly opposes his portrait of the fallen woman to other representations, carried over from seventeenth- and eighteenth-century misogynist and pornographic literature, that cast the prostitute as a wanton reveling in sensual delight.[9] Greg's rebuttal to this image draws upon the two vocabularies that characterized this phase of the prostitution debate: that belonging to the new project of social analysis, which highlighted the physical and emotional hardships the prostitute suffers; and the vocabulary of secular Evangelicalism, which depicted a normative domestic life, now preserved only in the prostitute's "dreams of a happy past." Greg's representation of female desire is central to this second image. Contrary to what the public imagines, Greg insists, women do not become prostitutes because of "lust, immodest and unruly desires," or "silly vanity." According to Greg, "women's *desires* scarcely ever lead to their fall" for the simple reason that "desire scarcely exists in a definite and conscious form [in women], till they *have* fallen. In this point," Greg continues, "there is a radical and essential difference between the sexes.

... In men, in general, the sexual desire is inherent and spontaneous, and belongs to the condition of puberty. In the other sex, the desire is dormant, if not non-existent, till excited; always till excited by undue familiarities; almost always till excited by actual intercourse" (p. 242). Instead of lust or vanity, Greg argues, the emotions that lead a woman into prostitution are versions of the same emotion that characterizes all women: a "positive love of self-sacrifice." "A vast proportion of those who . . . ultimately come upon the town," Greg explains,

> fall in the first instance from a mere exaggeration and perversion of one of the best qualities of a woman's heart. They yield to desires in which they do not share, from a weak generosity which cannot refuse anything to the passionate entreaties of the man they love. There is in the warm fond heart of woman a strange and sublime unselfishness, which men too commonly discover only to profit by,—a positive love of self-sacri-fice,—an active, so to speak, an *aggressive* desire to show their affection, by giving up to those who have won it something they hold very dear. . . . We believe, upon our honour, that nine out of ten originally modest women who fall from virtue, fall from motives or feelings in which sensuality and self have no share. (p. 244)

Greg's representation of the prostitute as innately moral ("a positive love of self-sacrifice") is the key to the ideological work of his argument, for it aligns the lower-class prostitute with—rather than in opposition to—the virtuous middle-class woman. This, in turn, decisively locates difference be-tween women and men, rather than among women, as did representations of the prostitute that emphasized her unruly appetites.[10] Greg's depiction of the prostitute as a victim is critical to stabilizing this polarity and helps explain why the discourse of domestic relations dominates the discourse of social analysis throughout his essay. Even his recognition that economic hardships drive women to the streets invokes a norm of middle-class domesticity in which men support women, and therefore implies that *any* woman who has to work is a victim. When Greg goes on to argue that increasing employment possibilities for women would not necessarily curtail prostitution, moreover, it becomes clear that his discussion of women's poverty does not initiate a sustained criticism of social arrangements but follows from his assumption that, because women are by nature selfless and susceptible, their proper place in the home must be guaranteed in order for society to function as it should.[11]

Representing all women—even the prostitute—as essentially asexual, self-sacrificing, and passive (or rather, aggressive only in the desire to "give up" independence for love) is therefore part of a model of society in which the class difference that might otherwise be seen as a *cause* of social unrest has been translated into a gender similarity that can ideally serve as the *solution* to immorality. That is, if all women are innately moral, then their sex matters more than their class, and women's morality can be counted on to control the "ready, strong, and spontaneous" drive of male sexuality. Three interdependent transformations are implicit in Greg's ideal: not only has class inequality been subordinated to gender similarity, but social distress and poverty have been subsumed into immorality, and immorality has become a function of sexual difference and unnatural domestic arrangements. The image of society that results from these transformations is a laissez-faire system of moral and class relations in which, if left alone, the natural difference between the sexes will "cure" social unrest by checking immorality, which causes both disorder and disease. Put women in their proper place, the argument suggests, and social stability will follow.

Greg's model of laissez-faire social relations depends upon the assumption that men and women are different by nature. But despite the fact that Greg insists upon and elaborates this claim, traces of the female sexuality he explicitly denies repeatedly appear in his essay—and these traces are not confined to members of the working class. In the same paragraph in which Greg insists on the difference between male and female sexuality, for example, he acknowledges that, although women may not be *conscious* of sexual impulses, they may still suffer from repressing them. "Those feelings which coarse and licentious minds are so ready to attribute to girls," he explains, "are almost invariably *consequences*. Women whose position and education have protected them from exciting causes constantly pass through life without ever [having] been cognizant of the promptings of the senses. Happy for them that it is so! We do not mean to say that uneasiness may not be felt—that health may not sometimes suffer; but there is no consciousness of the cause" (p. 242). Greg's insinuation that sexual desire festers in women even when they do not know it also surfaces in his repeated charge that the "coarse and licentious minds" that attribute lust to prostitutes most often belong to the very middle-class women whose position and education *have* protected them "from exciting causes" (p. 242). These allusions to female sexual desire undermine Greg's argument that the difference between the sexes is a function of the innate difference *of* sexed desire, but he retains them nevertheless because they are essential to another argument, whose logic actually governs his essay. This argument concerns the conditions that facilitate, not the moral relations of English society, but the prosperity of the middle class.

Traces of Greg's implicit argument surface in the limits of his conceptualization of prostitution. After explaining why the prostitute deserves more sympathy than she characteristically receives in England, Greg formulates "the practical and most painful question" of his essay: "Can prostitution be eradicated?" His answer is immediate and sure: "At present, *per saltum* and *ab extra*, certainly not" (p. 253). Greg provides a long catalogue of quasi-justifications for his position, but he devotes extensive attention only to what he calls "the knottiest, the saddest, and the most disturbing" question that can engage "the ethical inquirer"—the "question of the possibility of men in general leading a chaste life before marriage" (p. 254). Despite Greg's express wish that men learn to control their sexual desires, and despite offering three, admittedly wishful, suggestions for bolstering sexual self-restraint, he concedes that two characteristics of English society exacerbate the natural promiscuity of men: the tendency of middle-class men to marry only when they can emulate their parents' standard of living, and the dense congregation of the population in urban areas. The first of these social tendencies led many young middle-class men to develop habits of saving and investment that consolidated their own (and their class's) economic position[12]; the second meant that the workforce necessary to industrial and capital expansion was available for hire. Taken together, these two factors were instrumental in consolidating middle-class power and prosperity.

That these two features of mid-Victorian society were also associated with the flourishing prostitution trade suggests how intimately middle-class commentators considered their fortunes bound to this "great social vice." Given the assumption that men's sexual drive was "ready, strong, and spontaneous," a late marriage age meant that young middle-class men needed to seek premarital liaisons with available women; and given dense congregations of working-class populations and a finite number of jobs for women, prostitution was likely to remain a viable option for women who had to work in order to live. From this perspective, prostitution simply provided a valuable resource in the free-market system, supplying services in response to demand in a form that could protect the sanctity and economic prosperity of the middle-class domestic ideal.[13]

The contradictory position occupied by women in relation to these conditions largely explains the contradictory representation of woman in Greg's essay. On the one hand, because bourgeois prosperity seemed to depend on an unregulated system of economic relations in which class inequity was neutralized by its translation into moral terms, woman was represented as innately moral and different from man in being superior to both aggression and sexual desire. But on the other hand, because this prosperity also seemed to depend on the availability of a source of sexual supply for middle-class men, woman was also represented as always incipiently sexualized; Greg depicts her, for example, as a carrier of a sexual desire of which she is only belatedly and imperfectly aware. In Greg's argument about female nature, the concept of "sublime unselfishness" seems to resolve this contradiction, for it fits women simultaneously for moral superintendence and sexual availability. But this concept does not actually resolve anything, since it is never reconciled with the notion of "coarse and licentious [female] minds" that Greg also introduces. In fact, Greg preserves the contradiction in his representation of woman because the double function it assigns to women actually displaces and seems to resolve another contradiction—the contradiction inherent in the bourgeois image of laissez-faire social relations: the unregulated market relations celebrated by the middle classes did not actually entail equal access to available resources but institutionalized class exploitation. Greg's representation of woman seems to resolve this contradiction by moving it to the "natural" terrain of gender: as an asexual creature, woman is moral (and hence the guarantor of laissez-faire, because moralized, social relations); as an incipiently sexual creature, woman is always a sexual resource (hence both the symbol and site of "natural" class inequity and exploitation). The fact that this move, which entails separating female feeling from consciousness, goes unremarked simply suggests how amenable the figure of woman was to representational manipulation.

Other writers in the 1840s (Dickens prominent among them) articulated the same contradictory representation of woman by distinguishing between kinds of women: middle-class women were by nature moral and asexual; lower-class women were always morally suspect and the possessors of "coarser" appetites. But this rhetorical distinction was increasingly difficult to defend, partly because of the need to account for findings such as Duchatelet's, which showed prostitutes moving from the streets to marriage, and partly because the importance of neutralizing class inequity led more commentators to naturalize bourgeois morality by foregrounding the "natural" difference between the sexes. What interests me about Greg's essay is that it shows how articulating difference upon sex still entailed writing difference into female nature. Greg's essay shows a female nature implicitly divided against itself rather than being divided according to class, but this image serves the same function of underwriting middle-class identity as did the older class division.

The possibility that women really *are* more like than different from men, however, is potentially ruinous to Greg's underlying argument. Rhetorically, this possibility is linked to what Greg sees as the most dangerous threat to his ideal of a self-regulating society—syphilis. Syphilis is the excess that signals the limits of Greg's representational maneuvers: in transforming a natural sexual exchange into an assault upon public health, syphilis turns prostitution into a crime; in making the sublimely unselfish woman a carrier of disease, it transforms female susceptibility into an active agent of death; in defying the boundaries of class and gender, syphilis substitutes for the false equality promised by bourgeois rhetoric a true and hideous equality before an indiscriminate disease. Greg's representation of syphilis reveals how deadly he imagines this leveling of distinctions to be. "Where there are 50,000 prostitutes scattered over the country," Greg writes,

> (a vast majority of whom are, or have been diseased), spreading infection on every side of them, quarantines against the plague, and costly precautions against cholera, seem very like straining at gnats and swallowing

camels. It must not be imagined that the mischief of syphilis can be measured by the number of those who are ostensibly its victims, even could we ascertain this datum. We must take into account the sufferings of those innocent individuals in private life who are infected through the sins of others; we must take into account the happiness of many families thus irretrievably destroyed; the thousands of children who are in consequence born into the world with a constitution incurably unsound; the certain, but incalculable deterioration of public health and of the vigour of the race, which must ensue in the course of a generation or two more. (p. 253)

Whatever the actual effects of syphilis in the 1840s, the threat with which Greg associates the disease can best be appreciated in the context of the challenge it posed to the ideological work of gender that I have described. If syphilis leveled all distinctions, it wouldn't matter that women could be said to be different by nature from men; as long as they were available for sexual use, women would continue to spread the disease that made one man as helpless as another. Greg's attempt to detach the disease from its sexual origin can be understood as his symbolic defense against this possibility. When he refers to syphilis as a "malady more general, more constantly present, and more terrible than all other epidemics," for example, and when he compares the syphilic prostitute to "a plague-stricken sufferer who breaks through a *cordon sanitaire*" (pp. 260–61), Greg simultaneously emphasizes the danger of this disease and downplays the fact that it is initially spread by sexual contact. The effect of this representation is, on the one hand, to insist upon the importance of containing syphilis and, on the other, to confine this effort to something that will not jeopardize the source of sexual supply or the privilege of the middle-class male. Taken together, these two emphases mandate state intervention to stop the spread of syphilis—but they limit this intervention to the lives and bodies of women and members of the lower class.

Greg offers four proposals for containing syphilis. In addition to the expedient that he immediately discounts (increasing women's employment opportunities), he suggests building more lower-class housing, placing existing lodging-houses under police surveillance (p. 263), and "subjecting all prostitutes . . . to a periodical medical inspection, with the prompt sequestration or removal to the hospital of all who were found diseased" (p. 266). Greg does not suggest criminalizing or even limiting prostitution, nor does he examine the class and sexual inequities that his solutions preserve. His proposals simply remove infectious prostitutes temporarily from the free-market system while leaving both the economic and moral dimensions of that system intact. His plan, which was partially implemented by the Contagious Diseases Acts of 1864 and 1866, did not really solve the problem of syphilis, of course, for it both implicitly sanctioned prostitution and almost completely overlooked the fact that infected *men* also transmitted the disease—often to the very women from whom they claimed to have contracted it. Greg's proposals did not really even address prostitution, the putative subject of his essay, for to him prostitution was only a problem because syphilis had begun to expose the artificiality of the distinctions that were written into—and effaced by—the society he endorsed. Greg's assumptions—that "human progress" was equivalent to the triumph of the middle class, and that both were intimately bound to the sexual double standard—at once mark the limits of his proposals and determine what he could not say.

I have been arguing that the discussion about prostitution in the 1840s focused public attention on the "problem" of female sexuality more sharply than it had been focused since the 1790s, and, more specifically, that the relationship between gender and class in the bourgeois conceptualization of society set the limits to how this subject could be represented and understood. That this discussion was also the conduit through which women entered the Victorian debate about female sexuality is clear from the fact that what drew women like Josephine Butler into explicit public discussions of sex was the campaign to repeal the Contagious Diseases Acts. I will return briefly to Butler at the end of this essay, but I will focus here not on the polemical contributions women made in the late 70s and 80s to the prostitution debate, but on a novel about romantic love published by a woman in 1847. I have chosen to write about a novel partly because literature was the nineteenth-century discourse in which women participated in the greatest numbers and arguably with the least cultural restraint; because literature—and the novel in particular—was a forum in which women's sexual transgressions continued to be represented even after the mid-Victorian moralization of woman was under way; and because it was the genre that most readily accommodated mid-Victorian women's efforts to represent female sexual desire.[14] I have chosen *Jane Eyre* because in this novel Charlotte Brontë presents a more positive—if still internally conflicted—image of assertive female desire than did many of her contemporaries. My argument here is that the limits of Brontë's representation were given by terms established elsewhere, in the prostitution debate, and that identifying traces of this debate helps explain contradictions that remain unresolved in Brontë's novel itself. I will also argue, however, that Brontë's very different investment in the subject of female sexuality gave her contribution to this discussion the potential to undermine the ideological work performed by essays such as Greg's.

Jane Eyre is not about prostitution, needless to say, nor does it contain any streetwalking prostitutes. Nevertheless, Brontë's most explicit characterizations of female sexuality do invoke images of literal or metaphorical prostitutes: both Céline Varens, the French opera-dancer for whom Rochester once harbored a *"grande passion,"* and Bertha Mason, the beautiful Jamaican, are characterized as sexual commodities and as women of aggressive, illicit appetites. Of the two, Céline more explicitly barters sexual favors for money, but what Rochester calls Bertha's "giant propensities" marks her as the more sexually wanton of the two. Even after marriage should have harnessed her passions, Rochester explains with disgust, Bertha is "at once intemperate and unchaste."[15] Despite being purged from the novel, these representations infect its depiction of Jane herself.

While the subject of female sexuality most explicitly enters *Jane Eyre* in relation to characters associated with prostitution, Brontë initially cordons these characters off from the plain, unsophisticated heroine of the novel. Her rhetorical strategy, that is, at first seems to emphasize the differences among women rather than their similarities. Much of the Thornfield section of *Jane Eyre* is devoted to elaborating this contrast. When Rochester begs Jane to elope with him, for example, Jane's refusal takes the form of denying her likeness to the French dancer. "I will not be your Céline Varens," she exclaims. By the same token, when Jane first sees Bertha, both her description of the madwoman as a "clothed hyena" and Rochester's bitter comparison of his past with his would-be bride underscore the differences between the two women. "That is *my wife*," Rochester sneers, pointing to Bertha. "And *this* is what I wished to have" (pointing to Jane). "I wanted her just as a change after that fierce ragout. Wood and Briggs, look at the difference! Compare these clear eyes with the red balls yonder—this face with that mask" (p. 322).

Despite the characters' explicit assertions that Jane is not like these sexualized women, however, Brontë also repeatedly stresses the ways in which Jane *is* like them. When Jane falls in love with Rochester, for example, she becomes in one sense exactly what she vowed she would not be: "the successor of these poor girls" (p. 339). Not only is she just another in the series of Rochester's illicit loves, but Jane also bears an uncanny, textually elaborated likeness to the wife from whom Rochester insists she so dramatically differs. Bertha's laughter punctuates Jane's reveries about rebellion in Chapter 12 as if in ironic self-commentary, and when Bertha tries on Jane's wedding veil in Chapter 25, the madwoman's face appears in the mirror where the young girl's reflection ought to be (p. 311). As several feminist critics have pointed out, Bertha's literal imprisonment metaphorically figures the entrapment Jane's bigamous marriage would entail, and the lunatic's fiery revenge upon Rochester acts out a much more dramatic version of the resentment Jane elsewhere admits.[16] Bertha's rebellious fury can also be seen as adding another dimension to the aggressiveness dramatized in the child Jane, just as Céline's taunts about Rochester's *"beauté mâle"* give a more cynical twist to Jane's playful complaints about her master's face.

In the hands of a writer like Greg, as I have argued, emphasizing the likeness among women is part of a representation that denies sexuality and agency to all women so as to stress the natural difference between women and men. By contrast, Brontë highlights the similarities among Jane, Bertha, and Céline not to erase sexual desire but to insist that her middle-class heroine feels just as other, more obviously sexualized, women do. Juxtaposing St. John Rivers's marriage proposal with the mysterious summons of Rochester's voice explicitly foregrounds the alternative between self-sacrifice and self-assertion. When Jane obeys the latter despite her belief that Bertha is still alive, we are given to understand that Jane feels and acts upon some passion that is *not* just the "positive love of self-sacrifice." Jane's return to Rochester invokes both Céline and Bertha, for Jane can only imagine she will take his mistress's place, even though she is awarded that of his wife. Because the possibility of sexual desire has been admitted into the novel through these two characters, Jane's return draws out the hidden sexual aggression implicit in the young girl's advances. Brontë's descriptions of Jane's and Rochester's married life, which depict Jane becoming "ever more absolutely bone of [her husband's] bone and flesh of his flesh" (p. 476), further emphasize Jane's sexualized nature, making it clear that, in Brontë's eyes at least, female nature is neither passive nor passionless. So vivid was Brontë's image of female sexuality that a disapproving reviewer for the *Christian Remembrancer* singled out these scenes for remark. "The love-scenes glow with a fire as fierce as that of Sappho," he complained, "and somewhat more fuliginous."[17]

Locating sexual desire in women as diverse as Céline, Bertha, and Jane subordinates any differences that might be thought to exist between women and men to what Jane calls the "heterogeneity" within every individual. In Chapter 12, Brontë explicitly challenges the opposition upon which arguments like Greg's were based. "It is vain to say human beings ought to be satisfied with tranquillity," Jane muses:

> they must have action; and they will make it if they cannot find it. . . . Nobody knows how many rebellions besides political rebellions ferment in the masses of life which people earth. Women are supposed to be very calm generally: but women feel just as men feel; they need exercise for their faculties, and a field for their efforts as much as their brothers do; they suffer from too rigid a restraint . . . precisely as men would suffer. . . . It is thoughtless to condemn them, or laugh at them, if they seek to do more or learn more than custom has pronounced necessary for their sex. (p. 141)

Locating difference within every individual instead of between women and men problematizes the moral work Greg assumes women can perform, for it makes sacrificing personal desire to some abstract principle as difficult a task for women as both writers acknowledge it to be for men. Jane's struggle against Rochester's appeal, which Brontë details in Chapter 27, figures this difficulty explicitly; the fact that Jane's inner turmoil is only decisively resolved by a dream in which the mother-moon commands her to "flee temptation" represents how unnatural Jane's self-sacrifice feels (p. 346). Far from following from love and earning her domestic fulfillment, Jane's sacrifice entails a painful renunciation of both love and hope, and it culminates in her literal exile from domestic space.

For Brontë, then, self-sacrifice is not an effect of one's sexed nature, and the relation between the sexes cannot be expected to neutralize conflicts within the individual, much less in society as a whole. Despite Brontë's insistence on the difficulty of what Greg takes for granted, however, her novel shares with Greg's essay a version of the contradictory image of woman I have already examined. In Greg's essay, the contradiction written into female sexuality is signaled by his allusions to the pernicious effects of those impulses he claims women feel but do not know. In *Jane Eyre*, the contradiction is marked by a similar representation, which locates desire simultaneously inside woman's body and outside her consciousness. Like the middle-class women Greg describes, what Jane feels in Chapter 35 is not what she knows: what she *feels* is "an inexpressible feeling that thrilled [her heart] through"; what she *knows* is the sound of "a known, loved, well-remembered voice," the voice of Rochester summoning her to come home (pp. 444, 445).

This episode in the novel is marked by an extraordinarily dense concentration of narrative anomalies, which violate the realistic terms Brontë has otherwise generally established. Here, as elsewhere, Brontë offers a token explanation for the most egregious anomaly, Rochester's mysterious summons; but claiming that Rochester actually called Jane's name at the very moment she heard it does not really account for her hearing the voice. Nor can this voice fully account for the transformation that characterizes Brontë's description of Jane's feelings. Whereas Jane had previously referred to her desire for Rochester as a species of "insanity" (p. 386), as soon as she hears Rochester's call, Brontë explicitly rejects this psychological explanation for Jane's response and substitutes instead an elaborate religious analogy that purports both to explain and to "cure" Jane's feelings.

> I asked was it a mere nervous impression—a delusion? I could not conceive or believe: it was more like an inspiration. The wondrous shock of feeling had come like the earthquake which shook the foundations of Paul and Simon's prison; it had opened the doors of the soul's cell and loosed its bonds—it had wakened it out of its sleep, whence it sprang trembling, listening, aghast; then vibrated thrice a cry on my startled ear, and in my quaking heart and through my spirit, which neither feared nor shook, but exulted as if in joy over the success of one effort it had been privileged to make, independent of the cumbrous body. (pp. 446–47)

Why does Brontë attribute to "nature" and "inspiration" the same feelings she had previously castigated as "insane promptings"? Given the fact that, as far as Jane knows, nothing has changed in Rochester's domestic situation, her love for him would be as "delusive" as ever. Why, then, is this love suddenly dignified as spiritual "exultation"? The answer to these questions lies not in the nature of Jane's desire but in the teleological design of the plot, which is moving inexorably, conventionally, toward marriage. The problem this rhetorical transformation addresses is that middle-class marriage was conventionally represented as the inauguration, not the reward, for passion as assertive as Jane's. What Brontë's invocation of a religious vocabulary does is to allow her to preserve both sides of the contradictory image of woman at once: not knowing Bertha is dead, Jane still acts on an aggressive, assertive desire; because she feels this desire as an "inspiration," Jane's initiative becomes a response sanctioned by its religious cast. Translating Jane's desire into Rochester's voice and importing a religious analogy therefore function to separate Jane's feelings from her "cumbrous body" without denying the validity or intensity of those feelings. The morality of these feelings is then "proved" by the fact that Rochester turns out to be at once free to marry Jane and as dependent as a child.

I have been arguing that Brontë's novel and Greg's essay both participated in the mid-Victorian contest over the nature of female subjectivity, and that recognizing the contradictory image of woman produced by this context helps explain the contradictions that mark each text. Like Greg, Brontë initially links the possibility of female sexual desire to prostitution, but does so in such a way as to sanction female desire—which in turn necessitates that she somehow neutralize the pejorative connotations that accompany female self-assertion. Like Brontë, Greg insists that women can moralize men, but does so without losing women as a sexual resource—which means that he must marginalize and rewrite as susceptibility the sexuality he simultaneously retains and denies. In one sense at least, the difference between the two texts is a function of their own discursive status: without the constraints imposed upon her solution by the specter of syphilis, Brontë is able to represent love as an unproblematic arbitor, obliterating class difference, neutralizing the threat of Jane's aggression, and taming the excess of sexual desire. What love cannot solve, chance can; and by the end of the novel, Greg's fantasy of a self-regulating moral system has been perfected—with the striking difference that self-sacrifice, in the person of the ambiguously phallic and feminized St. John Rivers, has been exiled to India.

My last point suggests that the difference between these two texts is not simply a difference of genre but also a function of the differential placement of these two individuals in the mid-Victorian social formation. The first conclusion which juxtaposing these two texts enables us to draw, then, is that women were solicited differently by representations of gender than were men at mid-century.[18] By this, I do not mean simply that women had a different investment than men in the subject of female sexuality because they were women; rather, that because the "problem" of sexuality was articulated in relation *to* women and because women's roles were given initially *by* their sex, women's investment was first of all *in* the representation of gender and only secondarily in other determinants of identity such as class. For male writers such as Greg, gender was a transparent category because maleness was understood to be the norm; male identity seemed to be primarily a function of class position and individual achievement, and the aggression naturalized for men by contemporary definitions of masculinity made a man's struggle for money and power seem simply like natural self-expression. When a writer like Greg represented female subjectivity, then, his treatment of this issue was placed in the service of what was for him a more problematic issue—the issue of class. Greg reproduces a contradictory image of female subjectivity without exploring these contradictions because this double image answered to the complex conditions with which he associated middle-class prosperity. By contrast, for a woman to express or represent "herself," she had to foreground, and work through, the dominant representation of gender. For her, unexplored contradictions could be articulated much more unproblematically in relation to class issues, as when Jane's legacy magically transforms her into Rochester's social equal at the end of the novel.

The second point raised by this juxtaposition concerns the relative power of those individuals conceptualized as objects to alter the terms of the discourse that so defines them. Here, again, the concept of investment is crucial, both because it redefines power in such a way as to emphasize the agency (although not the choice) of individuals traditionally seen to lack power, and because it helps account for the differential sites of ideological work.[19] Because women's "nature" and social roles were dictated by sex at mid-century, any woman was likely to understand her own experience through the lens of gender; this, in turn, led women to view all social relations through this lens and to concentrate their attention initially (although not exclusively) on exploring or elaborating the terms of their gender definition. If the limits of female self-representation were initially set by the dominant representation of women, however, this representation could not finally dictate how individuals with a different investment in it would elaborate the contradictions it contained. When Brontë worked through the representation of woman, she simply elaborated the trace of female desire that remained marginal—but essential—to representations such as Greg's. This shifting of emphasis had the potential to undermine the ideological work Greg's image was designed to perform; insisting that "women feel just as men feel" obliterated the difference between women and men that Greg invoked to moralize and regulate class relations. The potential effect of Brontë's representation was to call attention both to the contradictory nature of images such as Greg's and to the artifice inherent in naturalizing any definition of gender. This, in turn, implicitly undermined the naturalistic rationale for a sexual double standard and the model of social relations which this difference was invoked to support. In Brontë's text, the elaborate narrative contrivances I have described—the intervention of a supernatural agent and religious terminology to moralize Jane's desire—constitute traces of the contradictory nature of the female subject; but, in calling attention to this contradiction, they make it that much more visible.

I am not suggesting that Brontë's contribution to the mid-Victorian discussion of female subjectivity was simply a woman's defense of some innate drive that men, but not women, could easily misrepresent because men did not know what women felt. Instead, I am proposing that the relationship between dominant representations such as Greg's and representations by the cultural "other" was one of productivity, not repression. The fact that Greg's investment in the conditions he considered essential to his class identity led him to reproduce a contradictory image of woman kept both terms of this contradiction available for individuals positioned differently in the social formation. Because women's treatment of this contradiction was not limited by their class investment in the same way as men's, when women entered the discussion about female sexuality (especially in a discourse as "recreational" as literature) they were able to reverse the emphasis of the contradiction that was constantly being reproduced so as to give a different—if still problematic—value to the idea of women's sexual desire.

Brontë's contribution to the construction of female sexuality was not the only logical expression of a woman's investment in the Victorian definition of gender. By the 1880s, in fact, feminists like Josephine Butler had begun to endorse Greg's definition of female subjectivity more frequently than Brontë's. The explanation for this is partly that the material and psychological investment of women as a group in altering gender definitions had been changed by the passage of the Contagious Diseases Acts. In institutionalizing the medical inspection of any woman suspected of prostitution, the Contagious Diseases Acts made the class and gender assumptions that had underwritten Greg's proposals more visible, because they made poor, sexually active women increasingly subject to state supervision. To defend women against both class and sexual double standards, Butler endorsed the idea that women's passionlessness should set the tone for social morality. That Butler explicitly endorsed passionlessness, however, was probably less important than the fact that her arguments were part of an explicit, public discussion of female sexuality in which women participated as passionately and vocally as men. If novels such as Brontë's began to exploit the contradiction written into female sexuality in the 1840s, by the 1880s women like Josephine Butler were able to take advantage of the opening produced by such early efforts. Given the fact that gender remained a site of cultural contestation, it matters less that the image of female sexuality generated by feminists like Butler was not necessarily a positive one, than that Butler's campaign meant that women had begun to participate actively in constructing the female subject—a subject that theoretically represented themselves.

Notes

1. Two recent discussions of the issue are Michele Barrett, "The Concept of Difference," *Feminist Review* 26 (Summer 1987):29–42; and Teresa de Lauretis, *Technologies of Gender: Essays on Theory, Film, and Fiction* (Bloomington: Indiana University Press, 1987), 1–26.

2. Examples of the first position include many studies of "images of women" produced during the 1970s; the second position is exemplified by many of the essays influenced by object relations theory, such as the articles collected in Shirley Nelson Garner, Claire Kahane, and Madelon Sprengnether, eds., *The (M)other Tongue: Essays in Feminist Psychoanalytic Interpretation* (Ithaca: Cornell University Press, 1985).

3. This phrase is used by Alice Jardine in *Gynesis: Configurations of Women and Modernity* (Ithaca: Cornell University Press, 1985), 26.

4. See Cora Kaplan, *Sea Changes: Culture and Feminism* (London: Verso, 1986), 31–56.

5. The best feminist study of nineteenth-century British prostitution is Judith R. Walkowitz, *Prostitution and Victorian Society: Women, Class, and the State* (Cambridge: Cambridge University Press, 1980).

6. This text is available in a facsimile edition: Henry Mayhew, *London Labour and the London Poor*, 4 vols. (New York: Dover, 1968), 4:35–272.

7. Walkowitz, 37.

8. W. R. Greg, "Prostitution," *Westminster Review* 53 (July 1850):238–68. All future references to this text will be cited by page numbers.

9. For examples of seventeenth-century misogynist texts, see Katherine Usher Henderson and Barbara F. McManus, eds., *Half Humankind: Contexts and Texts of the Controversy about Women in England, 1540–1640* (Urbana and Chicago: University of Illinois Press, 1985); eighteenth-century novels about prostitutes include John Cleland's *Fanny Hill*, and Daniel Defoe's *Roxana* and *Moll Flanders*.

10. When William Acton (who quotes passages from Greg's article) argues that prostitutes return to normal (married) life after a short period on the streets, he is reproducing this same position. See Acton, *Prostitution, Considered in its Moral, Social and Sanitary Aspects in London and Other Large Cities, &c.* (London: John Churchill, 1857). For an extended discussion of the mid-Victorian articulation of difference as sexual difference, see Mary Poovey, *Uneven Developments: The Ideological Work of Gender in Mid-Victorian England* (Chicago: University of Chicago Press, 1988), ch. 1.

11. See Greg, 262–63.

12. J. A. Banks, *Prosperity and Parenthood: A Study of Family Planning Among the Victorian Middle Classes* (London: Routledge & Kegan Paul, 1954).

13. Greg explicitly uses the image of supply and demand; see p. 259.

14. See Kaplan, *Sea Changes*, p. 3.

15. Charlotte Brontë, *Jane Eyre*, ed. Q. D. Leavis (Harmondsworth, Middlesex: Penguin, 1966), 334. All future references to this edition will be cited by page numbers.

16. See, for example, Sandra M. Gilbert and Susan Gubar, *The Madwoman in the Attic: The Woman Writer and the Nineteenth-Century Literary Imagination* (New Haven: Yale University

Press, 1979), 336–71; and Mary Poovey, "The Governess and *Jane Eyre*," in *Feminism and Psychoanalysis*, eds. Richard Felstein and Judith Roof (Ithaca: Cornell University Press, forthcoming).

17. Cited in Elizabeth K. Helsinger, Robin Lauterbach Sheets, and William Veeder, eds., *The Woman Question: Literary Issues, 1837–1883* (New York: Garland, 1983), 99.

18. See de Lauretis, *Technologies*, iv.

19. Ibid., 16, 20.

3

Female Circulation:
Medical Discourse and Popular Advertising in
the Mid-Victorian Era

Sally Shuttleworth

Popular medical advertisements, and the writings of the more august medical establishment in the nineteenth century, reveal a common obsession with female secretions, and in particular with those of menstruation. Although the accredited medical profession waged war on the quacks and their "purient advertisements," their discourses on the female body disclose markedly similar preoccupations. Focusing on the representations of menstruation, this paper traces the interconnected roles played by these two spheres of medical practice in promulgating the increasingly polarized views of gender identity that emerged in the Victorian era.

Although the physiology of pregnancy, childbirth, and lactation drew unprecedented medical attention in the early nineteenth century, it was the functioning of menstruation, whose processes remained threateningly mysterious well into the latter part of the century, that seemed to haunt the male imagination. According to the physician George Man Burrows in his *Commentaries on Insanity (1828),*

> Every body of the least experience must be sensible of the influence of menstruation on the operations of the mind. In truth, it is the moral and physical barometer of the female constitution.[1]

Menstruation acted as an external instrument, a barometer by which doctors could read the internal health, mental as well as physical, of their patients.[2] It was believed, moreover, to play a uniquely causative role in the unified circulating system of body and mind. The physiological, mental, and emotional economies of womanhood were all regarded as interdependent. Any aberration in the menstrual flow, Burrows continues, must inevitably create

47

an equivalent form of mental disorder. Similarly, strong emotions could cause menstrual obstructions leading in turn to insanity and death. Burrows cites two noted cases of women who literally died of shame. He distinguishes the mere blush of modesty from the "suffusion of shame": "The blood is here retained, in a peculiar manner, in the capillary vessels, as if the veins were constringed [sic]. This sensation will suppress the menses, or other secretions, has occasioned insanity, and in some instances has even produced death." Thus one woman "became insane on the wedding-night, from shame on sleeping with a man."[3] The medical and psychological literature of the period focused on the interrelations of the nervous and vascular systems in the enclosed system of the female economy. If the menstrual flow were obstructed, and thence denied its usual exit, it would, doctors warned, be forced to flood the brain and thus lead to irreparable psychological breakdown.

The physician's word was also matched by deed, as women increasingly became the subject of medical regulation and control. Public medical writings, along with private diaries and letters of the era, suggest that we must discard our customary image of Victorian middle-class women as isolated from physical contact and understanding of their own bodies, and in its place substitute a (perhaps even more disturbing picture) of women anxiously monitoring the slightest aspect of their bodily functions, constantly under threat of medical intervention in the most overtly physical forms. I will argue that this Victorian concern with regulating the circulation of the female uterine economy only takes on its full historical meaning when read as part of the wider social and economic ideologies of circulation that underpinned the emergent social division of labor within industrial England.

Despite their mutual enmity, both reputable medical writers and quack practitioners (the latter through their ubiquitous advertisements) participated in the social construction of popular images of womanhood that emphasized woman's subjection to the tyranous processes of the menstrual cycle. The significance of the advertisements for female remedies that peppered the pages of provincial mid-nineteenth-century newspapers lies not only in their reiterated message but also in their mode of address. Whereas medical texts constructed images of women for the consumption and direction of male practitioners or, as in the case of many of the domestic medicines produced, for the male clergy and heads of households, these advertisements were specifically addressed to a female audience—and were indeed the only elements within the newspapers of this era specifically targeted for female consumption.[4] The following study arises out of local research that I conducted for work on Charlotte Brontë and nineteenth-century discourses of psychology. The two newspapers from which examples of popular advertising are drawn, *The Leeds Mercury,* a liberal paper, and *The Leeds Intelligencer,* a Tory organ, were both taken by the Brontë family and avidly consumed (the Brontë juvenilia frequently imitates the format of the papers and their specific advertising copy). The sample runs between the years 1830 and 1855 and appears to be fairly representative of the provincial press as a whole during this period.

Both papers, in their coverage of local and national news and in their advertising copy, give a prominence to the material, sexual body which must necessarily undermine any generalized notions about Victorian prudishness. Graphic sexual details were included in court reports and also in the early advertising copy for venereal-disease remedies, which clearly showed no regard for the "cheek of the young person." The terrain of medical advertising, dominated initially by venereal-disease remedies, was increasingly devoted in the 1840s to cures for masturbation (or "certain delusive practices") and to medication for female complaints.[5] The 1840s also witnessed the beginnings, in the pages of *The Lancet,* of the wrathful onslaught of the medical establishment on these "quacks" and their "filth." But as the campaign heats up it becomes clear that the real ground of dispute is not indecency, rather professional territory, prestige, and material gains. All advertisements for medical remedies come under attack (even when the efficacy of the remedy is not disputed), and an extensive onslaught is launched against the use of doctors' names in the advertisements (whether pirated or authorized).[6] The debate offers useful evidence about the prevalence and extent of market penetration established by these remedies. A writer in *The Lancet* calculates that five well-known advertisements appeared throughout the country newspapers and magazines a total of 626 times a week, which would make the expenditure on advertising alone 16,000 pounds per year.[7] Although the advertisements could not achieve the same form of saturation as is now made possible by television, they clearly had a very wide and repetitive circuit of distribution. Some measure of their impact even on the educated public might be gleaned from the fact that the Reverend Brontë, who prided himself on his medical knowledge, recorded in his copy of Graham's *Domestic Medicine* (a standard household text) his family's use of, and response to, various of these remedies.

The advertisements directed specifically at a female audience were distinguished by lengthy preambles and "medical" justifications that reiterated and confirmed contemporary beliefs in the peculiar delicacy of the female system and the pernicious impact of menstruation. Thus an early 1837 advertisement for "Lady Huntingdon's female pills" proclaims that they have "rescued many thousand young persons from an early grave." Their particular efficacy was to be found in "cases of general Debility of the Constitution, in creating appetite, by strengthening the system, removing obstructions, giving relief to those troubled with fainting fits, nervous giddiness, pains in the head. . . ."[8] Such recitations of symptoms functioned almost as a prescriptive list for femininity. In each case, the various forms of female ailments were all associated with "obstructions," the suppression or irregularity of the menses. Pursuing a common practice, this advertisement reinforced its message with dire warnings drawn from contemporary medical opinion:

> A learned Physician very justly observes that the health of females depending on circumstances more complicated and uncertain than that of the other sex, it is the duty of persons entrusted with their care to instruct them in the course they ought to pursue at those periods of life which require the utmost attention to prevent consequences which may render them sickly, infirm, and miserable for the rest of their existence.[9]

Although the rhetoric is highly alarmist, it is no more than was to be found in contemporary medical texts. A possible source would have been William Buchan's *Domestic Medicine* (an eighteenth-century work, constantly reprinted during the nineteenth-century, which laid down the outlines within which the nineteenth-century medical specialization in "female diseases" would develop). Buchan's section on the "Menstrual Discharge" is included under the heading of "Diseases of Women." His argument is that the conduct of a woman at the beginning of her menses would determine both her future health and happiness. Such is her delicacy at this stage that "taking improper food, violent affections of the mind, or catching cold . . . is often sufficient to ruin the health, or render the female ever after incapable of procreation."[10] Buchan's warnings about the dangers of the commencement of the menstruation are supplemented in the advertisement by advice about the necessity of authoritative supervision of the helpless young female, at the mercy of her physical system. The same citation from a learned physician occurred eight years later in an advertisement for the aptly named "Croskell's female corrective pills" (phrasing that suggests it is the very condition of being female that the pills are trying to correct) which were "adapted to those morbid periodic affections peculiar to females."[11]

It is possible that, as was the case in some later American advertising, the condition of obstruction that some of these pills claimed to cure was also that of pregnancy. This association, however, does not feature in the rhetoric of medical opposition to such remedies in the 1840s and 1850s, an omission that suggests abortion was not perceived to be the dominant message of these particular advertisements. Their ambiguous wording, nonetheless, often left this interpretation open to women who were seeking such a remedy. In marketing their wares, the quacks skillfully took over the language and rhetoric of contemporary medicine, manipulating it for their own purposes and simultaneously reinforcing the dominant ideological projections of female weakness and subordination to the body.[12]

The constant refrain throughout the advertisements of this period is that of female vulnerability, and the determining impact of menstrual obstruction. Thus an 1850 advertisement for "Dr Locock's Female Pills," which prevent consumption, remove chlorosis and "all nervous and hysterical affections," cites the opinion of six doctors that "most of the diseases of women are caused by irregularities."[13] (The desire to gain the authority of medical respectability is evidenced by this product which pirated the name of the eminent accoucheur to Queen Victoria.) On a more folksy level, "Widow Welch's Female Pills" were recommended as a "safe and valuable medicine in effectually removing obstructions, and relieving all other inconveniences to which the female frame is liable."[14] The advertisement for Dr. Barker's Female Pills is quite specific on the causative role played by female secretions in provoking illness. His pills are "for regulating the secretions and keeping them in a healthy condition, and for removing all affections depending on irregularities, such as general weakness, nervousness, giddiness, pains in the head, breast, side or stomach."[15] All advertisements for female pills assume a direct continuity between the operation of the menstrual cycle and mental health. Their threats and warnings were supplemented by advertisements for remedies for nervous affections which, if left untreated, the readers are informed, are liable to result in insanity.[16]

Medical advertising did not offer its message in isolation, however; to appreciate its impact fully it must be read in conjunction with the social and political reporting that defined its context. The medical remedies and texts touted in the *Leeds Intelligencer* of January 4, 1851, for example, include *The Medical Adviser,* which offers help with extirpating the evils of masturbation and venereal disease, Kearsley's Original Widow Welch's Female Pills, "a safe and reliable Medicine in effectually removing obstructions, and relieving all other inconveniences to which the female frame is liable," and Holloway's Pills. These were billed as "an infallible cure for female complaints." They were "searching, cleansing, and yet invigorating" for "the maiden, the mother and the middle aged," swiftly undertaking their task to "remove every species of irregularity." Under the mellifluous three *m*'s lie the three biological stages of womanhood: puberty, pregnancy, and what was termed the "climacteric," or menopause. In each case the dark obstructions within the body that cause irregular flow are to be sought out and "cleansed"; invigorating purity will result from this ritual purgation that rids the body of "morbid blood," restoring the modest maiden to a state where surface appearance is not belied by the state of her bodily secretions.

Set against these advertisements was an account of the recent lectures at the Leeds Mechanics' Institute, including that by Dr. Samuel Smiles on "Self-Help in Man" and the Rev. W. M. Guest on "Mental Improvement and Discipline." In both instances, the activities of control and regulation are at issue; there is, however, a crucial gender distinction. Whereas the woman, rendered helpless by the tyranny of her body, must resort to external medication and supervision to regulate the flow of her secretions, and hence her physical and mental health, the man in Smilesian ideology needs nothing more than his own internal resources to bring about the requisite self-control that will enable him to climb the social ladder. With enough "self-help" the laborer will become the "self-made" man of mid-Victorian ideology—an expression that perpetuates the ideological erasure of female agency. These juxtaposed images of female helplessness and male self-help are indicative, I would suggest, of the increasingly rigid demarcation of gender roles that was taking place in the nineteenth century: a transformation over which the medical establishment presided, lending and indeed also in part deriving their growing prestige and authority from this process. With the development of the new specialty in women's diseases, the male medical profession arrogated to itself the exclusive right to diagnose the pathology of both the female mind and body, offering thus a forceful object lesson in the power of male science to read and control the mysteries of nature.[17]

A blatant ideological defense of this position, which in more subtle forms underpinned the assumption of authority in the medical profession as a whole, was offered by the obstetrician W. Tyler Smith in the pages of the *The Lancet*. According to Smith, "the state of the obstetric art in any country may be taken as a measure of the respect and value of its people for the female sex; and this, in turn, may be taken as a tolerably true indication of the standard of its civilization." Contemporary England, he claimed, placed a "value" on women that had never been equaled, a value that he focuses, significantly, on the image of women as a passive vehicle of reproduction: "It may be said that no life seems so valuable as that of a woman in childbirth." To preserve this "value," however, women had to be excluded from the labor market, restricted to the "natural" sphere of reproductive labor. For Smith, the profession of obstetrics was "degraded" as long as it permitted female midwives to participate; true "respect" toward women, and thus the triumph of civilization, was signaled by the transference of "the allegiance of the lying-in woman from Lucina to Apollo"—from the incompetent female midwife to omnicompetent male science.[18] Such a seemingly contradictory formulation, with its simultaneous elevation and abasement of the woman, reducing her from an active participant in the labor market to a passive bodily existence to be controlled by male expertise, is indicative of the ways in which the ideological deployment of gender roles operated to facilitate and sustain the changing structure of familial and market relations in Victorian England.

The social effectiveness of Victorian gender ideology derived to a large degree from the lack of apparent novelty in the formulations. Women were not for the first time being associated with the forces of the body; nor were they thereby being cast forth from their other ideological role of spiritualizing and civilizing force. Throughout Western culture, the male/female divide has operated as a crucial site of ideological deployment. Although it has been articulated through a fairly constant set of interrelated oppositions, most notably those of mind/body and culture/nature, its formulations are never stable. Woman, for example, though rarely identified with mind, can emerge on either side of the nature/culture divide, depending on the specific historical and social context of the argument. With changing economic and social formations, different aspects of these polarities are mobilized, often in seemingly contradictory conjunctions, their articulation both containing and contributing to wider social tensions and conflicts. From the late eighteenth century onward, we find that the traditional, rather undefined, associations between woman and the body are strengthened, particularized and codified in medical science. The introduction by Linnaeus of a sexual system of plant classification in the eighteenth century was indicative of a whole shift to a taxonomy of gender that was to emerge in the biological and social sciences in the nineteenth century. Victorian scientists and social theorists increasingly sought out and extolled biological evidence of the sexual division of functions in all forms of life, transforming the interpretative map of both natural and social existence into one continuous chart of gender polarity.

To try to explain why the study of biological differentiation should have been invested with such urgency at this period is to become involved in a complex network of determinants whose interconnections and formations have not yet been fully explored. Until we have a firmer grasp, for example, of the precise relations of women to the nineteenth-century labor market, any explanation of the Victorian preoccupation with biological differentiation must necessarily remain partial and exploratory. One obvious impetus for this interest was the changing structure of social relations under the emerging industrial economy: the increasing social division of labor that took place both on the factory floor and in the growing bureaucracy that sustained the industrial system, and the concomitant further domestication of the middle-class woman. The intersection of class and gender ideology during this era is peculiarly instructive. Although middle- and working-class women were clearly situated in different relations to the labor market, both were equally subject to the reigning ideology that operated across class lines, emphasizing domesticity, and woman's role as biological reproducer of labor, rather than as active participant in the labor market. While middle-class women were thus held firmly within the confines of the home, supplying (in accordance with Malthusian notions of underconsumption) a leisured class of consumers, women of the working class were transformed into a more docile workforce who could be slotted into or retired out of the labor market, in accordance with the specific demands of each industry and the cycles of trade. Within this ideological formation, woman was figured simultaneously as angel, divorced from the material realm of the marketplace, and as body, devoted to the uncontrollable processes of material reproduction. The potential contradictions between these two models emerge strongly within Victorian formulations of gender roles.

Until recently, feminist criticism has tended to argue that the Victorian ideology of female domesticity was designed to suppress and control the threat of female sexuality. The problem should, however, be posed the other way around: Why, at this specific historical period, should women have been perceived as being in possession of a disruptive sexuality that needed to be disciplined and controlled? Given that there was not an upsurge of female sexual rampancy at this period, and no more than the first murmurings of female social discontent, the answer would seem to lie outside the domain of female sexuality *per se*. Although many factors are once again in play (including the displacement of class antagonisms into gender terms), I would suggest that one strong impetus behind Victorian ideologies of womanhood springs not from the need to control women, rather from the problems involved in assimilating *men* to the new conditions of the labor market.

With the increasing social division of labor, the question of sexual difference became the focus of ideological attention; concern with the partitioning of economic roles was displaced metonymically onto the individual body. By the early-Victorian period gender demarcations in social and medical texts were mobilized within forms that responded directly to the contradictory formulations of laissez-faire economics. In the social and economic discourse of the era, man was figured both as a rational, self-interested actor, in full control of his own destiny, and also as a mere cog within the larger machinery of industrial labor, without free agency or self-determination. By the 1820s and 1830s the speed of industrial transformation had accelerated, and revivified notions of the division of labor were brought to bear on the disciplining of the labor force. Political economists such as Andrew Ure and Charles Babbage extolled the virtues of the machine as a corrective to the indiscipline of labor and portrayed in loving terms the industrial ideal as that of "a vast automaton, composed of various mechanical and intellectual organs, acting in uninterrupted concert for the production of a common object, all of them being subordinated to a self-regulated moving force."[19] Both Tory and radical opponents of contemporary developments in industrialism appropriated the notion of man as machine to voice their criticisms. Peter Gaskell expressed the fear that human labor would lose all social value under the industrial system: Man "will have lost all free agency, and will be as much a part of the machines around him as the wheels on cranks which communicate motion."[20] Critics and apologists of industrialism alike proposed a similar model of man as automaton, a model seemingly confirmed on the factory floor with its endless subdivision of manual tasks and the subordination of human labor to the requirements of machinery.

The early Victorians were thus forced to address, in terms very different from those employed by Descartes, the interface between man and machinery. Yet at the same time that man was spoken of as a mindless machine he was also being celebrated, in accordance with the ideology of laissez-faire economics, as a rational, independent actor, in full control of his own activities in the marketplace, and capable of rising upward through the social ranks solely through the exertion of his own powers. In the light of these social contradictions, I would suggest that Victorian ideologies of gender functioned as a displaced form of resolution. Notions of gender differentiation fulfilled the ideological role of allowing the male sex to renew their faith in personal autonomy and control. Unlike women, men were not prey to the forces of the body, the unsteady oscillations of which mirrored the uncertain flux of social circulation; rather, they were their own masters—not automatons or mindless parts of the social machinery but self-willed individuals, living incarnations of the rational individualists and self-made men of economic theory. The disruptive social forces that had to be so decisively channeled and regulated to ensure mastery and controlled circulation in the economic sphere were metonymically represented, however, in the domestic realm, in the internal bodily processes of the woman in the home.

We are all familiar with the Victorian trope of the angel in the house: The male returns from his contaminating material labors in the outer world to be spiritually refreshed by his angel within the inner sanctum of the home. This outer/inner polarity existed, however, in direct conjunction with another formulation of the inner/outer divide: women were outwardly fair, but internally they contained threatening sources of pollution. A representative example of the Victorian ability to maintain seemingly contradictory models of femininity is offered by Dr. J. G. Millingen's 1848 work, *The Passions; or Mind and Matter*:

> If the corporeal agency is thus powerful in man, its tyrannic influence will more frequently cause the misery of the gentler sex. Woman, with her exalted spiritualism, is more forcibly under the control of matter; her sensations are more vivid and acute, her sympathies more irresistible. She is less under the influence of the brain than the uterine system, the plexi of abdominal nerves, and irritation of the spinal cord; in her, a hysteric predisposition is incessantly predominating from the dawn of puberty.[21]

Two traditional tropes are here combined: Victorian medical textbooks demonstrated not only woman's biological fitness and adaptation to the sacred role of homemaker, but also her terrifying subjection to the forces of the body. At once angel and demon, woman came to represent both the civilizing power that would cleanse the male from contamination in the brutal world of the economic market and also the rampant, uncontrolled excesses of the material economy. The medical specificity of Millingen's terms, of uterine system and spinal irritation, gives scientific authority to notions of female pathology. Woman, with her constant predisposition to hysteria, is a figure of radical instability. As in the social economy, surface order rests on a precarious balancing of forces, ready to be disrupted and thrown into convulsions at the slightest disturbance of equilibrium.

A fictional representation of this duality is offered in one of Charlotte Brontë's juvenilia fragments, where the passionate Zenobia Percy is figured as "a noble creature both in mind and body, though full of the blackest defects: a flawed diamond; a magnificent landscape trenched with dark drains; virgin gold basely adulterated with brass."[22] The rhetoric of drains and sewers was not reserved for that outcast group of women, the prostitutes. Like the industrial social body itself, the body of woman promises virgin gold, but then contaminates prospectors with the muckiness of brass. The "magnificent landscape trenched with dark drains" stands as a figure of the industrial organism: the noble progress of industrial development carries with it a threatening inner pollution, spawned in the dark recesses of the slums, which has to be controlled, purged, and cleansed, or even removed by surgery. That prime ideologue of the Victorian economy, Herbert Spencer, observed with reference to the social disease engendered by the socially useless poor who were clogging and obstructing the system, that a surgeon would be foolish "to let his patient's disease progress to a fatal issue, rather than inflict pain by an operation." Indeed, in a natural social order, unencumbered by state interference in the form of poor laws, society would "excrete" its useless and unhealthy members."[23] Women, with their concealed inner recesses and harboring of polluted blood, contained naturally within them the sewers that so preoccupied the sanitary reformers of the mid-century and that figured in contemporary rhetoric as the breeding ground of social disease. One physician, for example, described the uterus as "the sewer of all the excrements existing in the body."[24] Calls for social sanitary reform were matched by those for "mental sanitary reform" of which women, with their unstable physical systems and thus predisposition to insanity were to be one of the primary targets.[25] The Victorian era witnessed the growth of a new medical speciality, the diseases of women and children (a category grouping suggestive of women's uncontrolled state), as well as unprecedented medical interference in the regulation of the female uterine economy—a regulation that extended at its most extreme into the sphere of surgical excision.[26]

Intuitively, one might assume that, as in other cultures, the sense of pollution associated with menstruation in Victorian England would be focused on the flow itself, on the mysterious outpouring of blood. Contrary to such expectations, however, it seems that it was not the menstrual flow *per se* that caused alarm, rather its suppression and retention. In this regard the marketing of female remedies mirrored the concerns of the medical establishment: the primary ill the pills were designed to alleviate was not the menstrual flow itself, and any accompanying physical pain, rather its obstruction and suppression. Whereas the primary categories of male sexual disfunction in the Victorian era, masturbation and spermatorrhoea, focused on the male need to retain vital force and to expend capital only in productive fashion, the primary form of female pathology was that of the *retention* of internal secretions.

Spermatorrhoea was itself an invention of the Victorian economic and sexual imaginary, a dreaded "disease" whose definitive symptom was the uncontrolled emission of semen. According to William Acton, it was "a state of enervation produced, at least primarily, by the loss of *semen*."[27] The medical elaboration of this disease drew on earlier strictures against the undisciplined "spending" of vital force in masturbation, a vice that functioned in turn as a primary ideological figure of the horrors awaiting men who violated the sacred economic and social rules of self-control.[28] As in the case of representations of female "obstructions," doctors and quacks alike participated in the social popularization of ideas of spermatorrhoea. Although some doctors dissented, and others tried to distance themselves from the unscrupulous ways in which quacks were manipulating worried males, both sides of medical practice basically collaborated in fanning the social fears focused on this particularly worrying disruption of self-control.[29]

The fashionable diseases of mid-nineteenth-century England were thus marked by a crucial gender distinction: While male health was believed to be based on self-control, woman's health depended on her very *inability* to control her body. Any exertion of the mind, whether of intellectual effort, or fierce emotion, might prove fatal, it was suggested, in creating a stoppage of menstrual flow. Women should therefore concentrate on dulling the mind, allowing the processes of their body to proceed unimpeded by mental obstruction. Indeed, the very possibility of female health depended on the woman's ultimate inability consciously to interrupt her menstrual flow. As in Brontë's vision of Zenobia, female identity was defined by the condition of *excess,* an excess that had to be sluiced away through her "dark drains" if it was not to flow back and pollute the entire system. Samuel Hibbert, writing on woman's predisposition to hysteria in the early part of the nineteenth century, observed that "when the growth of the form is nearly completed, the circulating fluid necessary for the future support of the body is in superabundance, and unless corrected in the delicate system of the female, must . . . necessarily acquire a power of rendering unduly intense the feelings of the mind."[30] The intensity of emotion associated with womanhood is directly aligned with the flow of bodily fluids; only if such "superabundance" is drained from the body can emotional tranquillity be preserved.

By the mid-century, this model of female "excess" was incorporated into the new theories of the relationship between the sympathetic and spinal nervous systems, and into physiological theories of the conservation of energy which, regarding the body as a closed system, suggested the ready translatability of emotional and physiological force. In his 1853 study of hysteria, Robert Carter argues that there existed a "natural tendency of an emotion to discharge itself either through the muscular, the secreting, or the sanguiferous system."[31] Following through this notion of the interchangeability of emotional and physiological energy, he suggests that if women lack social outlets for sexual expression, they will be thrown into a state of hysteria.[32] Although arguments have been made for the modernity of Carter's thought, his arguments are solidly based on a development of mid-Victorian theories on the "perversion of the secretions."[33] In common with his contemporaries, he believed that the mental and physical health of woman depended on ridding the body of any obstructions to the free circulation of internal energy.

The fears of obstruction, accumulated waste, and stockpiling that dominated Victorian theories of the female economy were not confined to this one arena of concern. Like the rhetoric of male self-control that spread across medical and economic discourse, these preoccupations also figured prominently in contemporary writings on laissez-faire economics. Herbert Spencer, one of the primary social spokesmen of the era, argued fiercely for a literal, rather than a simple metaphorical, relationship between the internal dynamics of a physiological and a social organism. The two organizing categories for the social, as for the bodily organism, were, he maintained, those of waste and repair: "What in commercial affairs we call *profit*, answers to the excess of nutrition over waste in a living body."[34] Taking his cue from the chemist Justus von Liebig he argues for a direct analogy between the circulation of blood and that of money, concluding that there is a homologous relation between "the blood in a living body and the consumable and circulating commodities in the body-politic."[35] Viewed within these terms, the retention of the menstrual discharge would thus be the overwhelming of profit and nutrition by the poisonous attributes of waste. Free, unimpeded flow is Spencer's primary category of social health; any blockage or interference would overthrow the system as a whole. Thus government action to prevent the issue of notes by local banks would lead to extensive disruption elsewhere—the excess of the local bankers' capital would give rise to wild unregulated forms of speculation which would threaten the stability of the entire system.[36] Just as blockage in the female economy would lead to hysteria and insanity, so in the wider social system it led to its equivalent economic form: uncontrolled speculation. Spencer's physiological theories of the social economy place on a material base the traditional associations between the fickle, uncontrollable operations of credit and the female sex.

Although Spencer himself did not explicitly address the relationship between the female and the social body, one finds throughout the medical and social rhetoric of the period an increasing intensity of focus on this issue. The cycles of production and reproduction are repeatedly aligned and compared. According to the obstetrician Tyler Smith in an article in *The Lancet,* the uterus was the "organ of circulation of the species."[37] The cycle of reproduction had to be policed and controlled to ensure the quality and continuity of social production. A woman's womb was figured both as a sacred font originating life, and as a crucial stage in the machinery of material social manufacture. Contemporary medical accounts emphasized the criteria of efficiency and the productive channeling of physiological force. Class anxieties fueled these discussions. The idle middle-class woman, a direct product of the increasing social division of labor, was yet made the subject of attack by the selfsame classes that had produced her. The alarming fertility of the working classes was contrasted with the supposed barrenness of the middle-class woman, whose idle and luxurious life-style, it was argued, created the internal obstructions of secretions that led both to insanity and sterility.[38]

William Buchan's *Domestic Medicine* outlined the complaint against the middle-class woman that was to a gain a groundswell of popular support in the Victorian era. Barrenness, which was "chiefly owing to an obstruction or irregularity of the menstrual flux," was to be regarded as a disease afflicting only the indolent and affluent female; the poor remained free from its effects.[39] Early-nineteenth-century accounts added the "savage" to this list, contrasting the seeming fertility and lack of labor pains of "primitive" females to that of their diseased, "civilized" counterparts. Buchan's observations on menstruation offer a perfect exemplum of the contradictory injunctions that were to govern Victorian prescriptions for womanhood. Women are simultaneously castigated for idleness and yet also warned that they must treat themselves with great delicacy during menstruation, making sure not only that they protected the body from cold and exertion, but that they also similarly protected the mind. The female should force herself to keep calm and cheerful during her menses since "every part of the animal economy is influenced by the passions, but none more so than this. Anger, fear, grief, and other affections of the mind, often occasion obstructions of the menstrual flux, which prove absolutely incurable."[40] The foundations of the cherished Victorian image of female placidity are here being laid. Woman's "mission" is to try and suppress all mental life so that the self-regulating processes of her animal economy can proceed in peace. Female thought and passion, like government intervention in the Spencerian model of the economy, created blockages and interference, throwing the whole organism into a state of disease.

With the development of medical specialization in the diseases of women during the Victorian era, the preoccupation with the functions and role of menstruation became more intense. Despite extensive research, however, the menstrual flow still remained, by the 1850s, threateningly inexplicable.[41] Perhaps more than the self-evident functions of childbirth, menstruation became an obsessive focus for the male imagination, symbolizing, with its bloody, uncontrollable flow, the dark otherness of womanhood, the suppressed term behind the ideological projections of female purity and spirituality. Many commentators still followed the traditional associations that linked menstruation with the state of sexual heat in animals. Thus C. Locock, in his article on menstruation in John Forbes's 1833 *Cyclopaedia of Practical*

Medicine, bases his theory of menstruation on the resemblance between the state of the uterus in a woman menstruating and the appearance in "rabbits killed during the state of genital excitement, usually called the time of heat." Even in the 1854 revised reprint there is no reference to the ovaries: the discharge is still described as the consequence of "a peculiar periodical condition of the blood-vessels of the uterus, fitting it for impregnation, which condition is analogous to "heat" in the inferior animals."[42]

Menstruation was regarded as an outward sign of the threatening sexual and reproductive excess of the female body, an excess that caused her to vibrate indiscriminately to all external stimuli, as in the account of the "enchantment" exercised by the sight of a soldier's red uniform on the body of "a young female just bursting into womanhood":

> This *enchantment*—which it literally is—this infatuation, is often due to the unrecognised reaction of the physical appearance of the tempter upon the mind of his victim, untrained to self-control, predisposed to the allurement by an excess of reproductive energy, and irresistibly impelled forward to the gratification of the obscure, deep-felt longings he excites by an overstimulated nervous system.[43]

The traditional scenario of the fairy tale is reversed: the princess is not lulled to sleep or imprisoned by enchantment, rather stimulated into frenetic activity. Overwhelmed by the uncontrollable processes of her own body, the young female must turn to male medical guidance (or popular remedies) if she is to avoid precipitating herself into a state of permanent nervous disease or insanity. The obstruction of menstruation, viewed as the outward sign of sexual heat, represented the damming up of sexuality, causing pollution and implosion throughout the entire mental, emotional, and physiological economy.

The double binds involved in these prescriptions for femininity are legion. Women were expected to be more controlled than men, but were also presumed to be physiologically incapable of imposing control. As vessels of receptivity, doomed to vibrate uncontrollably both to external stimuli and to the functions of their uterine system, they are helpless prisoners of their own bodies. All paths of active self-help also seem foreclosed: if the internal "excess" of reproductive enegy is suppressed or obstructed in its outward flow, then insanity will ensue. If, however, it is acted on, the resulting "immodest" behavior would immediately call for the certification of insanity. (Victorian psychiatric accounts cite the eruption of immodesty in a previously well-behaved girl as one of the most telling symptoms of insanity.)

For the Victorian woman, the threat of insanity loomed large, figuring in the rhetoric of some medical practitioners as almost the determining condition of womanhood. Psychiatrists, or "alienists" as they were known, frequently debated amongst themselves whether women were actually more prone to insanity, and whether they constituted a larger proportion of inmates in asylums; but such measured discussion was overbalanced by their own examples and illustrations, and indeed by the very categories of insanity they formulated. A list of forms of insanity, drawn up in the 1860s by Dr. Skae, includes as separate categories: hysterical mania, amenorrhoeal mania, puerperal mania, mania of pregnancy, mania of lactation, climacteric mania, ovariomania, and the intriguing category of "post-connubial mania."[44] The male reproductive system drew no equivalent listing; there was no form of insanity specifically theorized as a male disease. Throughout mid-Victorian discussions this gender discrepancy was maintained. Although spermatorrhoea became an obsessive concern in the 1850s, it never entered medical lists as an independent cause of insanity. Masturbation was specified as a prevalent cause, but the literature here referred both to male and female figures.[45]

In a table of the causes of insanity published in *The Lancet,* in 1845, the only sex-specific causes are associated with the physical processes of the female body, including, notably, the suppression of the habitual evacuation of menstruation.[46] According to J. C. Bucknill and D. H. Tuke, uterine disorders, and suppressed or irregular menstruation, accounted for 10 percent of all female admissions to asylums.[47] Even higher figures were offered in other works. Accounts by alienists of their female patients all gave extraordinary narrative prominence to the state of the menstrual flow. In cases where a theoretical connection is not drawn explicitly, it is nonetheless established by association, as in Esquirol's account of Madam de C who "at the period of menstruation, was attacked with hysterical monomania." Esquirol's diagnoses include a woman "who had become insane at her first menstrual period, and who was cured at forty-two years of age, at the disappearance of her menses" and a girl who was in a state of dementia for ten years with the suppression of her menses and was cured on the day that they flowed.[48]

A preoccupation with menstrual flow was not confined, however, to the arena of mental pathology. It was equally prevalent in the various *Domestic Medicines* produced for home consumption, and more general medical discussions of female health. I am going to take here, as a guide to mid-nineteenth-century perceptions of the female body, John Forbes's 1833 *Cyclopaedia of Practical Medicine.* The list of specific female diseases in Forbes, and particularly those connected with menstruation, is of impressive length. The *Cyclopaedia* offers separate articles on amenorrhoea (retention and suppression of the menses), dysmenorrhoea (acute pain during menstruation), menorrhagia (morbidly profuse menstruation), the pathology of menstruation, and leucorrhoea (white vaginal discharge) as well as discussions of chlorosis, pregnancy, hysteria, and puerperal diseases. To read through the entries is to gain an impression of a near-hysterical male anxiety focused on the flow of female secretions, and in particular those of menstruation—a hysteria whose impact on the female psyche must inevitably have been to create the sense of existing in an almost permanent state of pathology. The catamenia (or discharge) could be too thick or too thin, too profuse or too scanty, too frequent or too scarce; though when it ceased to flow, womanhood itself was at an end, since medical texts insistently told their readers that women were attractive to men (and thus truly female) only during the period of activity of their reproductive organs.[49] Womanhood itself is thus figured as a form of pathology: only when polluted and out of control (and thus not "feminine") could females be socially accredited with the title of true woman. Medical literature warned of the dangers surrounding the period of the climacteric or menopause which, it was believed, would often put an end not only to womanhood, but to life itself. Buchan observes that the "period of life at which the menses ceases to flow is likewise very critical to the sex. The stoppage of any customary evacuation, however small, is sufficient to disorder the whole frame, and often to destroy life itself. Hence it comes to pass, that so many women either fall into chronic disorders, or die about this time."[50]

Worry about menstruation for the Victorian woman could not be confined solely to its commencement or its surcease. Locock, the famous accoucheur to Queen Victoria, who contributed virtually all the articles on the female secretions in the *Cyclopaedia,* informs his readers that "during the menstrual period, when quite regularly and properly performed, no medical treatment is required."[51] The question of proper "performance" he continues, however, should always be the focus of careful attention of both the woman and her medical adviser who should always inquire as to their state. Despite Locock's disclaimer, the very suggestion that medical treatment might be required under normal circumstances offers some inkling of the degree of medical intervention to which middle-class Victorian women were subject. Given the innumerable criteria of quality control applied to the menstrual flow, and the difficulties of assessing normality, female anxiety could only be allayed by medical opinion, or by ingesting "female corrective pills." The medical rhetoric through which the doctors in the new specialist field of female diseases sought to make themselves indispensable also contributed, ironically, to the growing importance of their rivals, the purveyors of the so-called "quack" medicines.

The measures suggested by Locock for inducing normal flow in the female body might appear to us quite draconian, but his descriptions—for example, of treating amenorrhoea by applications of electricity or galvanism to the pelvis, and of applying leeches once a month to the groins, labia, as uteri, or (interestingly) the feet—are reiterated in the practical medical advice disseminated in the *Lancet* and W. Braithwaite's *Retrospect of Practical Medicine and Surgery* (a national journal which came out of the Leeds School of Medicine).[52] An 1847 article on uterine diseases in the *Retrospect* suggests that "When the menses are interrupted, a few leeches ought immediately to be applied to the uterus, and if the patient be plethoric, the lancet may be used; but the period ought not to pass over without detracting some blood, either from the uterus or its immediate neighbourhood." "Half-periods" should also be forestalled by the application of leeches a day or two before they were likely to occur.[53] The article suggests the terror aroused by the idea of obstructed, or, less importantly, indiscriminate flow. Blood should be drawn from even neighboring areas, rather than let a month pass by without flow.

The controversy surrounding the use of the speculum in the 1840s gives further indication of the degree of medical intervention to which middle-class Victorian women were subject. The more research was pursued, the more it seemed to be established that a majority of English women were in fact suffering from some form of uterine disease, particularly those of congestion of the uterus and inflammation of the cervix. Robert Lee's objections to the practice of using the speculum to cauterize the cervix gives an indication of its widespread nature. He writes in the *Retrospect,* 1850, to complain, that "it is impossible that any disease of the os uteri, or any other part of the body, can require twice or thrice a week for six or nine months, the alternate application of leeches and caustic through the speculum, in the manner which has recently been recommended and practised."[54] The speculum did have its enthusiastic supporters, however, as evidenced in Protheroe Smith's lyrical depiction of the virtues of his new design of speculum which "accomplishes the object, never heretofore attained, of employing *simultaneously* both visual inspection and tactile examination."[55] Technology here offers the fulfillment of the male erotic dream: the male gaze could follow the fingers and penetrate into the most hidden recesses of the female anatomy.

Carter's ill-humored observations on the use of the speculum in his study on hysteria confirm the widespread nature of the practice. Recent researches on uterine disease have revealed, he observes, that "a very large number of our countrywomen are invalided by some of its numerous forms. It is scarcely possible at present for an hysterical girl to have no acquaintances among the many women who are subjected to the speculum and caustic, and who love to discuss their symptoms and to narrate the sensations which attend upon the treatment."[56] Carter's vision is that of lascivious women, luring men on to examine their sexual organs, and to delight their feelings by applying caustic to their cervix. Such practices can lead respectable, middle-class and unmarried females, he observes, into the "mental and moral condition of prostitutes."[57] Subjected to such forcible medical penetration, women are doubly victimized—made to bear the burden of guilt evoked by male anxiety over their own erotic arousal. While no doubt exaggerated, Carter's claims do draw attention to the ways in which the rising medical industry devoted to investigating female diseases created and confirmed its object, establishing on medical authority that a majority of the female population of England was in a state of pathological disorder.

Although engaged in fighting a territorial dispute, the medical profession and the quacks, or purveyors of popular medical remedies, actually colluded in creating the justificatory grounds for their separate practices, producing and maintaining an ideological projection of woman held helplessly within the thralls of her own body. Both parties, I have argued, were concerned less with menstrual flow *per se* than with *obstruction*. The fashionable male diseases of the era, masturbation and spermatorrhoea, were concerned with the problems of loss, and the need to *conserve* vital force; in a physiological version of Freud's later theories of sublimation and displacement, medical discussions of spermatorrhoea argued that unused sperm could actually be absorbed back into the bodily economy.[58] Notions of female pathology, however, focused on woman's need constantly to sluice her internal drains, to ensure that she did not retain within her the polluting and disruptive forces of sexual energy.

The nineteenth-century obsession with the pathology of the uterine economy can only be fully understood, I have suggested, if viewed in the light of the increasing social division of labor under industrial capitalism, and the inherent contradictions within the ideological projections of laissez-faire economics. Ideologies of gender differentiation offered a displaced resolution to the contradictory economic figuration of man as both autonomous, rational actor, in control of his own destiny, and also as a mere unit controlled and determined by the wider operations of the social organism of which he formed a part. Manhood was articulated against and defined by its opposite: while the attributes of self-control and self-help were aligned with masculinity, woman was increasingly viewed as an automaton at the mercy of her body. Like the external economy, however, she also represented a threatening instability of physical forces that needed to be regulated and controlled. I would like, however, to end on a lighter note, which nonetheless suggests the continuing ideological force of these constructions of femininity throughout the nineteenth century. In a famous London trial in 1896, a wealthy American woman, Mrs. Castle, was let off from the charge of shoplifting on the grounds that she was suffering from kleptomania, a disease that one later psychological diagnosis traced back to the effects of "suppressed menstruation."[59] The hoarding of blood, it would seem, leads directly to a desire to hoard material goods, outside the legitimate circuit of the free-flowing monetary economy. Here Herbert Spencer's analogies between the flow of blood and the circulation of commodities are given literal embodiment.

Notes

1. George Man Burrows, *Commentaries on the Causes, Forms, Symptoms, and Treatment, Moral and Medical, of Insanity* (London: 1828; reprint. New York: Arno Press, 1976), 146.

2. For a discussion of earlier uses of the imagery of a thermometer and barometer, and its often overt sexual implications, see Terry Castle, "The Female Thermometer," *Representations* 17 (1987): 1–27.

3. Burrows, 12–13. The case cited is drawn from the work of J. E. D. Esquirol.

4. The *Domestic Medicine* owned by the Brontës, for example, states in the subtitle that it is "intended as a medical guide for the use of clergymen, families, and students in medicine." (T. J. Graham, *Modern Domestic Medicine* [London: Simpkin, Marshall et al. 1826])

5. In the early years of the sample there were comparatively few advertisements for products in the newspapers, and those we find, as throughout this period, were primarily medical, interspersed with announcements for recently published books. The real advertising industry only arises with the abolition of advertising tax in 1853, and of newspaper stamp duty in 1855. For further details of the rise of newspaper advertising see: Lucy Brown, *Victorian News and Newspapers* (Oxford: Oxford University Press, 1985); Alan J. Lee, *The Origins of the Popular Press in England 1855—1914* (London: Croom Helm, 1976); Diana and Geoffrey Hindley, *Advertising in Victorian England 1837—1901* (London: Wayland, 1972). Although it was possible to offer pictorial advertising from the 1840s, it was not until the 1870s that the real explosion occurred in that area. Advertisers until then tended to prefer the constant repetition of the same printed message. From 1846 the *Newspaper Press Directory* was produced which listed all the provincial papers where advertising might be placed (the *Leeds Mercury* was given a particularly favorable billing as the best advertising medium for Yorkshire and the northeast counties).

6. The unfortunate Dr. Basham, for example, who had happened to note the beneficial effects of Carrara Water is severely taken to task: "What if the Carrara Water have virtue? Is it not indisputably a patent, a quack medicine? . . . would Dr. Basham fasten a moral poison on the profession, for the sake of another palliative of dyspepsia?" (*The Lancet* 1[1846]; 257–8). The widespread nature of the practice of employing medical "testimonials" in advertising is suggested by the editorial complaint that "the public cannot drink bitter ale without having it invested with the eclat of a physician's prescription" (*The Lancet* 1 [1846]: 225).

7. *The Lancet* 2 (1845): 564.

8. *Leeds Intelligencer,* 25 February 1837.

9. *Leeds Intelligencer,* 25 February 1837.

10. William Buchan, *Domestic medicine: or a treatise on the prevention and cure of diseases by regimen and simple medicines,* 6th ed. (London: W. Strahan, 1779), 270.

11. *Leeds Mercury,* 11 January 1845.

12. For an account of the campaign against abortion, and the advertisement of abortifacients, in America during the latter half of the nineteenth century see Carl N. Degler, *At Odds: Women and the Family in America from the Revolution to the Present* (Oxford: Oxford University Press, 1980), 228–37. Sarah Stage, in *Female Complaints: Lydia Pinkham and the Business of Women's Medicine* (New York: W. W. Norton, 1979), suggests that while the Pinkham company did not overtly push the abortifacient potentiality of this all-purpose remedy, they also did not directly try to discourage such interpretations. In *Birth Control in Nineteenth-Century England* (New York: Holmes and Meier, 1978), Angus McLaren presents a detailed account of the upsurge of advertising for contraceptives and abortifacients in England in the 1890s. Richard Allen Soloway's work, *Birth Control and the Population Question in England, 1877–1930* (Chapel Hill: University of North Carolina Press, 1982) offers a general survey of the field in this later period, but does not focus on the role of advertising.

13. *Leeds Intelligencer,* 2 February 1850.

14. *Leeds Mercury,* 18 January 1845. Other variations on this theme include the "only genuine Widow Welch's pills prepared by Mrs. Smithers," which were "justly celebrated for all female complaints, nervous disorders . . . and particularly for irregularities in the female system" (*Leeds Mercury,* 3 January 1852); and "Frampton's Pills of Health: For Females these pills are most

truly excellent, removing all obstructions, the distressing headache so very prevalent with the sex; depression of spirits, dulness of sight, nervous affections" and problems with the complexion (*Leeds Mercury*, 5 June 1852).

15. *Leeds Intelligencer*, 15 March 1851.

16. Dr. Bennett offered to cure "all those distressing symptoms which betoken a disordered state of the Nervous system, and which too frequently result in confirmed insanity." (*Leeds Intelligencer*, 10 May 1851).

17. In the spheres of obstetrics, and psychiatry, female midwives and asylum keepers were subject to exceedingly hostile attacks in the medical literature. The nineteenth century witnessed the debasement of social prestige for the midwife, and the phasing out of women from positions of command in lunatic asylums. For details of these professional struggles see: Jean Donnison, *Midwives and Medical Men: A History of Inter-Professional Rivalries and Women's Rights* (London: Heinemann, 1977); and Elaine Showalter, *The Female Malady: Women, Madness, and English Culture, 1830–1980* (New York: Pantheon, 1985).

18. W. Tyler Smith, "Introductory Lecture to a Course of Lectures on Obstetricy, Delivered at the Hunterian School of Medicine, 1847–48," *The Lancet* 2 (1847), 371.

19. Andrew Ure, *The Philosophy of Manufactures,* quoted in, Maxine Berg, *The Machinery Question and the Making of Political Economy 1815–1848* (Cambridge: Cambridge University Press, 1980), 199.

20. Peter Gaskell, *Artisans and Machinery,* quoted in Berg, 265. I am indebted to this latter work for much of the material in this section.

21. J. G. Millingen, *The Passions; or Mind and Matter. Illustrated by Considerations on Hereditary Insanity* (London: J. and D. Darling, 1848), 157. Millingen had been a resident at the famous Middlesex Lunatic Asylum at Hanwell.

22. "A Peep into a Picture Book," in *The Miscellaneous and Unpublished Writings of Charlotte and Patrick Branwell Brontë,* ed. T. J. Wise and J. A. Symington (Oxford: Basil Blackwell, 1936), 358.

23. Herbert Spencer, *Social Statics* (London: John Chapman, 1851), 323–24.

24. Quoted in Stage, 70.

25. John Hawkes, "On the Increase of Insanity," *Journal of Psychological Medicine and Mental Pathology* 10 (1857):520. Although the emphasis in this article falls on the "mental sanitary reform" of the working classes, women, that other troublesome class, were also one of the ideological and practical targets.

26. For a detailed account of the Victorian practice of clitoridectomy, see Showalter, *The Female Malady,* 75–78.

27. William Acton, *The Functions and Disorders of the Reproductive Organs in Childhood, Youth, Adult Age, and Advanced Life Considered in Their Physiological, Social and Moral Relations* (Philadelphia: Lindsay and Blakiston, 1865), 206.

28. For an elaboration of the economic argument see, B. Barker-Benfield, "The Spermatic Economy: a Nineteenth Century View of Sexuality," *Feminist Studies* 1 (1972): 45–74.

29. Acton, for example, was particularly virulent against the quacks who played on male fears and tried to suggest that almost any symptom might be spermatorrhoea. There is, he maintained, "a fashion in diseases, just as there is in amusements or occupations" (p. 230). His attack on quack medicine was motivated, however, not by a desire to reveal the imaginary qualities of this disease, but to insist on his own superior powers of treatment.

30. Samuel Hibbert, *Sketches of the Philosophy of Apparitions; or, An Attempt to Trace such Illusions to their Physical Causes,* 2nd. ed. (Edinburgh: Oliver and Boyd, 1825), 81.

31. Robert Brudenell Carter, *On the Pathology and Treatment of Hysteria* (London: John Churchill, 1853), 15.

32. Ibid., 34.

33. See the discussion of Carter in Ilza Veith, *Hysteria: the History of a Disease* (Chicago: University of Chicago Press, 1965), Ch. 9.

34. Herbert Spencer, "The Social Organism," in *Essays: Scientific, Political, and Speculative,* 3 vols. (London: Williams and Norgate, 1891) i, p. 290.

35. Spencer, "The Social Organism," 294.

36. Spencer, "State-Tamperings with Money and Banks," in *Essays,* iii:350–52.

37. W. Tyler Smith, *The Lancet* 2 (1847):544.

38. This form of attack on the idle middle-class woman, which started in the latter part of the eighteenth century, became increasingly virulent in the nineteenth, as medical attention to woman's role as producer became ever more pronounced. Women were castigated not only for failing to reproduce (and thus opening the door to the social domination of the prolific working classes), but also for producing sickly infants who would pass hereditary defects down to future generations. For an example of this form of argument see "Woman in Her Psychological Relations," *Journal of Psychological Medicine and Mental Pathology* 4 (1851): p. 46.

39. Buchan, *Domestic Medicine,* p. 591.

40. Buchan, 273–74.

41. Although the basic connection with ovulation was more or less understood by the 1860s, it was not until well into the twentieth century that the precise relationship was articulated. Well into the 1920s contraceptive advice literature offered woefully mistaken definitions of the "safe" period. The state of medical ignorance surrounding menstruation in the 1840s is indicated by the claim by Robert Lee in *The Lancet,* 1845, that it is evident that "an ovum—by which is usually meant an embryo enveloped in membranes—does not pass from the ovarium during menstruation . . . from the fact that an ovum is never formed but as a consequence of impregnation." ("On the State of the Ovaries During Menstruation," *The Lancet* 1 (1845):p. 584).

42. C. Locock, "Menstruation, Pathology of," in *The Cyclopaedia of Practical Medicine,* eds. J. Forbes, A. Tweedie, and J. Conolly, 4 vols. (London: Sherwood et al, 1833), iii, p. 110. Also revised ed. by R. Dunglison (Philadelphia: Blanchad and Lea, 1854), iii:300.

43. "Woman in Her Psychological Relations," 25.

44. J. C. Bucknill and D. H. Tuke, *A Manual of Psychological Medicine* 3rd ed. (London: J. and A. Churchill, 1874), 53. Bucknill and Tuke question whether these categories are specific diseases in themselves, rather than different causes of insanity, but they accept unquestionably the role attributed to the uterine system.

45. Modern discussions of Victorian masturbation anxiety have tended to focus on this issue in relation to men. The medical literature was by no means solely concerned with men, however. The article on "Woman in Her Psychological Relations," for example, warns that by the age of seventeen a girl might already have ruined permanently her health: "It may be that vicious habits have already been acquired, and the ovaria have been unduly excited by lesbian pleasures" (p. 38).

46. M. Baillarger, "A course of lectures on Diseases of the Brain, Lecture II," *The Lancet* 1 (1845):109.

47. Bucknill and Tuke, p. 104.

48. J. E. D. Esquirol, *Observations on the Illusions of the Insane, and on the Medico-Legal Question of Their Confinement*, trans. W. Liddell (London: Renshaw and Rush, 1833), 19; and *Mental Maladies: A Treatise on Insanity*, tr. E. K. Hunt (1845; reprint New York: Hafner, 1965), 62.

49. See, for example, "Woman in her Psychological Relations," p. 19; and Burrows, p. 148.

50. Buchan, 577.

51. C. Locock, "Menstruation," in Forbes, ed. (1833), iii:111.

52. Forbes, ed. (1833), i:67–69.

53. E. Kennedy, "On Uterine Diseases," *The Retrospect of Practical Medicine and Surgery*, ed. W. Braithwaite, 15 (1847):350.

54. Robert Lee, "On the Uses of the Speculum," *The Retrospect of Practical Medicine and Surgery* 22 (1850):357.

55. *Lancet* 1 (1845):210.

56. Carter, 66–67.

57. Carter, 69.

58. Acton, for example, suggests that the reabsorption of semen into the body creates strength and vigour (p. 197).

59. For details of this case see, Elaine Abelson, "When Ladies Go A-thieving: The Department Store, Shoplifting and the Contradictions of Consumerism, 1870–1914," Ph.D. diss., New York University, 1986.

4

Science and Women's Bodies: Forms of Anthropological Knowledge

Emily Martin

Historically in the West, vision has been a primary route to scientific knowledge. We speak of "knowledge as illumination, knowing as seeing, truth as light"; throughout Western thought, the illumination that vision gives has been associated with the highest faculty of mental reasoning.[1] Recently, however, the role of vision has come to seem problematic. Some have singled out reliance on vision as a key culprit in the scrutiny, surveillance, domination, control, and exertion of authority over the body, particularly over the bodies of women. The use of visualization techniques for the fetus inside the mother's body, what Ann Oakley calls a "window on the womb," has been cited as a case in point.[2] Anthropologists have claimed that the privileging of the visual mode of knowledge is particularly likely to lead to forms of representation impoverishing the complex whole that actually exists. The emphasis on *observation,* on mapping, diagramming and charting, has meant that the "ability to 'visualize' a culture or society almost becomes synonymous for understanding it." "Visualism" connotes "a cultural, ideological bias toward vision as the 'noblest sense' and toward geometry qua graphic-spatial conceptualization as the most 'exact' way of communicating knowledge."[3]

In anthroplogy, a growing concern with the ways in which visual knowledge dominates the sciences, and how it affects the nature of what is known, has led to a new emphasis on hearing as a mode of perception. While "visualism" has been castigated as objectifying and limiting, the aural has been suggested as an alternative mode of perception which might avoid some of the problems associated with the visual. Quoting an earlier theorist, Walter J. Ong, Johannes Fabian deplores the "antipersonalist orientation of visualism." "Persons, who alone speak (and in whom alone knowledge and science exist), will be eclipsed insofar as the world is thought of as an assemblage of the sort of things which vision apprehends—objects or surfaces." Ong hopes that a move to auditory metaphors would mean a move to more personal, existential, and humane forms of knowledge; Fabian, however, cautions that there is no guarantee that aural perception and oral expression will lead to more personal use of knowledge, especially given new technologies that permit rapid translation of verbal signals to visual ones; he suggests merely that the aural and oral may provide a "better starting point for a *dialectical* concept of communication."[4]

To pursue this line of thought, I will look at an area of anthropology in which attention to "voices" is paramount, what some have called postmodern anthropology.[5] One of the major characteristics of this approach is that it privileges *hearing* overseeing as the mode for taking in knowledge. Stephen Tyler begins his "Post-Modern Anthropology" by saying "Post-modern anthropology is the study of man 'talking.' "[6] James Clifford, in the introduction to *Writing Culture,* calls for an anthropology in which

> cultures are no longer prefigured visually—as objects, theaters, texts—it becomes possible to think of a cultural poetics that is an interplay of voices, of positioned utterances. In a discursive rather than a visual paradigm, the dominant metaphors for ethnography shift away from the observing eye and toward expressive speech (and gesture). The writer's "voice" pervades and situates the analysis, and objective, distancing rhetoric is denounced.[7]

Instead of the ethnographic gaze, we should have the ethnographic ear. And presumably we will no longer be "participant observers," but "participant-auditors."

What are the characteristics of these voices? Primarily, they are multiple. They comprise a polyphony of different sounds: "Polyphony is a better metaphor because it evokes sound and hearing and simultaneity and harmony, not pictures and seeing and sequence and line," they comprise a heteroglossia.[8] As Clifford puts it, "Ethnography is invaded by heteroglossia," "a more radical polyphony that would 'do the natives and the ethnographer in different voices'."[9]

Further, these multiple voices cannot be related to any sort of organizing structure. There is no organizing whole, but rather fragmentary shreds, a verbal pastiche, "partial truths."[10] Since we have now become aware of the "fragmentary nature of the post-modern world," we can see that the societies in which we do field work are themselves fragmentary.[11] It is not that we have only partial evidence with which to guess the shape of an organizing structure; at least some postmodern anthropologists claim that no organized structures exist. In Tyler's words, "It is not just that we cannot see the forest for the trees, but that we have come to feel that there are no forests where the trees are too far apart, just as patches make quilts only if the spaces between them are small enough."[12]

Anthropology has much to learn from these insights. The new focus on the subtleties of voices in ethnographic descriptions has given us increased awareness of the need to identify the position from which we speak as ethnographers, and has enhanced the intricacy and sophistication of the ways in which we convey the voices of those whose cultures we study. Postmodern anthropology has also joined forces with the work of philosophers who have encouraged us to see even our most sacred form of knowledge, science, as one discourse among many.[13] In this view, scientific discourse is no more privileged in its relation to reality than any other form of description: there would be a "concrete absurdity" in "thinking that the vocabulary used by present science, morality, or whatever has some privileged attachment to reality which makes it *more* than just a further set of descriptions."[14]

Yet not all anthropologists are equally willing to embrace this new kind of ethnography. Its practitioners often remark on the puzzling fact that there seem to be no feminists (and hardly any women) at all doing this kind of anthropology. Clifford says that the absence of any feminist theory in *Writing Culture* "cries out for comment" and concludes that it is absent because feminist writing has not contributed much to the theoretical analysis of ethnographies as texts.[15] Recognizing the importance of this observation, Marilyn Strathern argues that between textual anthropology and feminist anthropology lie irreconcilable differences derived from incompatible views of the self and the world, and incompatible goals. As she sees it, in the feminist task

> the constant rediscovery that women are the Other in men's accounts reminds women that they must see men as the Other in relation to themselves. Creating a space for women becomes creating a space for the self, and experience becomes an instrument for knowing the self. Necessary to the construction of the feminist self, then, is a nonfeminist Other. The Other is most generally conceived as "patriarchy," the institutions and persons who represent male domination, often simply concretized as "men." Because the goal is to restore to subjectivity a self dominated by the Other, there can be no shared experience with persons who stand for the Other.[16]

In stark contrast, the postmodern anthropologist "constitutes himself in relation to an Other, vis-à-vis the alien culture/society under study. Its distance and foreignness are deliberately sustained. But the Other is not under attack. On the contrary, the effort is to create a relation with the Other, as in the search for a medium of expression that will offer mutual interpretation, perhaps visualized as a common text, or a dialogue." What *is* under attack is the part of the self that is embodied in the anthropologist's home cultural tradition and personal experience. The goal is to achieve multiple authorship with the Other, by presenting a monograph as a collaborative production, in which the separate dignity of each voice (the anthropologist's and the many Others') is preserved, but no one voice submerges any other.[17]

Strathern encapsulates the feminist response to this project as follows:

> There can be no collaboration with the Other. This anthropological ideal is a delusion, overlooking the crucial dimension of different social interests. There can be no parity between the authorship of the anthropologist and the informant; the dialogue must always be asymmetrical. Whether the prime factors are the colonial relations between the societies from which both anthropologists and informants come or the use to which the text will be put, the worlds of anthropologist and informant are different. They have no interest in common to be served by this purportedly common product.[18]

In my view, the underlying problem with postmodern anthropology is precisely in the treatment given by its proponents to the structures Strathern identifies—structures such as patriarchy or colonialism. In other words, because they often do not seem to recognize the existence of a world outside discourse, they cannot ask anything about such a world. While I would endorse the effort to dislodge science from its privileged position, and while I agree that the discourse of science (including the science of anthropology) is no more privileged than any other form of description, along with Strathern, I do not think this means we give up altogether the effort to define patriarchal, economic, or racial structures that exist independently of any particular discourse about them.

One fruitful way forward is to take on the dislodging of science from its privileged position by focusing on the historical conditions under which it is produced. In what follows I will treat a small piece of biology this way. We will see that a variety of different power structures have crucial roles to play in the form of this scientific knowledge at any given time. Without sidestepping the attempt to identify structures of power, I will also—taking an insight from postmodern anthropology—examine certain discourses *about* science, and in particular, discourses spoken by women, whose selves and bodies are oppressed in specific ways by biological knowledge.

I begin with an illustration from the one of the early-twentieth-century engineers of our system of scientific medicine, Frederick T. Gates.[19] In advising John D. Rockefeller on how to use his philanthropies to aid scientific medicine, Gates used a series of interrelated metaphors to explain the scientific view of how the body works:

> It is interesting to note the striking comparisons between the human body and the safety and hygienic appliances of a great city. Just as in the streets of a great city we have "white angels" posted everywhere to gather up poisonous materials from the streets, so in the great streets and avenues of the body, namely the arteries and the blood vessels, there are brigades of corpuscles, white in color like the "white angels," whose function it is to gather up into sacks, formed by their own bodies, and disinfect or eliminate all poisonous substances found in the blood. The body has a network of insulated nerves, like telephone wires, which transmit instantaneous alarms at every point of danger. The body is furnished with the most elaborate police system, with hundreds of police stations to which the criminal elements are carried by the police and jailed. I refer to the great numbers of sanitary glands, skillfully placed at points where vicious germs find entrance, especially about the mouth and throat. The body has a most complete and elaborate sewer system. There are wonderful laboratories placed at convenient points for a subtle brewing of skillful medicines. . . . The fact is that the human body is made up of an infinite number of microscopic cells. Each one of these cells is a small chemical laboratory, into which its own appropriate raw material is constantly being introduced, the processes of chemical separation and combination are constantly taking place automatically, and its own appropriate finished product being necessary for the life and health of the body. Not only is this so, but the great organs of the body like the liver, stomach, pancreas, kidneys, gall bladder are great local manufacturing centers, formed of groups of cells in infinite numbers, manufacturing the same sorts of products, just as industries of the same kind are often grouped in specific districts.[20]

Elements of the images that occurred to Gates are still commonplace in contemporary biology. For many years, the "imagery of the cell [has] been that of the factory . . .;" more recently, ATP (a molecule involved in energy exchange in the body) has been characterized as the body's "energy currency:" "Produced in particular cellular regions, it [is] placed in an 'energy bank' in which it [is] maintained in two forms, those of 'current account' and 'deposit account'." Development of molecular biology brought additional metaphors based on information science, management, and control. In this model, flow of information between DNA and RNA leads to the production of protein. Molecular biologists conceive of the cell as "an assembly line factory in which the DNA blueprints are interpreted and raw materials fabricated to produce the protein end products in response to a series of regulated requirements."[21] The cell is still seen as a factory, but, compared with Gates, there is enormous elaboration of the flow of information from one "department" of the body to another, and of the exertion of control from the center. Here is an example from a college physiology text:

> All the systems of the body, if they are to function effectively, must be subjected to some form of control. . . . The precise control of body function is brought about by means of the operation of the nervous system and of the hormonal or endocrine system. . . . The most important thing to note about any control system is that before it can control anything it must be supplied with information. . . . Therefore the first essential in any control system is an adequate system of collecting information about the state of the body. . . . Once the CNS knows what is happening, it must then have a means for rectifying the situation if something is going wrong. There are two available methods for doing this, by using nerve fibres and by using hormones. The motor nerve fibres . . . carry instructions from the CNS to the muscles and glands throughout the body. . . . As far as hormones are concerned the brain acts via the pituitary gland . . . the pituitary secretes a large number of hormones. . . . the rate of secretion of each one of these is under the direct control of the brain.[22]

This view of the body as a hierarchically organized bureaucratic system of control has profound implications for how a basic change in the system is perceived. In medical terms, for instance, menopause is seen as a failure or breakdown of central control: ovaries become "unresponsive"; the hypothalamus begins to give "inappropriate orders."[23]

Other implications for scientific descriptions of women's bodies also come from prevailing metaphors. At the cellular level, DNA communicates with RNA, all for the purpose of the cell's production of proteins. It is no surprise, therefore, that the system of communication involving female reproduction is also thought to be geared toward production. It is clear that the system is supposed to produce many good things: the ovaries produce estrogen, the pituitary produces FSH and LH, and so on. Follicles also produce eggs in a sense, although this is usually described as "maturing" them, since the entire set of eggs a woman has for her lifetime is known to be present at birth. Beyond all this, the system is seen as organized for a single preeminent purpose: "transport" of the egg along its journey from the ovary to the uterus and preparation of an appropriate place for the egg to grow if it is fertilized.[24]

This teleological view of the purpose of the process has direct implications for how menstruation is described. First of all, the action of progesterone and estrogen on the lining of the uterus is seen as "ideally suited to provide a hospitable environment for implantation of a fertilized ovum" intended to lead to "the monthly renewal of the tissue that will cradle [the ovum]."[25] As Guyton summarizes, "The whole purpose of all these endometrial changes is to produce a highly secretory endometrium containing large amounts of stored nutrients that can provide appropriate conditions for implantation of a fertilized ovum during the latter half of the monthly cycle."[26] Given this teleological interpretation of what the increased amount of endometrial tissue is for, it should be no surprise that when a fertilized egg does not implant, the next thing that happens is described in very negative terms. The fall in blood progesterone and estrogen "deprives" the "highly developed endometrial lining of its hormonal support," "constriction" of blood vessels leads to a "diminished" supply of oxygen and nutrients, and finally "disintegration starts, the entire lining begins to slough, and the menstrual flow begins." Blood vessels in the endometrium "hemorrhage" and the menstrual flow "consists of this blood mixed with endometrial debris." The "loss" of hormonal stimulation causes "necrosis."[27]

The construction of these events in terms of a purpose that has failed is beautifully captured in a standard text for medical students (a text otherwise noteworthy for its extremely objective, factual descriptions) in which a discussion of the events covered in the last paragraph (sloughing, hemorrhaging) ends with the statement: "When fertilization fails to occur, the endometrium is shed, and a new cycle starts. This is why it used to be taught that 'menstruation is the uterus crying for lack of a baby.' "[28] Clearly, just as conceputalizing menopause as a kind of failure of the authority structure in the body contributes to our negative view of it, so does the construction of menstruation as failed production contribute to our negative view of that process. Susan Sontag's work on metaphors in science draws attention to the horror we have of production out of control. But another kind of horror for us is *lack* of production: the disused factory, failed business, idle machine. Langdon Winner, for instance, terms the stopping and breakdown of technological systems in modern society "apraxia" and describes it as "the ultimate horror, a condition to be avoided at all costs."[29]

It may be that an element in the negativity attached to imaging menstruation as failure to produce is precisely that women are, in some sinister sense, out of control when they menstruate instead of getting pregnant. They are not reproducing, not continuing the species, not preparing to stay at home with the baby, not providing a safe, warm womb to nurture a man's sperm. Whether or not this suggestion can be supported, I think it is plain that the negative power behind the image of failure to produce can be considerable when applied metaphorically to women's bodies. A description of menstruation in one standard text confronts the reader in rapid succession with "degenerate," "decline," "withdrawn," "spasms," "lack," "weakened," "leak," "deteriorate," "discharge," and, after all that, "repair."[30] In another standard text, we are presented with imagery of catastrophic disintegration: "ceasing," "dying," "losing," "denuding," and "expelling."[31] And the accompanying illustration depicts this explosive decomposition exactly.

These are not neutral terms, but ones that convey failure and dissolution.

Consider, by contrast, this extract from a text that describes male reproductive physiology: "The mechanisms which guide the *remarkable* cellular transformation from spermatid to mature sperm remain uncertain. . . . Perhaps the most *amazing* characteristic of spermatogenesis is its *sheer magnitude*: the normal human male may manufacture several hundred million sperm per day."[32] Needless to say, this text has no parallel appreciation of female processes such as ovulation or pregnancy, and in terms of my argument, it is surely no accident that this "remarkable" process involves precisely what menstruation does not involve in the medical view—production of a product deemed valuable.

So we see that in this case the story science tells is a very concrete one, rooted in our particular social and economic history. Following along the lines advocated by postmodern anthropology, let us go farther in search of other stories, maintaining the search for polyphonic voices. The view of menstruation promulgated by scientific medicine is that it is failed (re)production. Do women whose stake in production and reproduction varies, along lines of class and race, also differ in how comfortable they feel about this view of menstruation, or how willing they are to offer it themselves?

Among middle-class women, both black and white, two questions in the interviews in my recent study elicited familiar versions of the scientific view of menstruation.[33] The questions were: "What is your own understanding of menstruation? and "How would you explain menstruation to a young girl who didn't know about it?" Accounts differed in details, but almost all began immediately with internal organs, structures, and functions:

> When you reach puberty, hormones in your body cause your—you have eggs in your ovaries—I'd explain the structures—the hormones in your body cause some of these eggs to ripen and it releases into your fallopian tubes and this is where pregnancy would occur. And your uterus has prepared the lining in case of fertilization and if there is not fertilization then the lining is sloughed off, comes out in a bloody sort of tissuey substance and that's what happens" (Tania Parrish).

Almost all who spoke of internal organs conveyed the sense that the purpose of the whole process is to provide key steps in reproduction, and that if menstruation occurs it is a waste product of an effort that failed: "All the blood that comes out with [the egg] was sort of like a home for the egg, so if the egg doesn't have to grow bigger into a baby you just say that it leaves with all that . . ." (Mara Lenhart). The central metaphor of failed production of a baby comes through vividly. Other middle-class women (particularly high-school-age women, who have heard this story a lot less often than older women) became somewhat uncomfortable in the interview when they couldn't remember to their satisfaction just what body parts were doing what

("Isn't it one egg from each tube every month and it changes, something like that, I don't remember, I don't know all about the stuff that's going on technically" [Julie Morgan]). But in spite of these hesitations, all of them managed to get out some version of the failed-production view.

Later in the interview, many of these women made remarks in passing about how this internal model was not relevant to them. "When I have my period I don't really think about what's going on inside. I think about what's coming out of me. I don't think about—the eggs are coming down—I just— it's just like I have my period and it's gone. Not like in the middle of the month and then well, like it's about time an egg is making its way into my fallopian tubes—I mean—!" (Kristin Lassiter). But despite this kind of dissatisfaction with the medical model, the interviews with middle-class women do not contain more than a glimmer of a different view of menstruation. Only one woman began her answer in a different mode, with what might be called the phenomenology of menstruation:

> "How would you explain menstruation to a young girl who knew nothing about it? What happens in menstruation is that something that looks like blood but isn't in fact because it's darker comes out of your vagina and it has to be kept clean because otherwise you make a mess. What comes out changes its appearance, you have a flow coming out of your body for anywhere from 3 to 7 days, and it changes. Sometimes it comes out very heavily, you can almost feel it coming out and sometimes it's very light and sometimes it stops during that time. And it changes consistency during the time it comes out, it looks very red and bloody, sometimes it's darker, sometimes it's almost brown" (Shelly Levinson).

This woman then proceeds directly to the scientific model, saying the process is caused by an egg that has died coming out with its fluids.

The disjunction between this woman's two versions of menstruation cannot be overemphasized. In her first version, she deals with: what menstruation feels like, looks like, smells like, what the immediate experience of being a "menstruator" is like, aspects of the process that are untouched by the medical model. Even women who describe only the scientific view of menstruation, and say it is satisfying in one context, find themselves at a loss with what it leaves out in another. One woman was given a "pretty good explanation" of "the mechanics" by a friend, her mother, and a fifth-grade sex-education class. But when she started menstruating, she had no idea what to do when she went to bed. "I didn't know how you are supposed to cope with it. You change during the day, how could you sleep all night?" (Shelly Levinson). She was very nervous about asking her mother, but when she eventually did she was told the flow slows down at night. The interviews are full of anguish surrounding first periods, when women wonder: Is the color of my blood all right? What do I wear? What if I skip a month? How often do I change pads or tampons?

If middle-class women readily incline toward the medical view of menstruation, even though this leads to difficulties dealing with the actualities of menstruating, how do working-class women explain menstruation? There the middle-class pattern is reversed: almost nobody—black or white—came out spontaneously with the failed-production model of menstruation, and almost everybody accounted for it either phenomenologically or in terms of a life change. Here are some examples in response to the question "How would you explain menstruation to a young girl who didn't know anything about it?"

> "I'd just tell her it's when your body's changing and you're ready to have children. Your body allows you to have children now and it's one of the first steps to becoming a woman" (Valerie Bartson).
> "I guess it's a part of your life. Growing up. [Could you give a description of menstruation itself?] Yeah. [What would you tell her?] Just red blood" (Patricia Henderson).
> "I don't know, it's part of Mother Nature, I guess. I guess I would explain it the same way my mother explained it to me [which was: it's just part of life, your body's changing and you're becoming a woman.]" (Kathleen Reardon).

These women—and all other working-class women interviewed, black and white—share an absolute reluctance to give the medical view of menstruation. This is so in spite of the interviewers' many efforts to give them a variety of opportunities to come up with it, and in spite of the fact that all of them have been exposed to it in classes in school. In fact many of the women mentioned how much attention was paid to menstruation in school: ". . . had films and everything, books and pamphlets given out." In spite of this only two of the women mention anything inside the body at all: "the eggs passing through" and "to clean out your insides." All other responses involve only what a woman sees and feels, or the significance it has in her life. This material would certainly be grist for the mill in looking for "radical polyphony" or "heteroglossia," and the search for different voices would have hardly begun.

My difficulty here is not with the search for different voices, but with the assertion that we cannot know what these various voices are talking *about*. I am not convinced that we are in fact hearing about trees unrelated to a forest, or patches unrelated to a quilt. The voices I describe talking about menstruation do not, in fact, strike me as random and disordered cacophony. They strike me as systematically related to certain material forces in our society. As a beginning analysis in this direction, we could suggest that the working-class women have simply been more able to resist one aspect of the scientific view of women's bodies, either because it is not meaningful to them or because it is downright offensive, phrased as it is in the negative terms we have seen. The ironies in this are many: middle-class women, much more likely to benefit from investment in the productive system, have swallowed a view of their reproductive systems which sees menstruation as failed production, and which is divorced from women's own experience. Working-class women, perhaps because they have less to gain from productive labor in the society, have rejected the application of models of production to their bodies. It is striking that in the working-class interviews there is none of the angst that runs through the heart of middle-class interviews: almost no one describes being mystified at the details of menstruating, at a loss about the mechanics of taking care of it, or the variety of forms menstruating can take.

In arguing against the possibility that certain "sorts of representations, certain expressions, certain processes are 'basic,' 'privileged,' and 'foundational,' " Richard Rorty proposes that the model of a conversation should replace structures "erected upon foundations."[34] As I argued earlier, I would agree that science should not be privileged as a description of "reality," but this does not mean that the discourse of science (indeed any discourse) may not in fact be *socially* privileged by its relation to structures of power. Nancy Hartsock has recently taken Rorty to task for suggesting that the best model for philosophical discussion is that of a conversation. She points out that this model ignores the power relationships among participants in a conversation: some of us may only now be struggling for a sense of self and a voice in which to speak because of the peripheral position we have had in our language and culture.[35] I would add that "conversations" between men and women in our culture are often highly hierarchical affairs. Sociolinguists have shown that women speak less in mixed sex groups than men, succeed in establishing the topic of conversations less often than men, and are far more likely to be interrupted by men than to interrupt.[36]

It is nearly impossible to imagine a "conversation" on menstruation among the voices I described above. Gynecologists would probably be threatened by the implied equality, while women would be intimidated, precisely because of the power relations involved in the codification and institutionalization of the science of women's bodies. One could imagine negotiating sessions, challenges, demands or even arbitrations, under the right circumstances. For the moment, conversations about menstruation that bring together differently positioned voices could only take place among women diversely affected by the same dominating structures. By listening to working-class women, for example, perhaps middle-class women could learn to escape the prevailing scientific view that internal invisible organs and structures in the body are what is central in menstruation. Ideally all women could learn to interpret the menstrual processes in accordance with their own needs and purposes. Menstruation could just as well be regarded as the making of life substance that marks us as women, or heralds our nonpregnant state, rather than as the casting off of the debris of endometrial decay or as the hemorrhage of necrotic blood vessels. The move to uncover various discourses about the body, where science is given only one voice among many, has revealed a rich diversity. These voices rarely come together as conversations; indeed they rarely come together even as challenge and rebuff. More often they exist in isolation from any effective contact with one another. Where this is so, I would argue it is because of the *existence* (not the *absence*) of hierarchical structures of domination, in this case structures that use cultural differences of gender and class to exert power and entrench social privilege.

Notes

1. See, for instance, Evelyn Fox Keller and Christine Grontkowski, "The Mind's Eye," in *Discovering Reality: Feminist Perspectives on Epistemology, Metaphysics, Methodology, and Philosophy of Science* (Dordrecht: D. Reidel, 1983), 208, and Richard Rorty, *Philosophy and the Mirror of Nature* (Princeton: Princeton University Press, 1979). For an analysis of the development of emphasis on the visual between Homer and Plato that went along with the development of individualism, see Eric Havelock, *Preface to Plato* (Cambridge, Mass.: Harvard University Press, 1963). My warmest appreciation to Evelyn Fox Keller and Sally Shuttleworth for their substantial editorial help.

2. See Ann Oakley, *The Captured Womb: A History of the Medical Care of Pregnant Women* (Oxford: Basil Blackwell, 1984), 156.

3. See Johannes Fabian, *Time and the Other: How Anthroplogy Makes Its Object* (New York: Columbia University Press, 1983), 106.

4. Ibid., 118–19; see also Walter J. Ong, *Ramus, Method, and the Decay of Dialogue* (Cambridge, Mass.: Harvard University Press, 1958), 9.

5. For brevity, my treatment must generalize somewhat and so will not do justice to variations among the positions represented in this enterprise.

6. Stephen A. Tyler, "Post-Modern Anthropology," in *Discourse and the Social Life of Meaning* (Washington, D.C.: Smithsonian Press, 1986), 23.

7. James Clifford, "Introduction: Partial Truths," in *Writing Culture: The Poetics and Politics of Ethnography,* ed. James Clifford and George E. Marcus (Berkeley: University of California Press, 1984), 12.

8. See Stephen A. Tyler, "Post-Modern Anthropology: From Document of the Occult to Occult Document," in *Writing Culture,* eds. Clifford and Marcus, 137; and see also Paul Rabinow, "Representations Are Social Facts: Modernity and Post-Modernity in Anthropology," ibid., 246.

9. James Clifford, "On Ethnographic Authority," *Representations* 1:2 (1983):140,139.

10. See Rabinow, *Writing Culture,* p. 249, and Clifford, ibid., 7.

11. Tyler, *Discourse and the Social Life of Meaning,* 132.

12. Ibid., 132.

13. See, for instance, Rorty, 382, Terry Eagleton, *Literary Theory: An Introduction* (Oxford: Basil Blackwell, 1983), 132, and Jane Flax, "Postmodernism and Gender Relations in Feminist Theory," *Signs* 12:4 (1987):621—43.

14. Rorty, 361.

15. Clifford, *Writing Culture,* 20.

16. Marilyn Strathern, "An Awkward Relationship: The Case of Feminism and Anthropology," *Signs* 12:2 (1987):288.

17. Ibid., 12:2. 289, 290.

18. Ibid. 12:2. 290.

19. The following sections are elaborated in Emily Martin, *The Woman in the Body: A Cultural Analysis of Reproduction* (Boston: Beacon Press, 1987).

20. Frederick T. Gates, quoted by Howard Berliner, "Medical Modes of Production," in *The Problem of Medical Knowledge: Examining the Social Construction of Medicine,* eds. Peter Wright and Andrew Teacher (Edinburgh: Edinburgh University Press, 1982), 170–1.

21. See R. C. Lewontin; Steven Rose, and Leon J. Kamin, *Not in Our Genes: Biology, Ideology, and Human Nature* (New York: Pantheon, 1984), 58, 59.

22. David F. Horrobin, *Introduction to Human Physiology* (Philadelphia: F. A. Davis, 1973), 7–8. See also Arthur C. Guyton, *Physiology of the Human Body.* 6th ed. (Philadelphia: Saunders College Publishing, 1984), 7.

23. See Allan Lein, *The Cycling Female: Her Menstrual Rhythm* (San Francisco: W. H. Freeman, 1979), 97.

24. See Arthur J. Vander, James H. Sherman, and Dorothy S. Luciano, *Human Physiology: The Mechanisms of Body Function.* 3rd ed. (New York: McGraw-Hill, 1980), 503.

25. See ibid., 501, and Lein, 43.

26. Arthur C. Guyton, *Textbook of Medical Physiology.* 6th ed. (Philadelphia: W. B. Saunders, 1981), 1013.

27. See Vander et al., p. 501, and Guyton (1981), 1013. See also very similar accounts in Lien, 69; Vernon B. Mountcastle, *"Medical Physiology,* vol. 2, 14th ed. (London: The C. V. Mosby Company), 1750; Eliot B. Mason, *Human Physiology* (Menlo Park, CA: Benjamin/ Cummings Publishing Co., 1983), 578; and Ralph C. Benson, *Current Obstetric and Gynecologic Diagnosis and Treatment* (Los Altos, CA: Lange Medical Publishers, 1982), 128–9.

28. See William F. Ganong, *Review of Medical Physiology.* 7th ed. (Los Altos, CA: Lange Medical Publications, 1975), 356.

29. Langdon Winner, *Autonomous Technology: Technics-Out-of-Control As a Theme in Political Thought* (Cambridge, Mass.: The MIT Press, 1977), 185, 187.

30. See Mason, 525.

31. See Guyton (1984), 624.

32. Vander et al., 483–4.

33. For details about the study, who was interviewed, the questions asked, and so on, see Martin, passim.

34. Rorty, 310, 319.

35. Nancy C. M. Hartsock, "Epistemology and Politics: Minority vs. Majority Theories," *Cultural Critique* 5 (1987): 17. Rabinow, *Writing Culture,* 239, 255, recognizes the absence of attention to power and to the "realities of socioeconomic constraints" on the part of both Rorty and textual anthropologists.

36. See Paula A. Treichler and Cheris Kramarae, "Women's Talk in the Ivory Tower," *Communications Quarterly* 31:2 (1983):118–32; and Candace West and Don H. Zimmerman, "Small Insults: A Study of Interruptions in Cross Sex Conversations Between Unacquainted Persons," in *Language, Gender, and Society.* eds. Barrie Thorne, Cheris Kramarae, and Nancy Henley (Rowley, Mass.: Newbury House Publishers, 1983), 103–17.

5
Reading the Slender Body
Susan Bordo

In the late-Victorian era, arguably for the first time in the West, those who could afford to eat well began systematically to deny themselves food in pursuit of an aesthetic ideal.[1] Certainly, other cultures had "dieted." Aristocratic Greek culture made a science of the regulation of food intake, in the service of the attainment of self-mastery and moderation.[2] Fasting, aimed at spiritual purification and domination of the flesh, was an important part of the repertoire of Christian practice in the Middle Ages.[3] These forms of "diet" can clearly be viewed as instruments for the development of a "self"—whether an "inner" self, for the Christians, or a public self, for the Greeks—constructed as an arena in which the deepest possibilities for human excellence might be realized. Rituals of fasting and asceticism were therefore reserved for the select few, aristocratic or priestly in caste, deemed capable of achieving such excellence of spirit. In the late nineteenth century, by contrast, the practices of body management begin to be middle-class preoccupations, and concern with diet becomes attached to the pursuit of an idealized physical weight or shape; it becomes a project in service of "body" rather than "soul." Fat, not appetite or desire, is the declared enemy, and people begin to measure their dietary achievements by the numbers on the scale rather than the level of their mastery of impulse and excess. The bourgeois "tyranny of slenderness" (as Kim Chernin has called it[4]) had begun its ascendancy (particularly over women), and

I would like to thank the Rockefeller Foundation and the American Council of Learned Societies/Ford Foundation for their generous support, and Le Moyne College, for graciously granting me early sabbatical leave to work on *Food, Fashion and Power,* of which this paper (in modified form) will be a chapter (Berkeley: University of California Press, forthcoming.) Thanks to Mary Jacobus, Sally Shuttleworth, and especially to Mario Moussa for comments and editorial suggestions.

with it the development of numerous technologies—diet, exercise, and, later on, chemicals and surgery—aimed at a purely physical transformation.

Today, we have become acutely aware of the massive and multifaceted nature of such technologies and the industries built around them. To the degree that a popular critical consciousness exists, however, it has been focused largely (and not surprisingly) on what has been viewed as pathological or extreme—on the unfortunate minority who become "obsessed," or go "too far." Television talk shows feature tales of disasters caused by stomach stapling, gastric bubbles, gastrointestinal bypass operations, liquid diets, compulsive exercising. Magazines warn of the dangers of fat-reduction surgery and lipo-suction. Books and articles about bulimia and anorexia nervosa proliferate. The portrayal of eating disorders by the popular media is often lurid and sensational; audiences gasp at pictures of skeletal bodies or at item-by-item descriptions of the volumes of food eaten during an average binge. Such presentations encourage a "side show" experience of the relationship between the ("normal") audience and those on view ("the freaks"). To the degree that the audience may nonetheless recognize themselves in the behavior or reported experiences of those on stage, they confront themselves as "pathological" or outside the norm.

Of course, many of these behaviors *are* outside the norm, if only because of the financial resources they require. But preoccupation with fat, diet, and slenderness are not.[5] Indeed, such preoccupation may function as one of the most powerful "normalizing" strategies of our century, ensuring the production of self-monitoring and self-disciplining "docile bodies," sensitive to any departure from social norms, and habituated to self-improvement and transformation in the service of those norms.[6] Seen in this light, the focus on "pathology," disorder, accident, unexpected disaster, and bizarre behavior obscures the normalizing function of the technologies of diet and body man-agement. For women, who are subject to such controls more profoundly and, historically, more ubiquitously than men, the focus on "pathology" (unless embedded in a political analysis) diverts recognition from a central means of the reproduction of gender.

This paper is part of a larger analysis of the contemporary preoccupation with slenderness as it functions within a modern, "normalizing" machinery of power in general, and, in particular, as it functions to reproduce gender-relations. For the purposes of this larger analysis, I make use of Foucault's distinction between two arenas of the social construction of the modern body—the "intelligible body" and the "useful body": (1) the representational, and (2) the practical, direct locus of social control, through which culture is converted into automatic, habitual bodily activity. The "intelligible body" includes scientific, philosophic, and aesthetic representations of the body, norms of beauty, models of health, and so forth. These representations, however, may also be seen as legislating a set of *practical* rules and regulations (some explicit, some implicit), through which the living body is "trained, shaped, obeys, and responds . . .;" becomes, in short, a socially adapted and "useful body."[7] So, for example, the seventeenth-century philosophic conception of body-as-machine arguably both mirrored and provided a metaphysical and technical model for an increasingly automated productive machinery of labor.

Understanding the "political anatomy" (as Foucault would call it) of the slender body requires the interrogation of both "useful" and "intelligible" arenas—interrogation of the practices or "disciplines" of diet and exercise which structure the organization of time, space, and the experience of embodiment for subjects; and, in our image-bedazzled culture, interrogation of the popular representations through which meaning is crystallized, symbolized, metaphorically encoded, and transmitted. My overall argument emphasizes the primacy of practice for evaluating the role of bodies in the nexus of power relations. In this light, we should certainly be "politically" disturbed by recent statistics on the number of young girls (80% of the nine-year-olds surveyed in one study[8]) who are making dedicated dieting the organizing principle of their days. This particular paper, however, will approach the normalizing role of diet and exercise via an examination of the representational body—the cultural imagery of ideal slenderness—which now reigns, increasingly across racial and ethnic boundaries, as the dominant body-standard of our culture.[9] More specifically, I wish to pursue here Mary Douglas's insight that images of the "microcosm"—the physical body—may symbolically reproduce central vulnerabilities and anxieties of the macrocosm—the "social body."[10] I will explore this insight by "reading" (as the text or surface on which culture is symbolically "written") some dominant meanings that are connected, in our time, to the pursuit of slenderness.[11]

Decoding cultural images is a complex business—particularly when one considers the wide variety of ethnic, racial, and class differences that intersect with, resist, and give distinctive meaning to dominant, normalizing imagery. Even on the level of homogenizing imagery (my focus in this paper), contemporary slenderness admits of many variants and has multiple and often mutually "deconstructing" meanings. To give just one example, an examination of the photographs and copy of current fashion advertisements suggests that today's boyish body ideals, as in the 1920s, symbolize a new freedom, a casting off of the encumbrance of domestic, reproductive femininity. But when the same slender body is depicted in poses that set it off against the resurgent muscularity and bulk of the current male body-ideal, other meanings emerge. In these gender/oppositional poses, the degree to which slenderness carries connotations of fragility, defenselessness, and lack of power over against a decisive male occupation of social space is dramatically represented.

Since it is impossible for any cultural analyst to do a full reading of the text of slenderness in the space of a single article, I will instead attempt to construct

an argument about some elements of the cultural context that has conditioned the flourishing of eating disorders—anorexia, bulimia, and obesity—in our time. The first step in that argument is a decoding of the contemporary slenderness ideal so as to reveal the psychic anxieties and moral valuations contained within it—valuations concerning the correct and incorrect management of impulse and desire. In the process, I will be describing a key contrast between two different symbolic functions of body shape and size: (1) the designation of social position, e.g., marking class status or gender role; and (2) the outer indication of the state of the "soul." Next, aided by the significant work of Robert Crawford, I will turn to the "macro-body" of consumer culture, in order to demonstrate how the "correct" management of desire in that culture, requiring as it does a contradictory "double-bind" construction of personality, inevitably produces an unstable bulimic personality-type as its norm, along with the contrasting extremes of obesity and self-starvation.[12] These symbolize, I will argue, the contradictions of the "social body"— contradictions that make self-management a continual and virtually impossible task in our culture. Finally, I will introduce gender into this symbolic framework, showing how additional resonances (concerning the cultural management of female desire, on the one hand, and female flight from a purely reproductive destiny on the other) have overdetermined slenderness as the current ideal for women.

Slenderness and Contemporary Anxiety

In a recent edition of the magazine show *20/20*, several ten-year-old boys were shown some photos of fashion models. The models were pencil thin. Yet the pose was such that a small bulge of hip was forced, through the action of the body, into protuberance—as is natural, unavoidable on any but the most skeletal or the most tautly developed bodies. We bend over, we sit down, and the flesh coalesces in spots. These young boys, pointing to the hips, disgustedly pronounced the models to be "fat." Watching the show, I was appalled at the boys' reaction. Yet I couldn't deny that I had also been surprised at my own current perceptions while re-viewing female bodies in movies from the 1970s; what once appeared slender and fit now seemed loose and flabby. *Weight* was not the key element in these changed perceptions—my standards had not come to favor *thinner* bodies—but rather, I had come to expect a tighter, smoother, more "contained" body profile.

The self-criticisms of the anorectic, too, are usually focused on particular soft, protuberant areas of the body (most often the stomach) rather than on the body as a whole. Karen, in *Dying to Be Thin*, tries to dispel what she sees as the myth that the anorectic, even when emaciated, "misperceives" her body as fat:

> I hope I'm expressing myself properly here, because this is important. You have to understand. I don't see my whole body as fat. When I look

in the mirror, I don't really see a fat person there. I see certain things about me that are really thin. Like my arms and legs. But I can tell the minute I eat certain things that my stomach blows up like a pig's. I know it gets distended. And it's disgusting. That's what I keep to myself—hug to myself.[13]

Or Barbara:

Sometimes my body looks so bloated, I don't want to get dressed. I like the way it looks for exactly two days each month: usually, the eighth and ninth days after my period. Every other day, my breasts, my stomach—they're just awful lumps, bumps, bulges. My body can turn on me at any moment; it is an out-of-control mass of flesh.[14]

Much has been made of such descriptions, from both psychoanalytic and feminist perspectives. But for now, I wish to pursue these images of unwanted bulges and erupting stomachs in another direction than that of gender symbolism. I want to consider them as a metaphor for anxiety about internal processes out of control—uncontained desire, unrestrained hunger, uncontrolled impulse. Images of bodily eruption frequently function symbolically in this way in contemporary horror movies—as in recent werewolf films (*The Howling, A Teen-Age Werewolf in London,*) and in David Cronenberg's remake of *The Fly*. The original *Fly* imagined a mechanical joining of fly parts and person parts, a variation on the standard "half-man, half-beast" image. In Cronen-berg's *Fly,* as in the werewolf genre, a new, alien, libidinous, and uncontrollable self literally bursts through the seams of the victims' old flesh. (A related, frequently copied image occurs in *Alien,* where a parasite erupts from the chest of the human host.) While it is possible to view these new images as technically inspired by special-effects possibilities, I suggest that deeper psycho-cultural anxieties are being given form.

Every year, I present my metaphysics class with Delmore Schwartz's classic "The Heavy Bear" as an example of a dualist imagination of self, in which the body is constructed as an alien, unconscious, appetitive force, thwarting and befouling the projects of the soul. Beginning with an epigraph from Alfred North Whitehead, "The witness of the body," Schwartz's poem makes "the heavy bear who goes with [him]" into "A caricature, a swollen shadow,/A stupid clown of the spirit's motive." Last year, for the first time, quite a few students interpreted the poem as describing the predicament of an obese man. This may indicate the increasing literalism of my students. But it also is suggestive of the degree to which the specter of "fat" dominates their imaginations, and codes their generation's anxieties about the body's potential for excess and chaos. In advertisements, the construction of the body as an alien attacker, threatening to erupt in an unsightly display of bulging flesh, is a ubiquitous cultural image. Until the last decade, excess weight was the target of most ads for diet products; today, one is much more likely to find the enemy constructed as bulge, fat, or "flab." "Now" (a typical ad runs), "get rid of those embarrassing bumps, bulges, large stomach, flabby breasts and buttocks. Feel younger, and help prevent cellulite build-up. . . . Have a nice shape with no tummy." To achieve such results (often envisoned as the absolute eradication of body: e.g., "no tummy") a violent assault on the enemy is usually required; bulges must be "attacked" and "destroyed," fat "burned," and stomachs (or, more disgustedly, "guts") must be "busted" and "eliminated." The increasing popularity of liposuction, a far from totally safe technique developed specifically to suck out the unwanted bulges of people of normal weight (it is not recommended for the obese), suggests how far our disgust with bodily bulges has gone. The ideal here is of a body that is absolutely tight, contained, "bolted down," firm (in other words, body that is protected against eruption from within, whose internal processes are under control). Areas that are soft, loose, or "wiggly" are unacceptable, even on extremely thin bodies. Cellulite management, like liposuction, has nothing to do with weight loss, and everything to do with the quest for firm bodily margins.

This perspective helps illuminate an important continuity of meaning between compulsive dieting and bodybuilding in our culture, and reveals why it has been so easy for contemporary images of female attractiveness to oscillate back and forth between a spare "minimalist" look and a solid, muscular, athletic look. The coexistence of these seemingly disparate images does not indicate that a postmodern universe of empty, endlessly differentiating images now reigns. Rather, the two ideals, though superficially very different, are united in battle against a common platoon of enemies: the soft, the loose; unsolid, excess flesh. It is pefectly permissable in our culture (even for women) to have substantial weight and bulk—so long as it is tightly managed. On the other hand, to be slim is simply not enough—so long as the flesh jiggles. Here, we arrive at one source of insight into why it is that the image of ideal slenderness has grown thinner and thinner over the last decade, and why women with extremely slender bodies often still see themselves as "fat." Unless one goes the route of muscle building, it is virtually impossible to achieve a flab-less, excess-less body unless one trims very near to the bone.

Slenderness and the State of the Soul

This "moral" (and, as we shall see, economic) coding of the fat/slender body in terms of its capacities for self-containment and the control of impulse and desire represents the culimination of a developing historical change in the social symbolism of body weight and size. Until the late nineteenth century,

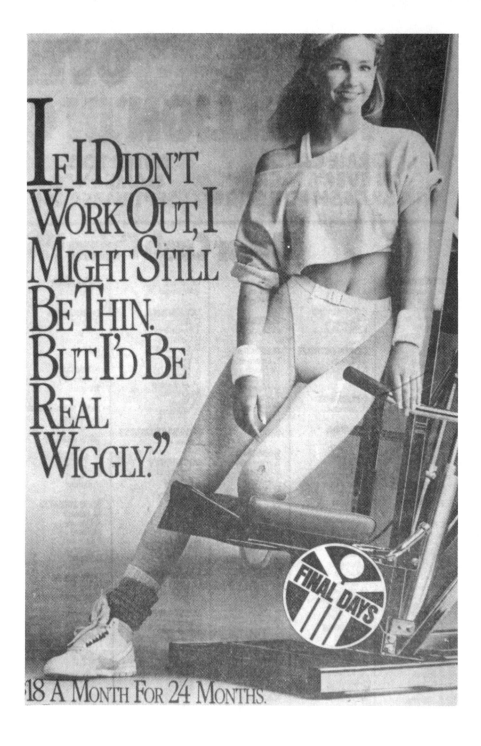

"Full Figure" Fashions

the central discriminations marked were those of class, race, and gender; the body indicated one's social identity and "place." So, for example, the bulging stomachs of successful mid-nineteenth-century businessmen and politicians were a symbol of bourgeois success, an outward manifestation of their accumulated wealth.[15] By contrast, the gracefully slender body announced aristocratic status; disdainful of the bourgeois need to display wealth and power ostentatiously, it commanded social space invisibly rather than aggressively, seemingly above the commerce in appetite or the need to eat. Subsequently, this ideal began to be appropriated by the status-seeking middle class, as slender wives became the showpieces of their husbands' success;[16] I will return to the gender symbolism of slenderness later.

Corpulence went out of middle-class vogue at the end of the century (even William Howard Taft, who had weighed over three hundred pounds while in office, went on a reducing diet); social power had come to be less dependent on the sheer accumulation of material wealth and more connected to the ability to control and manage the labor and resources of others. At the same time, excess body weight came to be seen as reflecting moral or personal inadequacy, or lack of will.[17] These associations are only possible in a culture of "overabundance" (that is, in a society in which those who control the production of "culture" have more than enough to eat). The moral requirement to diet depends upon the material preconditions that make the *choice* to "diet" an option and the possibility of personal "excess" a reality. Although slenderness has hitherto retained some of its traditional class-associations ("a woman can never be too rich or too thin"), the importance of this equation has eroded considerably over the last decade. Increasingly, the size and shape of the body has come to operate as a marker of personal, internal order (or disorder)—as a symbol for the state of the soul.

Consider one particularly clear example, that of changes in the meaning of the muscled body. Muscularity has had a variety of cultural meanings (until recently largely reserved for male bodies) which have prevented the well-developed body from playing too great a role in middle-class conceptions of attractiveness. Of course, muscles have symbolized masculine power. But at the same time, they have been associated with manual labor and chain gangs (and thus with lower-class and even criminal status), and suffused with racial meaning (via numerous film representations of sweating, glistening bodies belonging to black slaves and prizefighters). Given the racial and class biases of our culture, they were associated with the body as material, unconscious, or animalistic. Today, however, the well-muscled body has become a cultural icon; "working out" is a glamorized and sexualized yuppie activity. No longer signifying lower-class status (except when developed to extremes, at which point the old association of muscles with brute, unconscious materiality surfaces once more), the firm, developed body has become a symbol of correct *attitude;* it means that one "cares" about oneself and how one appears to others, suggesting willpower, energy, control over infantile impulse, the ability to "make something" of oneself. "You exercise, you diet," says Heather Locklear, promoting Bally Matrix Fitness Centre on television, "and you can do anything you want." Muscles express sexuality, but controlled, managed sexuality that is not about to erupt in unwanted and embarrassing display.[18]

To the degree that the question of class still operates in all this, it relates to the category of social mobility (or lack of it) rather than class *location*. So, for example, when associations of fat and lower-class status exist, they are usually mediated by qualities of attitude or "soul"—fat being perceived as indicative of laziness, lack of discipine, unwillinginess to conform, and absence of all those "managerial" abilities that, according to the dominant ideology, confer upward mobility. Correspondingly, in popular teen movies such as *Flashdance* and *Vision Quest,* the ability of the (working-class) heroine and hero to pare, prune, tighten, and master the body operates as a clear symbol of successful upward aspiration, of the penetrability of class boundaries to those who have "the right stuff." These movies (as one title explicitly suggests) are contemporary "quest myths"; like their prototype, *Rocky,* they follow the struggle of an individual to attain a personal grail, against all odds, and through numerous trials. But unlike the film quests of a previous era (which sent Mr. Smith to Washington and Mr. Deeds to town to battle the respective social evils of corrupt government and big business), *Flashdance* and *Vision Quest* render the hero's and heroine's commitment, will, and spiritual integrity through the metaphors of weight loss, exercise, and tolerance of and ability to conquer physical pain and exhaustion. (In *Vision Quest,* for example, the audience is encouraged to admire the young wrestler's perseverance when he ignores the fainting spells and nosebleeds caused by his rigorous training and dieting.)

Not surprisingly, young people with eating disorders often thematize their own experience in similar terms, as in the following excerpt from an interview with a young woman runner:

> Well, I had the willpower. I could train for competition, and I could turn down food any time. I remember feeling like I was on a constant high. And the pain? Sure, there was pain. It was incredible. Between the hunger and the muscle pain from the constant workouts? I can't tell you how much I hurt.
>
> You may think I was crazy to put myself through constant, intense pain. But you have to remember. I was fighting a battle. And when you get hurt in a battle, you're proud of it. Sure, you may scream inside, but if you're brave and really good, then you take it quietly, because you know it's the price you pay for winning. And I needed to win. I really felt that if I didn't win, I would die . . . all these enemy troops were coming at me, and I had to outsmart them. If I could discipline myself

enough—if I could keep myself lean and strong—then I could win. The pain was just a natural thing I had to deal with.[19]

As in *Vision Quest*, the external context is training for an athletic event. But here, too, that goal becomes subordinated to an internal one. The real battle, ultimately, is with the self. At this point, the limitations of the brief history that I presented in the opening paragraph of this paper are revealed. In that paragraph, the contemporary preoccupation with diet is contrasted to historical projects of body management suffused with moral meaning. In this section, however, I have suggested that examination of even the most "shallow" representations (teen movies) discloses a moral ideology—one, in fact, seemingly close to the aristocratic Greek ideal described by Foucault in *The Use of Pleasure*. The central element of that ideal, as Foucault describes it, is "an agonistic relation with the self"—aimed, not at the extirpation of desire and hunger in the interest of "purity" (as in the Christian strain of dualism), but at a "virile" mastery of desire through constant "spiritual combat."[20]

For the Greeks, however, the "virile" mastery of desire operated within a culture that valorized moderation. The culture of contemporary body-management, struggling to manage desire within a system that is dedicated to the proliferation of desireable commodities, is very different. In cultural fantasies such as *Vision Quest* and *Flashdance*, self-mastery is presented as an attainable and stable state; but, as I will argue in the next section of this paper, the reality of the contemporary agonism of the self is another matter entirely.

Slenderness and the Social Body

Mary Douglas, looking on the body as a system of "natural symbols" that reproduce social categories and concerns, has argued that anxiety about the maintenance of rigid bodily boundaries (manifested, for example, in rituals and prohibitions concerning excreta, saliva, and the strict delineation of "inside" and "outside") is most evident and intense in societies whose external boundaries are under attack.[21] Let me hypothesize, similarly, that preoccupation with the "internal" management of the body (i.e., management of its desires) is produced by instabilities in the "macro-regulation" of desire within the system of the social body.

In advanced consumer capitalism, as Robert Crawford has elegantly argued, an unstable, agonistic construction of personality is produced by the contradictory structure of economic life.[22] On the one hand, as "producer-selves," we must be capable of sublimating, delaying, repressing desires for immediate gratification; we must cultivate the work ethic. On the other hand, as "consumer-selves" we serve the system through a boundless capacity to capitulate to desire and indulge in impulse; we must become creatures who hunger for constant and immediate satisfaction. The regulation of desire thus becomes an ongoing problem, as we find ourselves continually besieged by temptation, while socially condemned for overindulgence. (It goes without saying that those who cannot afford to indulge, teased and frustrated by the culture, face different problems.)

Food and diet are central arenas for the expression of these contradictions. On television and in popular magazines with a flip of the page or barely a pause between commercials, images of luscious foods and the rhetoric of craving and desire are replaced by advertisements for grapefruit diets, low-calorie recipes, and exercise equipment. Even more disquieting than these manifest oppositions, however, are the constant attempts by advertisers to mystify them, suggesting that the contradiction doesn't really exist—that one *can* "have it all." Diets and exercise programs accordingly present themselves via the imagery of instant gratification ("From Fat to Fabulous in 21 Days," "Size 22 to Size 10 in No Time Flat," "Six Minutes to an Olympic-Class Stomach") and effortlessness ("3,000 Sit-Ups Without Moving an Inch . . . Ten Miles of Jogging Lying Flat on Your Back," "85 pounds Without Diet-ing," and even, shamelessly, "Exercise Without Exercise"). In reality, however, the opposition is not so easily reconciled. Rather, it presents a classic "double-bind," in which the self is torn in two mutually incompatible directions. The contradiction is not an abstract one but stems from the specific historical construction of a "consuming passion" from which all inclinations toward balance, moderation, rationality, and foresight have been excluded.

Conditioned to lose control at the very sight of desirable products, we can only master our desires through rigid defenses against them. The slender body codes the tantalizing ideal of a well-managed self in which all is "in order" despite the contradictions of consumer culture. Thus, whether or not the struggle is played out in terms of food and diet, many of us may find our lives vacillating between a daytime rigidly ruled by the "performance principle" while our nights and weekends capitulate to unconscious "letting go" (food, shopping, liquor, television, and other addictive drugs). In this way, the central contradiction of the system inscribes itself on our bodies, and bulimia emerges as a characteristic modern personality construction, precisely and explicitly expressing the ex-treme development of the hunger for unrestrained consumption (exhibited in the bulimic's uncontrollable food-binges) existing in unstable tension alongside the requirement that we sober up, "clean up our act," get back in firm control on Monday morning (the necessity for purge—exhibited in the bulimic's vomit-ing, compulsive exercising, and laxative purges).

The same structural contradiction is also inscribed in what has been termed (incorrectly) the "paradox" that we have an "epidemic" of anorexia nervosa in this country "despite the fact that we have an overweight majority."[23] Far from paradoxical, the coexistence of anorexia and obesity reveals the instability of the contemporary personality construction, the difficulty of finding homeo-stasis between the "producer" and "consumer" aspects of the self. While

bulimia embodies the unstable "double-bind" of consumer capitalism, anorexia and obesity embody an attempted "resolution" of that double-bind. Anorexia could therefore be seen as an extreme development of the capacity for self-denial and repression of desire (the work ethic in absolute "control"); obesity similarly points to an extreme capacity to capitulate to desire (consumerism in control). Both are rooted in the same consumer-culture construction of desire as overwhelming and overtaking the self. Given that construction, total submission or rigid defense become the only possible postures.[24]

Neither anorexia nor obesity is accepted by the culture as an appropriate response. The absolute conquest of hunger and desire (even in symbolic form) could never be tolerated by a consumer system—even if the Christian dualism of our culture also predisposes us to be dazzled by the anorectic's ability seemingly to transcend the flesh.[25] Anorectics are proud of this ability; but, as the disorder progresses, they usually feel the need to hide their skeletal bodies from those around them. If cultural attitudes toward the anorectic are ambivalent, however, reactions to the obese are not. As Marcia Millman documents in *Such a Pretty Face,* the obese elicit blinding rage and disgust in our culture, and are often viewed in terms that suggest an infant sucking hungrily, unconsciously at its mother's breasts—greedy, self-absorbed, lazy, without self-control or willpower.[26] People avoid sitting near the obese; comics feel no need to restrain their cruelty; socially, they are unacceptable at public functions (one man wrote to "Dear Abby," saying that he was planning to replace his brother and sister-in-law as honor attendants at his wedding, because "they are both quite overweight"). Significantly, the part of the obese anatomy most often targeted for vicious attack, and most despised by the obese themselves, is the stomach—symbol of consumption (in the case of the obese, unrestrained consumption taking over the organism; one of Marcia Millman's interviewees recalls how the husband of a friend called hers "an awful, cancerous-looking growth").[27]

Slenderness, Self-Management and Normalization

Self-management in consumer culture, I have been arguing, becomes more elusive as it becomes more pressing. The attainment of an acceptable body is extremely difficult for those who do not come by it "naturally" (whether aided by genetics, metabolism, or high activity-level) and as the ideal becomes firmer and tauter it begins to exclude most people. Constant watchfulness over appetite and strenuous work on the body itself are required to conform to this ideal, while the most popular means of "correction"—dieting—often ensures its own failure, as the experience of deprivation leads to compensatory binging, with its attendant feelings of defeat, worthlessness, and loss of hope. Between the media images of self-containment and self-mastery and the reality of constant, everyday stress and anxiety about one's appearance lies the chasm which produces bodies habituated to self-monitoring and self-normalization.

Ultimately, the body (besides being evaluated for its success or failure at getting itself in order) is seen as demonstrating correct or incorrect attitudes toward the demands of normalization themselves. The obese and anorectic are therefore disturbing partly because they embody resistance to cultural norms. Bulimics, by contrast, typically strive for the conventionally attractive body shape dictated by their more "normative" pattern of managing desire. In the case of the obese, in particular, what is perceived as their defiant rebellion against normalization appears to be a source of the hostility they inspire. The anorectic at least pays homage to dominant cultural values, outdoing them in their own terms:

> I wanted people to look at me and see something special. I wanted to look in the face of a stranger and see admiration, so that I would know that I accomplished something that was just about impossible for most people, especially in our society. . . . From what I've seen, more people fail at losing weight than at any other single goal. I found out how to do what everyone else couldn't: I could lose as much or as little weight as I wanted. And that meant I was better than everyone else.[28]

The anorectic thus strives to stand above the crowd by excelling at its own rules; in so doing, however, she exposes the hidden penalties. But the obese—particularly those who claim to be happy although overweight—are perceived as not playing by the rules at all. While the rest of us struggle to be acceptable and "normal," they must not be allowed to get away with it; they must be put in their place, humiliated, and defeated.

A number of recent talk shows make this abundantly clear. On one, much of the audience reaction was given over to disbelief, and the attempt to prove to one obese woman that she was *not* happy: "I can't believe you don't want to be slim and beautiful, I just can't believe it," "I heard you talk a lot about how you feel good about yourself and you like yourself, but I really think you're kidding yourself," "It's hard for me to believe that Mary Jane is really happy . . . you don't fit into chairs, it's hard to get through the doorway. My God, on the subway, forget it." When Mary Jane persisted in her assertion that she was happy, she was warned, in a viciously self-righteous tone, that it wouldn't last: "Mary Jane, to be the way you are today, you had better start going on a diet soon, because if you don't you're going to get bigger and bigger and bigger. It's true."[29] On another show, in an effort to subdue an increasingly hostile and offensive audience, one of the doctor-guests kept trying to reassure them the "fat and happy" target of their attacks did not *really* mean that she didn't *want* to lose weight; rather, she was simply tired of trying and failing. This is the construction that allows people to give their sympathy to the obese, assuming as it does the obese person's acknowledgment that to be "normal" is the most desired goal, elusive only because of personal inadequacy. Those who are willing to present themselves as pitiable, in pain, and conscious of their own unattractiveness—often demonstrated, on these shows, by self-admissions about intimate physical difficulties, orgies of self-hate or descriptions of gross consumption of food, win the sympathy and concern of the audience.

Slenderness and Gender

It has been amply documented that women in our culture are more tyrannized by the contemporary slenderness ideal than men, as they typically have been by beauty ideals in general. It is far more important to men than to women that their partners be slim.[30] Women are much more prone than men to perceive themselves as "too fat."[31] And, as is by now well known, girls and women are more likely to engage in crash dieting, laxative abuse, and compulsive exercising, and are far more vulnerable to eating disorders than males.[32] But eating disorders are not only "about" slenderness, any more than (as I have been arguing) *slenderness* is only—or even chiefly—about slenderness. My aim in this section, therefore, is not to "explain" facts about which so much has now been written from historical, psychological, and sociological points of view. Rather, I want to remain with the image of the slender body, confronting it now both as a gendered body (the slender body as female body—the usual form in which the image is displayed) and as a body whose gender meaning is never neutral. This "layer" of gender-coded signification, suffusing other meanings, overdetermines slenderness as a contemporary ideal of specifically *female* attractiveness.

The exploration of contemporary slenderness as a metaphor for the correct management of desire becomes more adequate when we confront the fact that hunger has always been a potent cultural metaphor for female sexuality, power, and desire—from the blood-craving Kali, who in one representation is shown devouring her own entrails, to the language of insatiability and voraciousness that marks the fifteenth-century discourse on witches, to the "Man-Eater" of contemporary rock lyrics: "Oh, oh, here she comes, watch out boys, she'll chew you up." This is a message, too, as I have argued elsewhere, that eating-disordered women have often internalized when they experience their battle with hunger in the gendered terms of a struggle between male and female sides of the self (the former described as "spiritual" and disciplined, the latter as appetitive and dangerous). In the anorectic's lexicon, and throughout dominant Western religious and philosophical traditions, the "virile" capacity for self-management is decisively coded as male. By contrast, all those "bodily" spontaneities—hunger, sexuality, the emo-

Even a woman in great shape is, on the average, 21% fat.

Which makes our salami look even better —you see, Hebrew National salami is only 17% fat.

That's not only less than our model, Kim Cooper; it's 50% less than the leading Genoa salami.

43% less than Oscar Mayer bologna.

And 8% less than even Best Kosher's "low-salt, low-fat, no-sugar" salami.

Mind you, this is no diet salami. This is good, old-fashioned, 100% beef, kosher salami.

So the next time you feel like a great-tasting, nutritional, low-fat lunch, skip the tuna and cottage cheese, and have some salami. That's what Kim does. How do you think she stays 79% fat free?

There's more fat on her than on our salami.

Kim Cooper
79% Fat Free

HEBREW NATIONAL

"You Should Be So Lean."

tions—seen as needful of containment and control have been culturally constructed and coded as female.[33]

The management of female desire becomes a particular problem in phallocentric cultures. Women's desires are "other," mysterious, threatening to erupt and challenge the patriarchal order. Some writers have argued that female hunger (as a code for female desire) is especially problematized during periods of disruption and change in established gender-relations and in the position of women. In such periods (of which our own is arguably one), nightmare images of what Bram Djikstra has called "the consuming woman" theme proliferate in art and literature (images representing female desire unleashed), while dominant constructions of the female body become more sylphlike—unlike the body of a fully developed woman, more like that of an adolescent or boy (images that might be called female desire unborn). Djikstra argues such a case concerning the late nineteenth century, pointing to the devouring sphinxes and bloodsucking vampires of *fin-de-siècle* art, and the accompanying vogue for elongated, "sublimely emaciated" female bodies.[34] A commentator at the time vividly describes the emergence of a new body-style, not very unlike our own:

> Women can change the cut of their clothes at will, but how can they change the cut of their anatomies? And yet, they have done just this thing. Their shoulders have become narrow and slightly sloping, their throats more slender, their hips smaller and their arms and legs elongated to an extent that suggests that bed, upon which the robber, Procrustes, used to stretch his victims . . .[35]

The fact that our own era has witnessed a comparable shift (from the hourglass figure of the fifties to the lanky, "androgynous," increasingly elongated slender look that has developed over the past decade) cries out for interpretation. This shift, however, needs to be interpreted not only from the standpoint of male anxiety over women's desires (Djikstra's analysis, while crucial, is only half the story), but also from the standpoint of the women who embrace the "new look." For them, it may have a very different meaning; it may symbolize, not so much the containment of female desire, as its liberation from a domestic, reproductive destiny. The fact that the slender female body can carry both these (seemingly contradictory) meanings is one reason, I would suggest, for its compelling attraction in periods of gender-change.[36]

To elaborate this argument in more detail: earlier, I presented some quotations from interviews with eating-disordered women in which they describe their revulsion to breasts, stomachs, and all other bodily bulges. At that point, I subjected these quotations to a "gender-neutral" reading. While not rescinding that interpretation, I want to overlay it now with another reading, which I have developed at greater length elsewhere.[37] The characteristic anorexic revulsion toward hips, stomach, and breasts (often accompanied by a disgust at menstruation, and relief at amenorrhoea) might be viewed as expressing rebellion against maternal, domestic femininity—a femininity that represents both the suffocating control the anorectic experiences her own mother as having had over her, *and* the mother's actual lack of position and authority outside the domestic arena. Here we encounter another reason for anxiety over soft, protuberant body-parts. They evoke helpless infancy and symbolize maternal femininity as it has been constructed over the last hundred years in the West. That femininity, as Dorothy Dinnerstein has argued, is perceived as both frighteningly powerful and, as the child comes increasingly to recognize the hierarchical nature of the sexual division-of-labor, as utterly powerless.[38]

The most literal symbolic form of maternal femininity is represented by the nineteenth-century "hourglass" figure, emphasizing breasts and hips— the markers of reproductive femaleness—against a wasp waist.[39] At the same time, the sharp contrast between the female and male form, made possible by the use of corsets, bustles, and so forth, reproduced on the body the dualistic division of social and economic life into clearly defined "male" and "female" spheres. It is not until the post-World War II period, with its relocation of women from factory to home and its coercive bourgeois dualism of the happy-homemaker-mother and the responsible, "provider" father, that such clear bodily demarcation of "male" and "female" spheres surfaces again. The era of the cinch belt, the pushup bra, and Marilyn Monroe could be viewed, for the body, as an era of "resurgent Victorianism."[40] It was also the last coercively normalizing body-ideal to reign before the beginnings of the ascendancy of boyish slenderness, in the mid-1960s.

From this perspective, one might speculate that the boys who reacted with disgust or anxiety to fleshy female parts were reacting to evocations of maternal power, newly threatening in an age when women can bring their desires out of the confinements of the home and into the public, traditionally male arena.[41] The buxom Sophia Loren was a sex goddess in an era when women were trained to channel their energy and desire into home, husband, and family. Today, it is required of that energy, loose in the public world, to be stripped of its psychic resonances with maternal power, and normalized according to the professional "male" standards of the public arena. From the standpoint of male anxiety, the lean body of the professional businesswoman today may symbolize such a neutralization. With her body and her dress, she declares symbolic allegiance to the professional, white, male world, along with her lack of intention to subvert that arena with alternative "female values." At the same time, insofar as she is clearly "dressing up," *playing* "male" (almost always with a "softening" fashion touch to establish traditional feminine decorativeness), she represents no serious competition (symbolically, that is) to the "real men" of the workplace.

The cultural association of slenderness with reduced power and contracted social space is strikingly revealed, as I mentioned earlier, in fashion poses that juxtapose the slender female body against the currently quite solid and powerful male body ideal. But for many women, this "androgynous" ideal, far from symbolizing reduced power, may symbolize freedom (as it did in the 1890s and 1920s) from a reproductive destiny and a construction of femininity seen as constraining and suffocating. Correspondingly, taking on the accoutrements of the white, male world may be experienced as empowerment by women themselves, and as their chance to embody qualities—detachment, self-containment, self-mastery, control—that are highly valued in our culture.[42] The slender body, as I have argued earlier, symbolizes such qualities. "It was about power," says Kim Morgan, speaking of her obsession with slenderness, "that was the big thing . . . something I could throw in people's faces, and they would look at me and I'd only weigh this much, but I was strong and in control, and hey *you're* sloppy . . . "[43] The taking on of "male" power-as-self-mastery is another locus where shedding pounds and developing muscles, for all their surface dissimilarities, intersect. Appropriately, the new "Joy of Cooking" takes place in the gym, in one advertisement that shamelessly exploits the associations of female bodybuilding and liberation from a traditional, domestic destiny.

In the intersection of these gender-issues and more general cultural dilemmas concerning the management of desire, we see how the tightly managed body—whether demonstrated through sleek, minimalist lines or firmly developed muscles—has been overdetermined as a contemporary ideal of specifically female attractiveness. The axis of consumption/production is gender-overlaid, as I have argued, by the hierarchical dualism which constructs a dangerous, appetitive, bodily "female principle" in opposition to a masterful "male" will. We would thus expect that when the regulation of desire becomes especially problematic (as it is in advanced consumer cultures), women and their bodies will pay the greatest symbolic and material toll. When such a situation is compounded by anxiety about *women*'s desires in periods when traditional forms of gender-organization are being challenged, this toll is multiplied. It would be wrong to suppose, however, that it is exacted through the simple *repression* of female hunger. Rather, here as elsewhere, power works also "from below," as women associate slenderness and self-management via the experience of newfound freedom (from a domestic destiny) and empowerment in the public arena. In this connection, we might note the difference between contemporary ideals of slenderness, coded in terms of self-mastery and expressed through

How to Make a Guy's Look Girlish

Add the right accents to handsome haberdashery and you can give it a frankly feminine air. Here are a few softening touches worth trying.

● **SCARVES** Drape a lacy scarf around your shoulders, tie a chiffon scarf in a floppy bow at your throat or let a lace-trimmed hanky peak out of your jacket or shirt pocket.

● **TIES** Knot a softly woven or paisley print tie and wear it the way no man would—with a strand or two of pearls.

● **JEWELRY** Gems are the definitive differentiating pieces. Try: long link chains with fake jewels, rhinestone pendants, pretty pins and elegant drop earrings.

● **BAGS** Carry a clutch in soft brightly colored leather—it has a businesslike shape with a casual flair.

● **SHOES** Go for mannish wing tip oxfords or Loafers with feminine details— pointed toes, under-slung heels, two-tone styling, leather bows or tassels—and wear them with bright or patterned tights or delicate crocheted socks. ●

Lace-trimmed pocket square

Red reptilian-leather clutch

Anne Klein II notch lapel shirt, V-neck sweater, blazer and pants. Amy Sinaiko

Advertisement for the "New Man" women's clothing line

traditionally "male" body symbolism, and mid-Victorian ideals of female slenderness, which symbolically emphasized reproductive femininity corseted under tight "external" constraints. But whether externally bound or internally managed, no body can escape either the imprint of culture or its gendered meanings.

Notes

1. See Keith Walden, "The Road to Fat City: An Interpretation of the Development of Weight Consciousness in Western Society," *Historical Reflections* 12:3 (1985):331–373.

2. See Michel Foucault, *The Use of Pleasure* (New York: Random House, 1986).

3. See Rudolph Bell, *Holy Anorexia* (Chicago: University of Chicago Press, 1985); and Carolyn Bynum, *Holy Feast and Holy Fast: The Religious Significance of Food to Medieval Women* (Berkeley: University of California Press, 1987), 31–48.

4. See Kim Chernin, *The Obsession: Reflections on the Tyranny of Slenderness* (New York: Harper and Row, 1981).

5. See Thomas Cash, Barbara Winstead, and Louis Janda, "The Great American Shape-up," *Psychology Today,* April 1986; "Dieting: The Losing Game," *Time,* 20 January 1986, among numerous other general reports. Concerning women's preoccupation in particular, see n. 41 below.

6. For Foucault on "docile bodies," see *Discipline and Punish* (New York: Vintage, 1979), 135–69. For an application of Foucault's ideas to the practices of diet and fitness, see Walden, "The Road to Fat City." For a Foucauldian analysis of the practices of femininity, see Sandra Bartky, "Foucault, Femininity, and the Modernization of Patriarchal Power," in *Feminism and Foucault,* ed. Irene Diamond and Lee Quinby (Boston: Northeastern University Press, 1988), 61–86.

7. Foucault (1979), 136.

8. "Fat or Not, 4th Grade Girls Diet Lest They Be Teased or Unloved," *Wall Street Journal,* 11 February 1986 (based on a University of California study.) A still more recent study conducted at the University of Ottawa concluded that by age 7, a majority of young girls are anxious about their weight, and convinced they are much fatter than they are. ("Girls, at 7, Think Thin, Study Finds," *New York Times,* February 11, 1988)

9. On the "spreading" nature of eating disorders, see Paul Garfinkel and David Garner, *Anorexia Nervosa: A Multidimensional Perspective* (New York: Bruner Mazel, 1982), 102–03; and George Hsu, "Are Eating Disorders Becoming More Common in Blacks?" *The International Journal of Eating Disorders* 6:1 (January 1987): 113–24. Despite these trends, resistance to the slenderness ideal persists, and should not be overlooked as a source of insight into different cultural models of beauty and the conditions that promote them.

10. See Mary Douglas, *Natural Symbols* (New York: Pantheon, 1982); and *Purity and Danger* (London: Routledge and Kegan Paul, 1966).

11. This approach presupposes, of course, that popular cultural images *have* meaning, and are not merely arbitrary formations spawned by the whimsy of "fashion," the vicissitudes of Madison Avenue, or the "logic" of postindustrial capitalism, within which (as it has been argued, by Frederick and others) a product or image's attraction derives solely from pure differentiation, from its cultural positioning, its suggestion of the novel or new. Within such a "postmodern" logic, Gail Faurschou argues, "Fashion has become the commodity 'par excellence.' It is fed by

all of capitalism's incessant, frantic, reproductive passion and power. Fashion *is* the logic of planned obsolescence—not just the necessity for market survival, but the cycle of desire itself, the endless process through which the body is decoded and recoded, in order to define and inhabit the newest territorialized spaces of capital's expansion;" "Fashion and the Cultural Logic of Postmodernity," *Canadian Journal of Political and Social Theory* 11:1–2 (1987):72. While I don't disagree with Faurschou's general characterization of "fashion" here, the heralding of an absolute historical break, after which images have become completely empty of history, substance, and symbolic determination, seems *itself* an embodiment, rather than a de-mystifier, of the compulsively innovative logic of postmodernity. More important to the argument of this piece, a "postmodern logic" cannot explain the magnetic cultural hold of the slenderness ideal, long after any novel juxtaposition with more fleshy forms from the 1950s has worn off. Many times, in fact, the principle of the "new" has made tentative, but ultimately nominal, gestures toward the end of the reign of thinness, announcing a "softer," "curvier" look, and so forth. How many women have picked up magazines whose covers declared such a turn, only to find that the images within remain essentially continuous with prevailing norms? Large breasts may be making a comeback, but they are attached to extremely thin, often athletic bodies. Here, I would suggest, there are constraints on the pure logic of postmodernity—constraints that this paper tries to explore.

12. See Robert Crawford, "A Cultural Account of 'Health'—Self-Control, Release, and the Social Body," *Issues in the Political Economy of Health Care,* ed. John McKinlay (New York: Methuen, 1985), 60–103. I want to stress that my own analysis is not intended to "explain" eating disorders, which, as I have argued elsewhere, are a complex, multidetermined formation requiring analysis and interpretation on many levels.

13. Ira Sacker and Marc Zimmer, *Dying To Be Thin* (New York: Warner, 1987), 57.

14. Dalma Heyn, "Body Vision?" *Mademoiselle,* April 1987, 213.

15. See Lois Banner, *American Beauty* (Chicago: University of Chicago Press, 1983), 232.

16. Ibid., 53–55.

17. See Walden, *Historical Reflections* 12:3. 334–35, 353.

18. I thank Mario Moussa for this point, and for the Heather Locklear quotation.

19. Ira Sacker and Marc Zimmer, 149–50.

20. Foucault (1986), 64–70.

21. See Mary Douglas, *Purity and Danger,* 114–28.

22. See Robert Crawford, "A Cultural Account of 'Health.' "

23. John Farquhar, Stanford University Medical Center, quoted in "Dieting: The Losing Game," *Time,* 20 February 1986, 57.

24. I discuss the construction of hunger in eating disorders more fully in "Anorexia Nervosa: Psychopathology as the Crystallization of Culture," *The Philosophical Forum* 17:2 (Winter 1985), 33–103.

25. While there has been controversy over the appropriateness of describing medieval saints as "anorexic" (see, for example, Bell, *Holy Anorexia,* and Bynum, *Holy Feast and Holy Fast* for different views on the subject), no one, as far as I am aware, has noticed that a stronger case can be made for focusing on the "spiritual" aspects of the asceticism of modern-day anorectics. As I suggest in "Anorexia Nervosa: Psychopathology as the Crystallization of Culture," it is striking how often the imagery of anorectics includes Christian/ascetic themes, with a dualistic construction of mind/matter and spirit/appetite coded in terms of purity/contamination, and the ultimate goal of cleansing the soul of desire/hunger. Thus, certain foods are seen by the anorectic as tainted, contaminating, and dangerous, while the practice of self-denial and, at times, self-

mortification, is seen as purifying. "Fasting," says Clement of Alexandria (d.ca. 215), "empties the soul of matter and makes it, with the body, clear and light for the reception of divine truth" (Bynum, p. 36). A similar war against matter, and the association of the de-materialized (i.e., thin) body with enhanced and purified vision, provides common images in the self-descriptions of anorectics, where comparisons with medieval asceticism are explicitly offered. Compare, for example, the words of "a certain Daniel" from the medieval *Sayings of the Fathers:* "As the body waxes fat, the soul grows thin; and as the body grows thin, the soul by so much waxes fat" (Bynum, p. 216) with those of a contemporary anorectic: "My soul seemed to grow as my body waned. I felt like one of those early Christian saints who starved themselves in the desert sun" (Bordo, "Anorexia Nervosa," p. 88).

26.   See Marcia Millman, *Such a Pretty Face: Being Fat in America* (New York: Norton, 1980), esp. 65–79

27.   Ibid., 77.

28.   Ira Sacker and Marc Zimmer, 32.

29.   These quotations are taken from transcripts of the Phil Donahue show, provided by Multimedia Entertainment, Cincinnati, Ohio.

30.   The discrepancy emerges very early, according to recent studies. "We don't expect boys to be that handsome," says a nine-year-old girl in the California study cited above. "But boys expect girls to be perfect and beautiful. And skinny." Her male classmate agrees: "Fat girls aren't like regular girls," he says. Many of my female students have described in their journals the pressure their boyfriends place on them to stay or get slim. They have plenty of social support for such demands. Sylvester Stallone told Cornelia Guest that he liked his woman "anorexic"; she immediately lost 24 pounds (*Time*, 18 April, 1988, 89). But few men want their women to go that far; Actress Valerie Bertinelli reports (*Syracuse Post*) how her husband, Eddie Van Halen, "helps keep her in shape": "When I get too heavy, he says, 'Honey, lose weight.' Then when I get too thin, he says, "I don't like making love with you, you've got to gain some weight."

31.   The most famous of such studies, by now replicated many times, appeared in *Glamour*, February 1984; a poll of 33,000 women revealed that 75 percent considered themselves "too fat," while only 25 percent of them were above Metropolitan Life Insurance standards, and 30 percent were *below*. ("Feeling Fat in a Thin Society," p. 86). See also Kevin Thompson, "Larger than Life," *Psychology Today*, April 1986; Dalma Heyn, "Why We're Never Satisfied With Our Bodies," *McCalls*, May 1982; Daniel Goleman, "Dislike of Own Body Found Common Among Women," *New York Times*, 19 March, 1985.

32.   90 percent of all sufferers from eating disorders are female, a fact that has been explored from many clinical, historical, psychological, and cultural angles. Some of the most profound insights—insights that have become incorporated, often without adequate acknowledgement, into more recent clinical and scholarly literature—have come from Kim Chernin, *The Obsession, the Hungry Self* (New York: Harper and Row, 1981) and Susie Ohrbach, *Hunger Strike: The Anorectic's Struggle as a Metaphor for Our Age* (New York: Norton, 1986).

33.   See Bordo, "Anorexia Nervosa." On female hunger as a metaphor for female sexuality in Victorian literature, see Helena Michie, *The Flesh Made Word* (New York: Oxford, 1987). On cultural associations of male/mind and female/matter, see, for instance, Dorothy Dinnerstein, *The Mermaid and the Minotaur* (New York: Harper and Row, 1977), Genevieve Lloyd, *The Man of Reason* (Minneapolis: University of Minnesota Press, 1984), and Luce Irigaray, *Speculum of the Other Woman* (Ithaca: Cornell University Press, 1985).

34.   Bram Djikstra, *Idols of Perversity* (New York: Oxford University Press, 1986), 29.

35.   "Mutable Beauty," *Saturday Night*, 1 February, 1902, 9.

36.   Mary Jacobus and Sally Shuttleworth, pointing to the sometimes boyish figure of the "new woman" of late-Victorian literature, have suggested to me the appropriateness of this

interpretation for the late-Victorian era; I have, however, chosen to argue the point only with respect to the current context.

37. Bordo, "Anorexia Nervosa."

38. See Chernin, for an exploration of the connection between early infant experience and attitudes toward the fleshy, female body. For the impact on clinical literature of the feminist/cultural argument about anorexia, see Susan Wooley, "Intensive Treatment of Bulimia and Body-Image Disturbance," in *Handbook of Eating Disorders,* ed. Kelly D. Brownell and John P. Foreyt (New York: Basic Books, 1986), 476–502.

39. Historian LeeAnn Whites has pointed out to me how perverse this body-symbolism seems when we remember what a pregnant and nursing body is actually like. The hourglass figure is really more correctly a symbolic "advertisement" to men of the woman's reproductive, domestic *sphere* than a representation of her reproductive *body.*

40. See Banner, 283–85.

41. It is no accident, I believe, that Dolly Parton, now down to 100 pounds and truly looking as though she might snap in two in a strong wind, opened her new show with a statement of its implicitly antifeminist premise: "I'll bust my butt to please you!" (Surely she already has?) Her television presence is now recessive, beseeching, desiring only to serve; clearly, her packagers are exploiting the cultural resonances of her diminished physicality. Parton, of course, is no androgynous body-type. Rather, like *Wheel of Fortune's* Vanna White (who also lost a great deal of weight at one point in her career, and is obsessive about staying thin) she has tremendous appeal to those longing for a more "traditional" femininity in an era when women's public presence and power have greatly increased. Parton and White's large breasts evoke a nurturing, maternal sexuality. But after weight-reduction regimens set to anorexic standards, those breasts now adorn bodies that are vulnerably, breakably thin, with fragile, spindly arms and legs like those of young colts. Parton and White suggest the pleasures of nurturant female sexuality without any encounter with its powers and dangers.

42. See my essay, "The Body and the Reproduction of Femininity: A Feminist Appropriation of Foucault" in *Gender/Body/Knowledge: Feminist Reconstructions of Being and Knowing,* ed. Susan Bordo and Alison Jaggar (New Jersey: Rutgers University Press, 1989), for elaboration of these points.

43. "The Waist Land: Eating Disorders in America," 1985, Gannett Corporation, *MTI* Teleprograms. The analysis presented here becomes more complicated with bulimia, in which the hungering "female" self refuses to be annihilated, and feminine ideals are typically not rejected but embraced. See also Bordo, "How Television Teaches Women to Hate Their Hungers," *Mirror Images* (Newsletter of Anorexia/Bulimia Support, Syracuse, N.Y.), 4:1 (1986): 8–9.

6

Feminism, Medicine, and the Meaning of Childbirth

Paula A. Treichler

> Language is not an abstract system of normative forms but rather a concrete heteroglot conception of the world. All words have the "taste" of a profession, a genre, a tendency, a party, a particular work, a particular person, a generation, an age group, the day and hour. Each word tastes of the context and contexts in which it has lived its socially charged life—M. M. Bakhtin[1]

> "Who gives [birth]? And to whom is it given? Certainly it doesn't feel like giving, which implies a flow, a gentle handing over, no coercion. . . . Maybe the phrase was made by someone viewing the result only. . . . Yet one more thing that needs to be renamed.—Margaret Atwood[2]

Whatever else a culture does or does not do, if it wishes to reproduce itself, it must produce new members. Because cultural reproduction depends upon human reproduction, questions of childbearing are invariably significant in the life of a culture, and significant changes in childbearing patterns often signal broad cultural change. The purpose of this essay is to examine the current crisis in childbearing in the United States and specifically to explore its complexities and contradictions. I use the term *crisis* conventionally, to mean a turning point in a sequence of events after which things get better or worse. The term *childbirth crisis*—widely used by feminists, along with *childbirth revolution*—refers to significant recent challenges to long-standing, medically managed, hospital-based childbirth. These challenges involve sometimes uneasy alliances among alternative movements, including feminism, midwifery, the consumer movement, and the home-birth movement. Initially perceived by organized medicine as a kind of wild and crazy conglomeration of nonprofessionals, these alternative groups have nonetheless threatened standard medical practice, mounting a challenge that medicine has had increasingly to address. Accordingly, childbearing patterns in the United States are being disrupted at many levels: through legislative battles over who can legally deliver babies (professional scope-of-practice acts), malpractice and other forms of litigation, rising insurance rates and health-care costs, lobbying contests, and market competition. As these disruptions are played out in

Research for this essay was supported in part by grants from the National Council of Teachers of English and the Graduate College Research Board of the University of Illinois at Urbana-Champaign and by a residency at the Ragdale Foundation. My thanks for comments or research assistance to Anne Balsamo, Daniel K. Bloomfield, Edward M. Bruner, Mary Jacobus, Lawrence Grossberg, Sally McConnell-Ginet, Laura O'Banion, Cary Nelson, and Sally Shuttleworth.

113

language, they embody the tensions and contradictions of the health-care system and the culture in which they occur.

A commonsense deduction from current statistics suggests neither tension nor contradiction but consensus: for of the more than three million babies born in the United States each year, the overwhelming majority of them (more than 98 percent) are delivered in hospitals by physicians.[3] A 1982 Institute of Medicine study of birth settings takes the conventional medical view that this demonstrates the success of hospitals in making birth safe and reflects the steady scientific progress of modern obstetrics. But the feminist interpretation is different. Childbirth takes place in hospitals because there are few alternatives: yes, obstetrics has been successful—not in creating safe childbirth but in creating a monopoly; for its own professional gain, organized medicine in the U.S. has "medicalized" childbirth, a process that in other cultures and other countries frequently takes place outside hospitals with little medical intervention.[4]

The feminist claim is convincing in many respects: scientific evidence lends support to a view of childbirth as a normal, "natural" event that calls for medical intervention only under certain circumstances. For an industrialized country, U.S. maternal- and infant-mortality statistics are nothing to be proud of and show a widening discrepancy between white and minority women and infants; and beyond the quantitative evidence, many women have eloquently expressed their dissatisfaction with traditional obstetric care and called publicly for alternatives.[5] The Institute of Medicine study notes that although the percentage of annual out-of-hospital births has remained steady in recent years, the number of freestanding birth centers has grown dramatically. Medicine's increasingly overt bid to maintain its share of the childbirth market indicates the presence of a third perspective on the "childbirth revolution," a strictly economic one. Recent changes in the financing and regulation of health care are acting to dislodge medicine from its position as a (loosely speaking) regulated monopoly; freer market competition with its supposedly more diversified consumer options inevitably subjects childbearing as well to the forces of the market. Certainly the language of the marketplace pervades discussions of childbearing even among those to whom the market approach is repugnant.

Yet the elusiveness of resolution and acceptable compromise suggests that childbirth continues to be a site of contestation. We do not yet know whether childbearing will ultimately be "better" or "worse." Perhaps it could not have been otherwise: ideological polarization is a major historical legacy of earlier debates on childbirth. Like them, today's debates also turn on pressing cultural questions: What has been the impact of industrialization and modernization on social and cultural life? Has technology disrupted what is taken to be "natural"? Should health care then be openly acknowledged as a broad social responsibility instead of a quasi-commodity like other commodities in a marketplace economy?[6] These questions provide the context in which the nature of childbirth as an event is overtly contested. One's position on the nature of childbirth in turn shapes corollary debates on more restricted questions, each with its own points of confrontation and scholarly literature: Where should birth take place? Who is best qualified to supervise it? Who should decide? How should pain be managed? How much technological intervention should be available? Who should profit from it? How much should childbirth cost? Who should pay? Who should be paid?

There are distinct positions in the United States on all these questions. To add to the complexity, as the childbirth revolution moves toward the end of the twentieth century, it finds the twenty-first century already there to greet it. The recent "Baby M" case revealed widespread confusion even among politically sophisticated groups and individuals. It also made clear that U.S. policy toward human sex and reproduction—including sex education, pregnancy, childbirth, maternity, surrogacy, *in vitro* (even *in vivo*) fertilization, teen pregnancy, and so-called "fetal distress syndrome"—remains an inconsistent patchwork of federal and state laws, initiatives, clinical practice acts, programs, lobbying efforts, and ideological pronouncements that involve such concepts as individual rights, free enterprise, market forces, God's will, and the family. Not unexpectedly, contradictions abound. Some states have laws, for example, that allow surrogacy but ban prostitution, raising the question of why a woman can legally rent out her womb but not her vagina; laws of other states ban the one but allow the other. A 1987 cartoon by Marlette, reprinted in *Newsweek* (16 Feb. 1987) shows a bemused woman facing a rack of greeting cards arranged by categories: BIRTHDAYS — MOTHER'S DAY — SURROGATE MOTHER'S DAY — TEST-TUBE BABIES — FROZEN EMBRYOS — ANONYMOUS SPERM DONORS. Another cartoon captures the national spirit of utter confusion as one lawyer asks another, "what did the judge decide to do in that surrogate motherhood case?" The other replies, "To take early retirement."

It is not surprising that in a pluralistic society positions should be diverse and debates fierce. And yet decades can go by with little external change. Then a crisis arrives—a turning point—and contests for meaning are waged everywhere, eventually dislodging the taken-for-granted and calling even widely accepted practices and assumptions into question. A crisis that continues long enough may at last destabilize established views of reality. It is quite likely we are witnessing such a destabilization at present, though its final outcome is far from clear. What is of immediate interest in the present debate is the existence of three divergent accounts of this crisis: the medical, the feminist, the economic. Each is coherent, each compelling, each has its nononsense definition of "reality," each appeals to what is "best for women." The crux of the problem is that childbirth is not a uniform event whose true meaning and real nature are universal and potentially accessible to everyone. Childbirth *is* what it means, and its meanings are so diverse as to be virtually infinite. It is meaning that is at the core of this crisis: what childbirth means, to whom, and under what circumstances a given meaning may come to constitute an official definition of reality. The problem of traditional childbirth for women is rooted not in "medicalization" *per se* but in monopoly: monopoly of professional authority, of material resources, and of what may be called linguistic capital—the power to establish and enforce a particular definition of childbirth. Childbirth in the United States takes place in hospitals because a definition of childbirth as a medical event is powerful enough to determine its physical location for nearly three million women each year. Thus it is of interest to ask how some meanings come to function as official definitions within a culture, with considerable power to influence material conditions. And what is the relationship of existing social arrangements—including cultural authority, scientific expertise, political activism, and economic incentives—to the construction and deployment of these definitions?

In this essay, I first identify a diversity of meanings attached to childbirth in current U.S. discourse. I next distinguish meanings from definitions, using a concrete case study to illustrate the distinction. The case study dramatically illustrates how "contests for meaning" go public. But again, the success or failure of a given definition is less my concern than the processes involved. How, in other words, is "linguistic capital" accrued? In conclusion, I try to point out some of the things, with regard to childbirth, that definitions do. This analysis, drawing upon some of the concerns and strategies of feminist cultural studies, seeks to illuminate how linguistic processes intersect with social structures, professional authority, economic resources, and political activism to produce gendered representations of social life and specifically of childbirth and women's health. Its ultimate aim is to propose a more complex theoretical understanding of how definitions of childbirth come to be constructed, codified, and mobilized. This in turn seems an essential prerequisite for developing more intelligent childbearing policies and practices in this country.

Some of the Meanings of Childbirth

> The history of obstetrics is the history of civilization itself.—David Danforth

> Throughout history, the woman's body is the terrain on which patriarchy is erected.—Adrienne Rich

> The high risk birth unit is booming.—Rochelle Green

> What [ideology] suppresses is its own construction in signifying practice.—Catherine Belsey[7]

When a word pervades the history of a language and the multiple discourses of a culture, it typically accumulates diverse meanings and representations.

To state this is not merely to assert the obvious but to suggest that the coexistence of multiple and often contradictory meanings of the word *childbirth* is significant and complicates the task of identifying a "dominant" meaning or ideology.[8] Historically, and as defined in many standard dictionaries today, the word *birth* refers both to the bearing of offspring, an act of the mother, and to being born, an act pertaining to the offspring. Childbirth establishes the offspring's independent existence and simultaneously transforms the woman into a particular kind of social being, a mother. Childbirth is also seen as having a dual existence as both a biological and a social event. Social scientists, especially anthropologists, have demonstrated that as a social and cultural institution, birth can take diverse forms. The social expression of childbearing is often assumed to be an overlay, as it were, upon a biological reality which is, in contrast, unchanging and universal. But current discourses make clear that even the biological dimension of birth is diversely perceived, defined, described, and managed.

Stedman's Medical Dictionary, for example, defines birth as "the passage of the offspring from the uterus to the outside world," focusing on the journey of the offspring rather than the labor of the mother. But *Stedman's* definition of birth continues: "specifically, in the human, the complete expulsion or extraction from its mother of a fetus weighing 500 gm. or more. . . ."[9] This implicit inclusion (via the word *extraction*) of the physician within the birth process is in keeping with an involvement of physicians in childbearing that goes back at least to the late eighteenth century but has become particularly intense and aggressive in the twentieth century.[10]

The contribution of physicians and modern obstetrics to childbearing is a contested one. Current versions of the nature and history of childbirth are laced with key words that figure in these contests and need to be unpacked. *Safety* is one example. Modern medicine is often credited with making childbearing safe: "There is no doubt," writes the British obstetrician Peter Huntingford, "that childbearing is safer today, both for mothers and babies, than ever previously, and that further improvements can be expected."[11] Huntingford, who is known for a relatively noninterventionist stance toward the delivery process, made this remark in the context of citing the collective debits and credits of modern childbirth. Quite different in motive is the statement of obstetrician George Little: "Being born is one of the most dangerous times of one's life."[12] Though Little likewise seeks to emphasize the contributions of modern obstetrics, his more far-reaching goal is to characterize birth as an inherently "high risk" event which can suddenly develop complications that require medical intervention (as Lindheim notes, this means that a pregnancy and birth can only be diagnosed as "normal" retrospectively, when both mother and infant are discharged in good health).[13]

The history of obstetrics is another contested site. When a standard obstetrics text proclaims that "the history of obstetrics is the history of civilization itself," it suggests that obstetrics embodies the broader triumphs of civilization over death and disease.[14] But the history that Danforth refers to is a history written by men for men which erases women's contributions to obstetrics and healing and gives men the credit. From a feminist perspective, there is an ironic double meaning here—for this erasure does indeed reproduce the history of civilization.

In contrast, there is a feminist version of "the history of civilization" in which women healers champion the natural, resist technology, and are instinctively in sympathy with the childbearing woman; Adrienne Rich suggests such a history in *Of Woman Born* and Ina May Gaskin elaborates it in *Spiritual Midwifery*. Yet as a number of critics and historians demonstrate with regard to the late nineteenth century (when "modern obstetrics" was in the process of being born), no absolute delineation of positions existed in relation to profession or gender. Regina Markell Morantz-Sanchez, for example, notes the strength of the debate in medical journals and dissertations of this period over whether childbirth required the obstetrician to "wait on nature" or to initiate vigorous intervention; both male and female physicians could be found on both sides.[15] In Great Britain, as Mary Poovey shows in her analysis of the British medical journal *Lancet,* the debate about the use of chloroform as an anesthetic in childbirth was represented as an argument about the nature of women in labor and, hence, medicine's proper relation to them. Poovey emphasizes that during this mid-nineteenth-century period, physicians were in sharp disagreement on these questions which in turn ended up being about medicine's own professional struggles—struggles that were crucial in shaping the medical analysis of childbirth.[16] As we observe the ideology of modern medicine evolving over the last century, we note that the medical position was not monolithic but emerged gradually in the course of key debates, federal initiatives, strains between private practitioners and academic physicians, and debates within medicine over what its professional hierarchy was to be. What we can point to today as "the dominant position" is an outcome, not a determinant, of these historical developments. Physicians did not uniformly declare a war on nature, nor decide that they should adopt an ideology of intervention and subordination of women. Ideology is lived, not simply created and flung out over society like a great net. Thus for physicians already oriented toward scientific progress, decisive clinical action, and professional sovereignty, the representation of childbirth as "natural" was simply a false and outmoded interpretation of reality. A view of childbirth as a scientific event not only opened an appropriate territory for medical specialization and professional development (including monetary gain) but also provided clear conceptual ground for conceding some territory to other practitioners. Poovey and Jean Donnison suggest that in Britain this demarcation between science and nature was ultimately class linked: "natural labor" was linked to "manual labor" and declared fit only for midwives (and GPs), while "scientific childbirth," with forceps, anesthesia, and other forms of intervention, was the realm of specialists.[17]

In the United States, this line of argument was fortified by a celebrated—or infamous—1920 essay by the influential obstetrician Joseph B. DeLee, who proposed to redefine the birth process as pathological and abnormal: We do not call it "normal," he argued to his colleagues, when a baby's head is crushed in a door and it dies of cerebral hemorrhage; yet "when a baby's head is crushed against a tight pelvic floor, and a hemorrhage in the brain kills it, we call this normal, at least we say that the function is natural, not pathogenic."[18] Though DeLee's specific purpose was to argue for the use of forceps and for the routine performance of episiotomy (an incision in the skin and muscles between the vagina and the anus to enlarge the opening through which the baby will pass), his work more broadly legitimated a medical definition of childbirth as pathological and diseaselike, providing a theoretical grounding for a high degree of medical intervention and corollary definitions of the pregnant woman as a patient and of childbirth as a dangerous and pathological event—even as "a double medical emergency" in which the lives of both mother and infant are seen as being at risk.

This medical view of childbirth "as a potentially diseased condition that *routinely* requires the arts of medicine to overcome the processes of nature" has been identified as the central and unique aspect of the development of childbirth in the U.S.[19] Indeed, in *Surfacing,* Margaret Atwood uses childbirth American style as a symbol for U.S. imperialism. Here is Atwood's vision of medicalized (American) childbirth:

> They shut you in a hospital, they shave the hair off you and tie your hands down, and they don't let you see, they don't want you to understand, they want you to believe it's their power, not yours. They stick needles in you so you won't hear anything, you might as well be a dead pig, your legs are up in a metal frame, they bend over you, technicians, mechanics, butchers, students clumsy or sniggering, practising on your body, they take the baby out with a fork like a pickle out of a pickle jar. After that they fill your veins up with red plastic, I saw it running down the tube. I won't let them do that to me ever again.[20]

The violent language of this passage equates a hospital with a slaughterhouse or a prison and the diseased technology of medical childbirth with the unnatural and dehumanizing tortures carried out on prisoners. But most striking is the issue of control: "they" is repeatedly the active subject of the sentences in this passage, embodying in language the narrator's claim that "they want you to believe it's their power, not yours." The series of run-on sentences emphasizes the narrator's loss of control. Her final statement, "I won't let them do that to me ever again," characterizes the entire process as something done by "them"—the medical system—to women. The abstract language of *Stedman's* and other medical discourse, reducing the role of the mother to focus on fetus and physician, perhaps facilitates childbirth practices which, as in Atwood's description, systematically undermine the vision, understanding, and power of the childbearing woman.

In Atwood's vision, technological childbirth enables medical professionals to extract the baby out of the mother "like a pickle out of a pickle jar." The simile seems at first a less accurate representation than, say, extracting an egg or a ripened pecan from a shell; but a pickle in a pickle jar in fact offers a powerful image of the high-tech baby as pickled commodity, plentifully stocked—there's more where that came from—in a container of brine like the bottled fetuses in an embryology lab. From the mother's perspective, this extraction may seem to violate what is naturally "hers." But it reminds us that a baby is more than an individual "possession" of its parents, for children are an important human resource in any society, fundamental to its ongoing social and economic existence: "No life seems so valuable as that of a woman in childbirth," proclaimed the British physician W. Tyler Smith in the mid-nineteenth century, voicing the concerns of industrialized capitalism.[21] Certainly productivity in childbearing was linked to the labor-intensive needs of both colonialism and capitalism, interests that have at once placed childbirth within the realm of the public interest and given the state certain oversight responsibilities. In turn, the health of childbearing becomes a signal of the health of a state: mortality and morbidity statistics for women and infants, for example, are standardly used to evaluate a given society's social and economic development; and in the U.S., high mortality rates have frequently been the catalyst for mobilizing social and government childbearing initiatives. Many decisions about pregnancy, childbirth, and maternity have therefore long been concerns of the state as well as of the childbearing woman and her family.

The definition of childbearing as a medical event has had scientific, ideological, and economic support. Scientific support has included specific educational reforms and technological developments in obstetrics; for example, the 1910 Flexner Report's conclusion that medical students should deliver babies under supervision before doing so as obstetricians in the "real world" encouraged hospital birth, to provide the necessary "teaching material" for student practice.[22] More broadly, a spectrum of scientific knowledge and scientific practices derived from the germ theory were increasingly incorporated into twentieth-century U.S. medicine. Ideological support I take, broadly, to include the growing role of scientific thinking and of the medical profession's authority to define the realities of illness and disease.[23] In addition, widespread ideas about women's bodies, about safety and cleanliness, about what was "progressive"—all played a part. And as Emily Martin convincingly shows, reproduction was closely linked to a pervasive scientific metaphor of the body as a production factory, with physicians the technicians who keep it running efficiently and profitably.[24] Thus is ideology linked, in turn, to capitalism, industry, and the free market—which provided economic support for medicalized childbirth, a money-making enterprise, particularly when coupled with state and federal support for maternal- and child-health programs including, later, retrospective reimbursement.

But in the last fifteen years, in all three areas, medicalized childbirth has come under increasing attack. The feminist movement and women's health movement, the consumer movement, and a broad spectrum of government policymakers have come together in calling the medical definition of childbearing into question. Feminists have generally emphasized the woman's right to be informed, fully conscious, and to experience childbirth as a "natural" process. "The normal human experience of childbirth," writes feminist Carol Downer, "has been entirely removed from daily life, so that most of us have no direct knowledge of it, and it has been transformed into a dangerous, pathological event, so much so that normal birth is no longer even taught in medical schools."[25] Feminists also have challenged the scientific claim that obstetrical intervention has made childbearing safer: "Childbearing can be qualitatively different from what the medical world offers us, much richer than we ever imagined and as free as possible from medical interventions. . . ."[26] The midwifery model, seeking to restore a sense of childbirth as a "normal human experience," defines birth as a normal, natural physiological process; though high risk conditions and/or medical complications may occur and necessitate medical solutions, most pregnant women are considered to be essentially healthy beings who usually need little medical management during the birth process. The home-birth movement also seeks the restoration of "the natural." The 1983 "Declaration of Independence" of the National Association of Parents for Safe Alternatives in Childbirth (NAPSAC) places the pregnant woman and her family at the center of the birth process and proclaims their presence an "unalienable right":

> We hold these truths to be self-evident, that all men, women, children, parents and professionals are created equal; that they are endowed by their creator with certain unalienable rights; that among these are life, liberty, the pursuit of happiness, the right to a safe, natural birth assisted by and in the company of those who love them, the right to be well nourished in their mother's wombs, and the right to be breastfed.[27]

The physician and emergency medical backup are merely implicit (via the word *safe*) rather than essential. The ideal underlying this declaration is not only that maternity and childbirth should be healthy and "natural" but also that individual rights should transcend the practices of the state.

Near the end of *Surfacing,* Atwood describes in fairly radical form a birth that is "natural" and independent from state interference. The birth event involves no one but mother and baby, alone in the woods:

> This time I will do it by myself, squatting on old newspapers in a corner alone; or on leaves, dry leaves, a heap of them, that's cleaner. The baby will slip out easily as an egg, a kitten, and I'll lick it off and bite the cord, the blood returning to the ground where it belongs; the moon will be full, pulling. In the morning I will be able to see it: it will be covered with shining fur, a god, and I will never teach it any words.[28]

Here—transformed in both situation and language—both mother and baby are active participants in the birth event (and in the sentence structure), in dramatic contrast to the high-tech birth where the baby is taken out of its maternal receptacle "like a pickle out of a pickle jar." Further, it is the mother who actively visualizes the child rather than herself serving as what Mary Ann Doane, in her discussion of women as patients in Hollywood films, calls "the specular object."[29] And it is the mother who by withholding language (civilization's symbolic order) will consciously prevent the child's entry into the diseased social life of global imperialism.

As challenges to the medical model of childbirth gain strength and legitimacy, and medicine in turn organizes to address them, the crisis in childbirth intensifies. At the core of this struggle is not only the question of what the term *childbirth* means, and to whom, but also how a given meaning comes to constitute an official "definition." As we have seen, the definition of *childbirth* as simultaneously "the act of giving birth to a child," and "the act of bringing forth offspring" leaves possibilities for a wealth of diverse meanings and experiences. Yet most U.S. medical discourse focuses on the act of the fetus alone, and further represents it as an act in which the physician's presence is crucial. Indeed, in some obstetrics and gynecology textbooks the woman is erased altogether:

> [Normal] labor is the physiologic process by which the uterus expels, or attempts to expel, its contents . . . through the cervical opening and vagina to the outside world. Normal labor is characterized by periodic, involuntary uterine contractions which produce gradual cervical efface- ment and delatation, as well as descent of the fetal presenting part.[30]

Atwood's dream of female solitude seems one this language shares: she seeks female autonomy without doctors; doctors seek medical autonomy without mothers. But neither dream exists in a social vacuum: the power to exercise autonomy requires the existence of supporting cultural, institutional, and economic structures. Thus despite diverse dreams, meanings, and experiences attached to childbirth within U.S. culture and its myriad subcultures, the medical definition has until quite recently almost universally determined actual cultural practices, structural alternatives, and economic incentives.

Meanings and Definitions: The MCA Case

> Distinctions current in language can never be safely ignored.—Cook Wilson

> He who has the power has the money, and he who has the money has the power.—Quoted by Ruth Watson Lubic

> Truth is defined by those professionally certified to name it.—Charles Sanders Peirce[31]

By the early 1970s, childbirth had accumulated a diversity of meanings for various groups and individuals in the United States—an unsurprising characteristic of discourse in a complex and pluralistic democracy. At the same time, the medical profession had established a highly successful monopoly on the organizational structures within which childbirth could actually take place: effectively mobilizing both ideological and material resources, physicians maintained official authority to diagnose the health of the pregnant woman and manage labor and delivery; childbirth, within the framework of this official, medical definition, was strikingly uniform.

Though the terms *meaning* and *definition* are often equated, a distinction between them may be useful in identifying the terrain as well as the limits of medical linguistic imperialism. The word *meaning* comes from an Indo-European base signifying "to have in mind," "to have as an opinion"; it is defined as "what is meant"—what is intended to be or in fact is signified, referred to, or understood—and incorporates the notions of signification, purport, import, sense, and significance. *Meaning,* then, leaves room for the workings of individual subjectivities in the formation of meanings, in their communication, and in their interpretation. Multiple meanings may coexist in a culture—even in a single room or a single head. But a *definition* is much less democratic. It sets limits, determines boundaries, distinguishes. Unlike meanings, which are bound up in what people *think* and *have in their minds* and *intend,* definitions claim to state what *is.* A definition is a meaning that has become official and thereby appears to tell us how things are in the real world.

Note that the distinction is not that between what is symbolic and what is real, between subjective meaning and objective meaning, between arbitrary meaning (red light means stop) and natural meaning (storm cloud means rain). I am also not discussing here how things acquire meaning for us in the first place.[32] Rather, the distinction enables us to look at the construction of definitions as a complex cultural process in which there occurs, at some point, legislation among existing meanings that shapes their official entry into discourse in the form of a constructed definition. An actual case will illuminate the complex ways in which this process actually works; I will therefore briefly sketch the establishment of an out-of-hospital childbearing center in New York City in the mid-1970s.[33]

On September 15, 1975, Jane Brody's health column in the *New York Times* announced that the Maternity Center Association (MCA) of New York City would soon open "a new non-hospital child-bearing center where a woman can give birth in a home-like setting surrounded by her family and go home with her baby within 12 hours of delivery." The MCA Childbearing Center, housed in a town house on Manhattan's Upper East Side but minutes away from a hospital emergency room, was intended to serve as a national model for improved maternity care. Brody quotes the director of MCA: "For too many women, normal childbirth turns out to be a harrowing, unpleasant experience." Dissatisfied with "the impersonal, dehumanizing and costly maternity care characteristic of hospitals," some of these women were having their babies at home; the MCA Childbearing Center is designed as a safe alternative that combines the best features of home and hospital.

Brody's straightforward announcement in no way suggested the storm of controversy that preceded the opening of the MCA Center and was to surround its continued operation—controversy so intense that the center became the subject of a detailed case study by Lazarus et al. which in turn served as evidence in the Federal Trade Commission's 1979 determination that the medical profession was guilty of engaging in restraint of trade.[34] While the center's opening was hailed by feminists and others as a progressive experiment in woman-centered birth, physicians denounced it vigorously, linking its practices to home birth ("child abuse"), spreading rumors about "baby-killing" during its trial period, and calling the center itself "a disgrace to modern obstetrics." At a key point, insurers—notably Blue Cross/Blue Shield—attracted by the center's record and its low costs, agreed to reimburse parents for childbirth costs, often against the advice of physicians on their boards. In the words of the researchers who conducted the FTC study, this "flagship case" revealed "the barriers typically encountered by non-physicians who attempt to provide services traditionally offered by physicians and who represent potential physician substitutes in certain well-defined circumstances."[35] Ruth Lubic, a nurse-midwife who was the center's executive director, analyzed the case as the classic unfolding of a "social drama" (in Victor Turner's sense) and based her doctoral dissertation on it.[36] It is a drama that has since been repeatedly replayed elsewhere over the past decade and whose final outcome— despite the more than ten years in which the MCA Center has successfully operated—remains unknown.

For present purposes, we can use this complex case to highlight several points. The MCA Center was developed in consultation with physicians and other authorities and established as a modest pilot project: its philosophy was not new, nor could its operation realistically challenge the well-entrenched and powerful obstetric market. Two questions emerge. First, why was the center's existence so controversial? But second, given the controversy, together with the broad authority and multiple resources of the powerful and well-organized medical community, how was the center able to survive at all? Despite any number of "obvious" explanations (e.g., a changing economic marketplace, the women's movement, the consumer movement, rising obstetrical costs, new political alliances, the involvement of particular individuals) they do not explain what happened in New York: why a freestanding birth center was successfully established there and then.

One way to understand the MCA case is to see it in terms of meanings and definitions. The center succeeded because it identified, articulated, and capitalized upon a variety of meanings that diverse individuals and groups attached to the idea of childbirth. While at least some of these meanings were discouraged by the medical model, more crucially these meanings were skillfully *mobilized* and *deployed*—primarily under the direction and execution of Ruth Lubic—in the form of a competing official definition of childbirth and an alternative set of organizational arrangements. New meanings were legitimated, but at the same time existing meanings were not discredited: thus the center legitimated comfort and the presence of family but did not downplay concerns about safety or middle-class standards; in Jane Brody's column Lubic emphasized the nearness of emergency facilities while Brody signaled to her readers that this was no Bay Area/hippie operation but a legitimate center in a fashionable "town house." Members of the medical community never fully understood this; rather they repeatedly stressed the illegitimacy of meanings and understandings constructed outside their own area of scientific expertise, a strategy that backfired more than once. At one crucial congressional hearing, for example, a physician began his testimony against the center by suggesting that babies born outside hospitals without medical supervision were at high risk; "I am one of five kids," replied the congressman chairing the hearing, "and we were all born at home. We all turned out to be fine."

The new (non-medical) definition opened a space compatible with a variety of existing discourses, including the meanings of feminists, consumers, the women's health movement, organized midwifery, and the home birth movement. At the same time, with the shifting rules and incentives of a volatile economy moving under Jimmy Carter (and of course this would intensify under Ronald Reagan) toward the growing deregulation of health-care provision, the MCA model became attractive to policymakers and insurers as well as to childbearing women: the definition of birth as a normal, non-technological, non-interventionist, process is appealingly economical. But a definition that happens to serve the changing interests of the competitive marketplace is not necessarily secure, for the "invisible hand" that gives can just as easily take away. It was therefore important for Lubic to consolidate MCA's definition through practices and organizational structures. This strategy included translating MCA's philosophy and definition of birth into city and state regulations, reimbursement policies, contracts with ambulance services and emergency rooms, public debates, congressional testimony, print and electronic media, reports, records of safety and accomplishments, conferences, and a substantial written record which encompassed published studies. These processes involve codifying a definition by literally affixing it to existing codes and practices. What is important here, again, is not that Lubic—in this case—succeeded but that cultural and semantic work are required to amass linguistic capital: the political, social, discursive, and economic weight required to transform a given meaning into an official definition.

To understand the childbearing center's challenge to medicine in terms of how a given definition comes to be constructed, we may find it useful to explore several issues in more detail. Where does the definition originate, for example? Who are its constituents? In whose name and in whose voice does it claim to speak? From what position are they speaking? Throughout the 1960s and 1970s, childbirth clearly had a diversity of meanings—including, increasingly, that of a "natural process"—for many women who nevertheless underwent classic hospital births because they had no alternative. If they expressed a sense of contradiction or even complained, their voices presented no real threat to medical authority. For they were—*by definition*—unqualified to define. Even when the nurse-midwives of MCA proposed to establish a freestanding out-of-hospital childbearing center, the local medical establishment was not unduly alarmed. But when Blue Cross/Blue Shield—a private insurer long dominated by physicians—decided to reimburse parents for their costs at the center, it sent shock waves through the whole New York City medical community. In doing so, they were agreeing to define childbirth as a normal, natural process and to modify rules, practices, and reimbursement schedules accordingly. Of course, the cost-containment climate encouraged Blue Cross/Blue Shield to seek economical practices. But Lubic skillfully emphasized the semantic rather than the economic implications of this new definition of childbirth, reasserting its origin with MCA and nurse-midwifery, so that decision looked enlightened, not opportunistic.

Social and economic contexts are crucial determinants nonetheless. In addition to the social debates described earlier, dramatically escalating costs since World War II (health care now constitutes eleven percent of the GNP and costs $400 billion per year) had brought medicine by the early 1970s under continuing scrutiny from insurers and other third-party payers, health-care policy analysts, and government officials increasingly desperate for ways to contain costs. The Blue Cross/Blue Shield decision represented a shift that in many respects demonstrates current thinking about health-care costs. What is now happening is a massive deregulation of the health-care system which has proceeded more rapidly than even its most optimistic proponents had envisioned. These economic forces are bringing dramatic changes to the health-care system and to even the most canonized of medical practices. With a competitive model comes increased focus on cost-effectiveness, larger units of production (e.g., group practices and health-maintenance organizations rather than solo practices), greater competition among alternative models of health-care financing and delivery (especially prepaid health plans and for-profit health-care corporations); greater competition for healthy, middle-class patients; and less interest than ever in patients who are poor, sick, and/or financially or medically risky otherwise. Though it may be possible for progressive social theory to capitalize on competitive economic practices—the MCA childbearing center is a clear example—those practices are not themselves allied with such theory or intrinsically progressive. The economic stakes attached to definitions in the childbearing struggle are not insignificant. Of the three million births per year, about 85 percent are estimated to be "low risk" or "normal" and thus could appropriately be attended by trained midwives or nurse-midwives. If even 75 percent of this population gave birth outside hospitals—for example, in alternative birth centers staffed by nurse-midwives, at about one third the cost—this would represent savings to individual consumers, to insurers, and to the state of several billion dollars per year. Both on the grounds of cost and on the grounds of consumer choice, alternatives to high-technology birth are appealing. There is therefore enormous competition—economic and ideological—for the low-risk birth market.[37] Because the definition of childbearing in the U.S. as a medical event has clearly served the interests of health-care providers, it is not surprising that many physicians have individually and collectively opposed out-of-hospital birth. The head of the American College of Obstetricians and Gynecologists in 1980 chose a revealing metaphor when he pleaded for an end to competition over deliveries between obstetricians and family practitioners in order successfully to unite against the common enemy—nurse-midwives:

> [It] is important for all of us in medicine to remember that the Indians are all outside the stockade and to avoid taking shots at each other.[38]

As external competition exerts increasing pressure, defenses become hysterical, a given position fragments into competing versions, people decamp from the position, language is carefully policed, every word is charged with ideological destiny. During a period in which a definition is at stake, lines are drawn: if you're not in the stockade, you're the enemy outside with a bow and arrow. Yet language itself may undergo various transformations during such a period. Just a few years after the statement above was made, many physicians had learned to be more subtle. Hence another physician used quite a different argument to oppose out-of-hospital birth: "Childbirth [is] a natural process and where nature [is] involved nothing [can] ever be risk-free."[39] Here the overtly adversarial territory of the stockade is forsaken for the linguistic high ground of safety of mother and baby; indeed, the term *natural* has been appropriated from the enemy.

A further issue involves the cultural history, tradition, or context in which a new definition originates. Whose interests does it represent? Women are currently represented in multiple and often contradictory ways—contradictions that discourses about childbirth intensify and exploit. Medical discourse still typically represents women as subordinate, irrational, passive, and incompetent; competitive economic theory represents women as independent consumers with rights and free choice; in Marxist economics, childbearing women contribute both to production and reproduction; in writings about motherhood, both from the radical left and the radical right, childbearing is often represented as the central meaningful event in women's lives; state interests in maternity care often use the language of safety and paternalism; and in feminist writing, women are represented as autonomous, healthy, and intelligent. Contradictions impel people to seek resolution: thus childbearing women, for example, may seek compromises in the form of hospital-based birth centers that link the services of midwives (what is "natural") with the presence of obstetricians and technological backup equipment (what is "safe").

The cultural context may influence the domains of data that are honored. Economists and physicians stress that studies involving large numbers of subjects are needed to amass meaningful morbidity and mortality statistics. But such statistics have been debated since the 1920s with no resolution; further, large volume is just what midwives in alternative childbearing centers are not equipped to handle; thus they are incapable of assembling the data base that both biomedical science and economics require as "evidence." Sociologist Ann Oakley has repeatedly argued that our understanding of birth must go beyond "hard outcomes" research to incorporate other evidence.[40] But anthropologist Brigitte Jordan argues that where childbirth is concerned scientific data do not function to disguise or reveal discrepancies and contradictions in existing practices. Rather, the practices are supported or challenged on other grounds: scientific data are then assembled to support the challenge or defend against it.[41]

We may also explore whether a definition is really "new," and whether it is really "deviant." The New York City childbearing center mentioned above was able to capitalize on a considerable reservoir of feminist ideological commitment by institutionally legitimizing a definition of childbirth as normal and non-medical. Yet its definition was not so deviant that the center could not operate within the existing health-care system. In similar fashion, medical providers attempt to market the hospital as a homelike, family-oriented setting expressly suited to enhance the meaningful experience of normal birth—in other words, selected (and some would say often comically cosmetic) features of the midwifery/feminist model (like chintz curtains) are coopted for the hospital setting. "We look upon the miracle of birth as an event to be celebrated, not a mere medical procedure," runs a 1986 newspaper advertisement for a community hospital in central Illinois, and continues:

> As a result of the changes that have occurred in recent years, we have recently completed remodeling of our Family Life Center. All seven of our birthing rooms are private, as are our seventeen post-partum rooms. You get homelike surroundings at the same cost as a semi-private room. These rooms have all been decorated with the warm touches of home— delicate wallpaper prints, the subtle presence of oak furniture and trim, and carpeting throughout, even in the hallways. What used to be a 'father's waiting room' is now a family room, where friends and relatives can wait while mom and dad deliver their new baby together. And, the newborn nursery has been relocated to allow more convenient access to family and friends who wish to see the new baby.[42]

This ad appeared just over ten years after the Jane Brody article in *The New York Times,* demonstrating, on the one hand, that some of the MCA Center's uniquely innovative features were nevertheless able to be accommodated within more traditional settings—and, on the other hand, that "the warm touches of home" remain innovative enough in hospital settings to be used in a marketing campaign. Here we see that a definition is constructed within a particular linguistic context and plays into existing systems of similarity and difference. Sexual difference is, of course, the most obvious, but there are others. I have noted the linguistic distinction between a woman's giving birth to a child and having a child "expelled" or "extracted." The verb *deliver* as an active transitive verb is another medical creation: the sentence "She was delivered [i.e., liberated] of her child" might have been uttered several hundred years ago; but "he delivered her child" is an invention of late-nineteenth-century obstetrics. Whereas the first is semantically equivalent to "she gave birth to her child" or "she bore her child" and leaves ambiguous the presence of birth attendants, the second makes clear that the male is the one who has delivered [liberated] the child.[43] The term *natural* in existing childbirth discourses is another example. Sometimes it means birth without the panoply of hospital procedures—shaving, drugs, enema, fetal monitoring. But it can also mean birth with Lamaze and/or without anesthetic, birth outside the hospital, vaginal delivery as opposed to cesarean section, or the outcome of "natural" rather than *in vitro* (test tube) fertilization. Marilyn Moran argues for natural birth at home from a conservative perspective that sees reproduction as the crucial bond between husband and wife and childbearing as the holy consummation of the nuclear family that the presence of the physician disrupts and corrupts.[44] In contrast, feminist Terrell Seltzer calls the "natural" philosophy espoused by a Berkeley birth center as tyrannical and prescriptive as the medical model—perhaps more so, because it pretends to be ideologically free and supportive of individuality.[45] How, then, do such linguistic dichotomies as "natural" and "medical" play into sexual, cultural, economic, and scientific ideologies? What does it signify about the meaning of the word *natural* when an eminent obstetrician can say that "childbirth is as much a natural event as is death, but whether it should be allowed to be so is a different matter."[46] Just a few terms from recent newspapers and other printed sources signal the further disintegration of any essentialist notions of motherhood: *egg mother, birth mother, name mother, surrogate mother, terry-cloth mother, gene mother, biomother, biomom, adoptive mother, legal mother, foster mother, mother of rearing, property mother, lab mother, blood mother, organ mother, tissue mother, nurturant mother, earth mother,* and *den mother.* A move into the world of *Alien, Aliens, Terminator,* even *Rosemary's Baby,* would generate perhaps a hundred more.[47]

Unless women can find ways to achieve greater control over their childbearing options at present, there are real dangers in the future when, perhaps, women will become not merely invisible in discourse but truly absent from the reproductive process. Because for some male professionals, one way to resolve current challenges to their authority is to match the discursive erasure of women in medical textbooks by erasing them from reproduction and childbearing quite literally: such erasure is quite possible through the development of *in vitro* fertilization, alternative "growing mediums" (now "surrogate mothers," tomorrow artificial wombs), and procedures for cloning human beings. From the perspective of a feminist subculture, this is not science fiction but a genuinely feasible version of the alchemists' old dream of reproducing the seed of The Father with no help from females.[48]

Many women may welcome the new freedoms and flexible structures becoming available as the health-care system deregulates. But an open marketplace also provides opportunities for economic exploitation and abuse, particularly of women with few material resources. Problematic as state regulation and professional supervision may be, they may offer more operating space and autonomy than letting the "free" market of a capitalist society decide.

Conclusion: Childbirth and Cultural Crisis

> The future is not female. But feminism . . . has a crucial role in its construction.—Lynne Segal.[49]

Multiple factors are presently operating in the United States to challenge, support, or alter the control over childbirth achieved and long maintained by the dominant medical culture. These changes are called, variously, the "childbirth crisis," the "childbirth debate," and the "childbirth revolution." In current discourse, at least three perspectives on this "revolution" are significant: the medical, the feminist, and the economic. But discourse does not merely furnish the script for this revolutionary production: it is the staging area, it influences ticket prices, it is the very material of the drama itself. As Poovey says,

> All such debates are inevitably as bound up with the representation of reality as with material social relations and practices. As the arena for negotiating values, meanings, and identities, representation authorizes ethics and social practices; it stages the workings through of the dominant ideology. But opposition can *also* emerge within representation. . . .[50]

The feminist self-help movement of the 1960s and 1970s was not only the genesis of "alternative health care" for women: it was also a free-speech movement that gave women the power to define reality. Its contributions, its articulation of feminist meanings, its publications, its popularity: all these created linguistic capital that gave weight to a non-medical definition of childbirth. Ironically, perhaps, this "demedicalization" moved childbirth out of the private sphere where women's reproductive and domestic labor have traditionally been positioned: more overtly visible in the public sphere, childbirth can more easily be represented as a commodity, not only in the economic marketplace but in the ideological and social marketplace as well. As I have tried to demonstrate, each of these definitions of childbirth—as medical event, as natural process, as market commodity—has powerful cultural backing (capital accumulation, let us say); none is innocent. As Bakhtin tells us, in the epigram that opens this essay, "Language is not an abstract system of normative forms but rather a concrete heteroglot conception of the world. . . . Each word tastes of the context and contexts in which it has lived its socially charged life."[51] The language of the childbirth debates maps the complex intersections among linguistic constructions and professional authority, economic interests, institutional structures, politics, money, and ideological positionings with regard to health care. In this essay I have tried briefly to suggest some of the difficulties and even dangers of believing we can define *childbirth* easily or unambiguously. The complexity in actual practice of such dichotomies as "natural" versus "technological" is only one problematic example among many. The following comments, for example, demonstrate how two different physicians have come to represent what is "natural." For the first, it remains worthless, bankrupt, even criminal:

> I think every baby . . . is entitled to have the safest kind of delivery possible. And when somebody denies him that by crawling into a cave or a log cabin without a telephone or electricity or running water—as we've seen happen—they are just not considering that infant's right to an intact birth.[52]

But the second physician appears to have invested linguistic currency in "the natural," having checked it out and found it less risky than rumor suggested; yet he does not altogether forsake the world of his texts and mentors, nor (we would assume) current market realities:

> [Natural childbirth] does not mean that you deliver in a cornfield, unattended, while out rounding up the cattle, but rather that you are awake, alert, aware, and able to participate in and enjoy the birth of your baby. It does not mean that you can't use analgesics or anesthetics, but that the selection of such is done wisely to minimize the effects on you and your baby.[53]

Thus paradoxically, as struggle and counter-struggle seek to define their own limits, they may grow closer together. An innovative structure—or a deviant definition—lives a double life, for it has grown out of a struggle with a dominant structure which continues to shape it, even cannibalize it. Counter-discourse does not arise as a pure autonomous radical language embodying the purity of a new politics. Rather it arises from within the dominant discourse and learns to inhabit it from the inside out.

In the case of childbirth, we see that meanings depend, among other things, on scientific evidence, personal experience, professional training, economic incentives, and ideological convictions. All these domains of "data" are in turn used to anchor and authorize given definitions. To claim this is to claim that definitions are social, cultural, and political as well as linguistic and that they are constructed by specific speakers with specific aims and interests. Like capital, language is liquid, not fixed, undecidable. We will not ultimately be able to resolve the controversies of the "childbirth revolution" by seeking the "true nature" or "real meaning" of childbirth as it exists in "external reality." The word *childbirth* is not merely a label, provided us by language, for a clear-cut event that already exists in the world; rather than describe, it *inscribes,* and makes the event intelligible to us. We cannot look *through* discourse to determine what childbirth "really" is, for discourse itself is the site where such determination is inscribed.

The "childbirth revolution" itself is such a site, though I have not fully focused on the scope of contradictions embodied in this term. In fact, feminists use it to mean the successful *challenges* to the medical model; obstetricians use it to mean the *triumph* of the medical model, both in knowledge and technology; and economists use it to mean the shift in health-care delivery toward deregulation, prospective reimbursement, and the "free market" that has turned "birthing centers" into big business. When these discourses intersect—as they do in this essay but rarely elsewhere—and these meanings are pressed into service as definitions, what is starkly revealed is the extent of contradiction, the nonexistence of dialogue, and the fundamental impossibility of any such thing as a *definitive* definition. To understand *this* is a beginning, and a crucial one. For I do not doubt for a moment that there is a crisis in childbirth, and my own discourse has not been innocent. The definition we hold is the one that tells our story. That is why it is ours.

To talk of language, discourse, and definitions sometimes evokes desire for a return to certainty about what is real, but the retrogressive protectionism of certainty is no more the answer than the nostalgic return to a pre-Cyborg, pre-surrogate female maternal body that never was and never will be. The real is always linguistic, unsentimental, and political. Thus a definition is not, as conventional wisdom assumes, the set of necessary and sufficient conditions that constitute a known, fixed starting point for political, economic, and ideological struggles. Rather a definition represents the *outcome* of such struggles—an unstable, negotiated, and often quite temporary cultural prescription. In turn, however, embodied in laws, policies, and everyday practices, definitions may have great power to determine material consequences. This knowledge enables us to approach the problem of defining childbirth with a more accurate understanding of what such a definition process entails and what its consequences may be. Childbirth entails the existence of multiple meanings, ideological commitments, and material resources. The real revolution will involve forsaking the notion that gender binds women in a magical ineluctable unity and rejecting definitions that ground the reality of birth in what is presumed to be natural and maternal. Instead we need to strengthen *feminist political aims*: women's right to economic resources, information, self-determination, strategic alliances across race and class, access to appropriate resources, and participation in decision-making about the reproductive process. In this essay I have tried to suggest a more complex theoretical understanding of how definitions of childbirth come to be constructed, codified, and mobilized. Such an understanding seems an essential prerequisite for using the childbirth crisis—this turning point in the evolution of childbearing policies and practices—to make childbirth better for women, not worse.

Notes

1. M. M. Bakhtin, *The Dialogic Imagination*, ed. Michael Holquist (Austin: University of Texas Press, 1981), 292.

2. Margaret Atwood, "Giving Birth," in *Dancing Girls and Other Stories* (New York: Simon and Schuster, 1978), 225.

3. See the annual reports of the National Center for Health Statistics. In 1900 fewer than 5 percent of births took place in hospitals; by 1940 it was 50 percent, and by 1980 it was more than 95 percent. The Institute of Medicine/National Research Council observes that although 1 pecent of births (planned and unplanned) takes place outside hospitals nationally (some home-birth groups cite higher figures), this varies considerably from state to state: in Oregon, for example, where accurate data are kept for all birth locations, 4.4 percent of births in 1981 took place outside hospitals. Roslyn Lindheim ("Birthing Centers and Hospices: Reclaiming Birth

and Death," *Annual Review of Public Health* 2 [1981], 1–29) discusses the way such statistics are gathered and what they mean.

4. Richard W. and Dorothy C. Wertz, *Lying-In: A History of Childbirth in America* (New York: The Free Press, 1977), x, provide one version of the claim that in the U.S. childbirth has been "medicalized"; they suggest that this can be considered the uniquely American contribution to cross-cultural diversity. The term "medicalization" in the context of childbirth is usually taken to encompass standard surgical preparation (enema, shaving), fetal monitoring, ultrasound, analgesic and anesthetic medications, induced labor, forceps delivery, episiotomy, and cesarean section. Challenges to medicalized childbirth, representing a variety of several perspectives, include Doris Haire, *The Cultural Warping of Childbirth* (Milwaukee: International Childbirth Education Association, 1972); Nancy Stoller Shaw, *Forced Labor: Maternity Care in the United States* (New York: Pergamon, 1974); Suzanne Arms, *Immaculate Deception: A New Look at Women and Childbirth in America* (Boston: Houghton Mifflin, 1977); Yvonne Brackbill, June Rice, and Diony Young, *Birth Trap* (New York: Warner Books, 1984); Gena Corea, *The Hidden Malpractice: How American Medicine Mistreats Women* (New York: Jove/Harcourt Brace Jovanovich, 1977); Ina May Gaskin, *Spiritual Midwifery* (Summertown, Tenn.: The Book Publishing Company, 1978); and Raymond G. DeVries, *Regulating Birth: Midwives, Medicine, and the Law* (Philadelphia: Temple University Press, 1985). More theoretically oriented discussions include Ann Oakley, *Women Confined: Towards A Sociology of Childbirth* (New York: Schocken, 1980); Les Levidow with Janet Jennings and Shelley Day, "Unnatural Childbirth?" *Radical Science Journal* 12 (1982):2–8; Evan Stark, "What Is Medicine?," *Radical Science Journal* 12 (1982):46–89; and William Ray Arney, *Power and the Profession of Obstetrics* (Chicago: University of Chicago Press, 1982).

5. For discussions of morbidity and mortality statistics in the U.S., see C. Arden Miller, in "Infant Mortality in the U.S.," *Scientific American* 253.1 (July 1985):31–37; Institute of Medicine Division of Health Sciences Policy and National Research Council Commission on Life Sciences, *Research Issues in the Assessment of Birth Settings: Report of a Study by the Committee on Assessing Alternative Birth Settings* (Washington, D.C.: National Academy Press, 1982); Wertz and Wertz, *Lying-In;* Lindheim, "Birthing Centers"; Dorothy C. Wertz, "What Birth Has Done for Doctors: A Historical View," *Women and Health* 8.1 (Spring 1983), 7–24.

6. See, for instance, discussions in Frances E. Kobrin, "The American Midwife Controversy: A Crisis of Professionalization," in *Women and Health in America,* ed. Judith Walzer Leavitt (Madison: University of Wisconsin Press, 1984), 318–26; Paul Starr, *The Social Transformation of American Medicine* (New York: Basic Books, 1982); Nancy Schrom Dye, "Mary Breckinridge, the Frontier Nursing Service, and the Introduction of Nurse-Midwifery in the United States," in *Women and Health in America,* ed. Leavitt; Wertz, "What Birth Has Done for Doctors"; DeVries, *Regulating Birth;* and James Black, "The Sentimental Marketplace," in *Money, Power, and Health,* eds. Evan Melhado, Walter Feinberg, and Harold M. Swartz (Ann Arbor: Health Administration Press, 1988).

7. See David N. Danforth, ed., *Obstetrics and Gynecology,* 4th ed. (New York: Harper and Row, 1982); Adrienne Rich, *Of Woman Born: Motherhood as Experience and Institution* (New York: W. W. Norton, 1976); Rochelle Green, "Birthing Alternatives: A Matter of Choice and Turf," *Medical World News,* 24 May 1984; Catherine Belsey, *Critical Practice* (London: Methuen, 1980).

8. Theoretical perspectives on the nature of childbirth (including pregnancy and maternity), for example, are articulated in Arney, *Power;* Boston Women's Health Book Collective, *The New Our Bodies Ourselves* (New York: Simon and Schuster, 1984); Mary Kelly, *Post-Partum Document* (London: Routledge and Kegan Paul, 1983); Sheila Kitzinger and J. A. Davis, eds., *The Place of Birth* (New York: Oxford University Press, 1978); Levidow with Jennings and Day, "Unnatural Childbirth?"; Mary O'Brien, *The Politics of Reproduction* (Boston: Routledge and Kegan Paul,

1981); Rich, *Of Woman Born;* Lynne Segal, *Is the Future Female? Troubled Thoughts on Contemporary Feminism* (London: Virago, 1987); and Terrell Seltzer, "The Berkeley Family Health Center: A Negative View," Printed flyer distributed in Berkeley, California, dated November 30, 1976. Investigation in the social sciences includes Brigitte Jordan, *Birth in Four Cultures: A Crosscultural Investigation of Childbirth in Yucatan, Holland, Sweden and the United States* (St. Albans, Vermont: Eden Press, 1978); Margaret Mead and Niles Newton, "Cultural Patterning of Perinatal Behavior," in *Childbearing: Its Social and Psychological Aspects,* ed. Stephen A. Richardson and Alan Guttmacher (Baltimore: Williams and Wilkins, 1967), 142–244; Oakley, *Women Confined;* Shelley Romalis, ed., *Childbirth: Alternatives to Medical Control* (Austin: University of Texas Press, 1981); Sheryl Burt Rusek, *The Woman's Health Movement: Feminist Alternatives to Medical Control* (New York: Praeger, 1979); and Shaw, *Forced Labor.* Representations (linguistic, literary, and visual) are explored by Carol Cohn, "Sex and Death in the Rational World of Defense Intellectuals," *Signs* 12.4 (1987):687–718; Brian Easlea, *Fathering the Unthinkable: Masculinity, Science, and the Nuclear Arms Race* (London: Pluto Press, 1983); Susan Stanford Friedman, "Creativity and the Childbirth Metaphor: Gender Difference in Literary Discourse," *Feminist Studies* 13:1 (Spring 1987):49–82; Cynthia A. Huff, "Chronicles of Confinement: Reactions to Childbirth in British Women's Diaries," *Women's Studies International Forum* 10.1 (1987):63–68; Robbie Pfeufer Kahn, "The Language of Birth," *Socialist Review* 80 (March/April 1985):185–98; Emily Martin, *The Woman in the Body: A Cultural Analysis of Reproduction* (Boston: Beacon, 1987); Constance Penley, "Time Travel, Primal Scene, and the Critical Dystopia," *Camera Obscura* 15 (1986):67–84; Rosalind Petchesky, "Fetal Images: The Power of Visual Culture in the Politics of Reproduction," *Feminist Studies* 13.2 (Summer 1987): 263–92; Mary Poovey, "'Scenes of an Indelicate Character': The Medical 'Treatment' of Victorian Women", in *The Making of the Modern Body,* eds. Catherine Gallagher and Thomas Laqueur (Berkeley: University of California Press, 1987), 137–68; Vivian Sobchack, "Child/Alien/Father: Patriarchal Crisis and Genetic Exchange," *Camera Obscura* 15 (1986):7–34; see also Jo Anne Brown, "Professional Language: Words that Succeed," *Radical History Review* 34 (1986):33–51. Historical background is provided by Black, "The Sentimental Marketplace" (1988); Margaret Llewelyn Davies, ed., *Maternity: Letters from Working Women,* collected by the Women's Co-operative Guild (New York: W. W. Norton, 1978; originally published 1915); Peter Huntingford, "Obstetric Practice: Past, Present, and Future," in *The Place of Birth,* ed. Sheila Kitzinger and John A. Davis (Oxford: Oxford University Press, 1978); Judith Walzer Leavitt, "Birthing and Anesthesia: The Debate over Twilight Sleep," in *Women and Health in America,* ed. Judith Walzer Leavitt (Madison: University of Wisconsin Press, 1984), 175–84; Regina Markell Morantz-Sanchez, *Sympathy and Science: Women Physicians in American Medicine* (New York: Oxford University Press, 1985); and Wertz and Wertz, *Lying-In.*

9. *Stedman's Medical Dictionary,* 24th ed. (Baltimore: Williams and Wilkins, 1982), 173.

10. Many current medical dictionaries define *birth* as an accomplishment of the fetus (and/ or physician) rather than of the mother: "The emergence of a new individual from the body of its parent (*McGraw-Hill Dictionary of Scientific and Technical Terms,* 3rd ed., ed.-in-chief Sybil P. Parker [New York: McGraw-Hill, 1984], p. 186); "The act or process of being born" (*Dorland's Illustrated Medical Dictionary,* 24th ed. [Philadelphia: 1965], 200); "The act of being born" (*Melloni's Illustrated Medical Dictionary,* 2nd ed. [Baltimore: Williams and Wilkins, 1985]; and Barbara F. Cape and Pamela Dobson, *Baillière's Nurses' Dictionary,* 18th ed. [Baltimore: Williams and Wilkins, 1974], 45; "the offspring's emergence from the womb of the mother" (*Blakeston's Gould Medical Dictionary,* 4th ed. [New York: McGraw-Hill, 1979], 174). British medical dictionaries are more likely to include the notion of "bringing forth" (e.g., *Butterworths' Medical Dictionary,* 2nd ed. [London: Butterworths, 1978], 231: "1. the act of being born; the fact of having been born. 2. The process of bringing forth. 3. That which is produced.") British physician Peter Wingate, in *The Penguin Medical Encyclopedia* (Harmondsworth, Middlesex: Penguin, 1972), 62, is even more explicit in noting under his entry on *birth* that "the process is considered

from the mother's point of view under *labour*." *Stedman's* definition of *labor*, however (p. 753), which we might expect similarly to reflect the mother's role, continues to subordinate or even negate her: "the process of expulsion of the fetus and the placenta from the uterus" (the subject of the sentence is not "the mother" but "the process"; nor is the mother even semantically—as opposed to grammatically—involved in the prepositional phrase, for the fetus is expelled not "from the mother" but "from the uterus").

11. Huntingford, "Obstetric Practice," 227.

12. Quoted in Green, "Birthing Alternatives," 44.

13. Lindheim, "Birthing Centers and Hospices," 2.

14. Danforth, ed., *Obstetrics and Gynecology*, 2.

15. Morantz-Sanchez, *Sympathy and Science*, 222–23.

16. Poovey, "Scenes of an Indelicate Character"; Jean Donnison, *Midwives and Medical Men: A History of Inter-Professional Rivalries and Women's Rights* (New York: Schocken, 1977); and Wertz ("What Birth Has Done for Medical Men") suggest ways that childbirth/obstetrics questions are linked to public debates on the violation of free trade, usurpation of women's labor, encouragement of prostitution, and destabilization of the labor market. As these debates continued, historical changes in the U.S. and Great Britain—industrialization, urbanization, modernization—favored the production of new or exaggerated representations of sexual difference (see Barrett, "The Concept of 'Difference' "; Leonore Davidoff and Catherine Hall, *Family Fortunes: Men and Women of the English Middle Class 1780–1850* [London: Hutchinson, 1987]; Ludmilla J. Jordanova, "Gender, Generation and Science: William Hunter's Obstetrical Atlas," in *William Hunter and the Eighteenth Century Medical World*, eds. W. F. Bynum and Roy Porter [Cambridge: Cambridge University Press, 1985]; and Martin, *The Woman in the Body*).

17. For discussion of the relations among women, medicine, and midwifery, see Arney, *Power and the Profession of Obstetrics;* DeVries, *Regulating Birth;* Donnison, *Midwives and Medical Men;* Green, "Birthing Alternatives"; Institute of Medicine/National Research Council Commission, *Research Issues;* Lindheim, "Birthing Centers and Hospices"; Ruth Watson Lubic, *Barriers and Conflicts in Maternity Care Innovation*, E. D. Dissertation, Teachers College, Columbia University, 1979; Maternity Center Association, *The Next Fifty Years of Nurse-Midwifery Education: Report of a Seminar Celebrating the Fiftieth Anniversary of Nurse-Midwifery Education in the United States* (New York: Maternity Center Association, 1983); Barbara Katz Rothman, *Giving Birth: Alternatives in Childbirth* (New York: Penguin, 1984); and Shaw, *Forced Labor.*

18. Joseph B. DeLee, "The Prophylactic Forceps Operation," *Journal of Obstetrics and Gynecology* 1 (1920):34–44.

19. Wertz and Wertz, *Lying-In*, x.

20. Margaret Atwood, *Surfacing* (New York: Simon and Schuster, 1972), 92.

21. Quoted in Poovey, "Scenes of an Indelicate Character," 145.

22. Abraham Flexner, *Medical Education in the United States and Canada*, Bulletin no. 4 (New York: Carnegie Foundation for the Advancement of Teaching, 1910).

23. See Starr, *The Social Transformation of American Medicine.*

24. Martin, *The Woman in the Body.*

25. Carol Downer, "Through the Speculum," in *Test-Tube Women: What Future for Motherhood?*, eds. Rita Arditti, Renate Duelli Klein, and Shelley Minden (London: Pandora, 1984), 419–26.

26. Boston Women's Health Book Collective, *The New Our Bodies Ourselves,* 362.

27. David and Lee Stewart, *The Childbirth Activists' Handbook: How to Get the Childbirth Options You Want . . . in Less Than Nine Months* (Marble Hill, Mo.: NAPSAC Reproductions, 1983), 21.

28. Atwood, *Surfacing,* 187.

29. Mary Ann Doane, "The Clinical Eye: Medical Discourses in the 'Woman's Film' of the 1940s," in *The Female Body in Western Culture: Contemporary Perspectives,* ed. Susan Rubin Suleiman (Cambridge: Harvard University Press, 1986), 152–74.

30. Tom P. Barden, "Perinatal Care," in *Gynecology and Obstetrics: The Health Care of Women,* eds. Seymour L. Romney, Mary Jane Gray, A. Brian Little, James A. Merrill, E. J. Quilligan, and Richard W. Stander (New York: McGraw-Hill, 1981), 596.

31. See Cook Wilson, quoted in Paul Edwards, ed.-in-chief, *Encyclopedia of Philosophy* (New York: Macmillan and the Free Press, vols. 5 and 6, 1967) (entry on meaning, pp. 2333–41, authored by Walter Alston); Ruth Watson Lubic, "Reimbursement for Nursing Practice: Lessons Learned, Experiences Shared," *Nursing and Health Care* 6.1 (January 1985); Charles Sanders Peirce, 1940, cited by Stanley Aronowitz, "The Production of Scientific Knowledge: Science, Ideology, and Marxism," in *Marxism and the Interpretation of Culture,* ed. Cary Nelson and Lawrence Grossberg (Urbana: University of Illinois Press, 1988).

32. While childbirth has provided obstetricians with evidence of their profession's scientific progress, it has provided the feminist movement with evidence of the universality of the female experience across societies, historical periods, and cultures. Useful discussions that problematize this view by stressing factors (including class) that influence social and cultural constructions of knowledge about childbirth include Barry Barnes, "Understanding Natural Order," Miller Committee Lecture, University of Illinois at Urbana-Champaign, October 1987; Elizabeth Fee, "The Language and Politics of Reproductive Freedom," Presented at the Third International Interdisciplinary Congress on Women, Dublin, July 1987; Jordan, *Birth in Four Cultures;* Kelly, *Post-Partum Document;* Martin, *The Woman in the Body;* Poovey, " 'Scenes of an Indelicate Character' "; and Segal, *Is the Future Female?* Science fiction also provides a salutary antidote to commonsense assumptions by subverting with ease the positioning of childbirth and maternity as "natural." Constance Penley's discussion ("Time Travel, Primal Scene, and the Critical Dystopia") of impregnation across time in *The Terminator* is a seminal example.

33. For detailed accounts of this case, see Wendy Lazarus, Ellen S. Levine, and Lawrence S. Lewin, *Competition Among Health Practitioners: The Influence of the Medical Profession on the Health Manpower Market*—Volume II: *The Childbearing Center Case Study* (Washington, D.C.: Federal Trade Commission, 1981); Lubic, *Barriers and Conflicts;* and Ruth Watson Lubic, "Alternative Maternity Care: Resistance and Change," in *Childbirth: Alternatives to Medical Control,* ed. Shelley Romalis (Austin: University of Texas Press, 1981), 217–49.

34. Lazarus et al., Volume I: Executive Summary and Final Report.

35. Lazarus et al, Volume II.

36. See Victor Turner, *Dramas, Fields, and Metaphors: Symbolic Action in Human Society* (Ithaca: Cornell University Press, 1974); Lubic, *Barriers and Conflicts.*

37. Economic debates about the U.S. health-care system remain intense. Accounts that favor free-market competition and deregulation include Clark C. Havighurst, "Health Care Cost Containment Regulation: Prospects and an Alternative," *American Journal of Law and Medicine* 3 (1977):309–22; Clark C. Havighurst, "More on Regulation: A Reply to Stephen Weiner," *American Journal of Law and Medicine* 4 (1978):243–53; Paul M. Ellwood, Jr., "Alternatives to Regulation: Improving the Market," in *Controls on Health Care,* Institute of Medicine, Papers of the Conference on Regulation of the Health Industry, January 7–9, 1974 (Washington, D.C.:

National Academy of Sciences, 1975), 49–72; Alain C. Enthoven, *Health Plan: The Only Practical Solution to Soaring Health Costs* (Reading, MA: Addison-Wesley, 1980); and Jack A. Meyer, *Market Reforms in Health Care: Current Issues, New Directions, Strategic Decisions* (Washington D.C.: American Enterprise Institute, 1983).

38.   Quoted in Lazarus et al, Volume II, 8.

39.   Robert Dingwall, "Malpractice Issues in Childbirth 1985," *Health Policy* 6 (1986): 104.

40.   Oakley, *Woman Confined;* "Social Consequences of Obstetric Technology"; and "The Importance of Measuring 'Soft' Outcomes," *Birth* 10:2 (1985):49–108.

41.   Jordan, *Birth in Four Cultures.*

42.   *Champaign-Urbana News Gazette,* 23 February 1986.

43.   In *The Penguin Medical Encyclopedia* Wingate defines "delivery" as "childbirth," and notes: "It is the mother who is delivered of the child, and not, as some medical jargon would have it, the child that is delivered (like a parcel at the door)" (p. 118). Like many British physicians, Wingate is more sympathetic to midwifery than U.S. obstetricians and consequently more likely to credit the work that women do in childbearing.

44.   Moran, *Birth and the Dialogue of Love.*

45.   Seltzer, "The Berkeley Family Health Center."

46.   Ian Craft, head of obstetrics and gynecology at the Royal Free Hospital, London; quoted by Levidow with Jennings and Day, "Unnatural Childbirth?", 5.

47.   See Sobchack, "Child/Alien/Father."

48.   See, for example, Rita Arditti, Renate Duelli Klein, and Shelley Minden, eds., *Test-Tube Women: What Future for Motherhood?*; and Gena Corea, *The Mother Machine: Reproductive Technologies from Artificial Insemination to Artificial Wombs* (New York: Harper and Row, 1985). Attempts to illuminate contradictions and/or reconcile the benefits and hazards of childbearing technologies include Arney, *Power and the Profession of Obstetrics;* James Brooke, "Third World Worry: Fatal Childbirth," *New York Times,* 14 February 1987, 4; Tim Chard and Martin Richards, eds., *Benefits and Hazards of the New Technology* (London: Heinemann, 1977); "Expensive Babies," Editorial, *New York Times,* 17 December 1986, 26; Denise Grady, "Preemies: A $2 Billion Dilemma," *Discover* (August 1985):53–65; Peter Huntingford, "Obstetric Practice: Past, Present, and Future," in *The Place of Birth,* eds. Kitzinger and Davis; Levidow, with Jennings and Day, "Unnatural Childbirth?"; Maternity Center Association, *The Next Fifty Years of Nurse-Midwifery;* Oakley, "Social Consequences of Obstetric Technology"; Deborah S. Pinkney, "Group Urges New Maternal Health Benefits in South," *American Medical News,* 24 April 1987, 12; M. C. Shapiro, J. M. Najman, A. Chang, J. D. Keeping, J. Morrison, and J. S. Western, "Information Control and the Exercise of Power in the Obstetrical Encounter," *Social Science and Medicine* 17.3 (1983):139–46; and Stark, "What is Medicine?"

49.   Segal, *Is the Future Female?* 246.

50.   Poovey, " 'Scenes of an Indelicate Character,' " 138.

51.   Bakhtin, *The Dialogic Imagination,* 292.

52.   Jerold Lucey, 1978; quoted in Arney, *Power and the Profession of Obstetrics,* 228.

53.   Larry R. Lane, *You and Your Pregnancy: Manual for Prenatal Lecture Series* (Champaign, Ill.: Christie Clinic Association, c. 1980).

7

Investment Strategies for the Evolving Portfolio of Primate Females

Donna Haraway

> "It was the high drama of their lives, the next episode of the colubine soap opera that got me out of bed in the morning and kept me out under the Indian sun, tramping about their haunts for eleven hours at a stretch."[1]—Sarah Blaffer Hrdy

> "[T]he central organizing principle of primate social life is competition between females and especially female lineages. Whereas males compete for transitory status and transient access to females, it is females who tend to play for more enduring stakes."[2]—Sarah Blaffer Hrdy

> "Besides, she continued, why call me sexually receptive anyway? That's one of those human words with an opinion written all over it. Call me sexually interested if you will, for I am . . . I'm about as receptive as a lion waiting to be fed!"[3]—Josie, the Chimpanzee

> "[T]he natural body itself became the gold standard of social discourse."[4]—Thomas Laqueur

In primatology as in its other genres, feminist discourse is characterized by its tensions, oppositions, exclusions, complicities with the structures it seeks to deconstruct, as well as by its shared conversations, unexpected alliances, and transformative convergences. Many of the major themes in modern feminism are elaborated in contemporary debates in primatology. Echoing each other across the disciplinary chasms dug to protect the human and natural sciences from each other and across the fortified wall erected to keep genres of science and politics from illicit congress, such twinned symbolic discourses are highly mediated expressions of pervasive, unresolved social contradictions and struggles.[5] This is not the same thing as reducing the oddly duplicated arguments to a governing, homogenizing ideology; each discourse has its specific practices for seeking to establish the authority of its accounts of the world. Marilyn Strathern defined feminist discourse as a field structured by shared yet power-differentiated and often contentious conversations, but not by agreements and, unhappily, not by equality.[6] The discourse is not a series of doctrines, but a web of intersecting and frequently contradictory inquiries and commitments, where gender is inescapably salient and where personal and collective dreams of fundamental change and of bridging the gap between

This essay is a revised version of a chapter in my book, *Primate Visions: Gender, Race, and Nature in the World of Modern Science* (New York: Routledge, 1989).

theory and other forms of action remain alive. In its feminist senses, gender cannot mean simply the cultural appropriation of biological sexual difference. Sexual difference is itself a fundamental—and scientifically contested—construction. Both "sex" and "gender" are woven of multiple, asymmetrical strands of difference, charged with multifaceted dramatic narratives of domination and struggle.

So it is not surprising to find that feminist discourse within primatology is heterogeneous and disharmonious, even as each knot in the field is tied to a resonating strand of feminist argument outside primate studies. Consider four prominent Euro-American women writing primate studies in North America in the 1970s and 1980s. Jeanne Altmann insisted on muted drama; Linda Fedigan deconstructed narratives empowered by anisogamy and its consequence of escalating sexual opposition; Adrienne Zihlman had no patience for evolutionary plots built on hypertrophied competition or sharp sexual difference.[7] But Sarah Blaffer Hrdy has built her scientific narratives and primatological feminist theory on foundations of popular high drama, originary sexual asymmetry and opposition, and the bedrock importance of competition, especially among females. All four women primate scientists engage in a complicated dance in their textual and professional politics around constructing isomorphisms or non-congruences among the potent entities that emerge as actors in their accounts, called female, woman, and scientist. All four engage in problematizing *gender* by contesting for what can count as *sex*; that is, their reinventions of nature are part of their cultural politics. And all four set on stage a different kind of female primate self or subject to enact the crucial dramas. Jeanne Altmann proposes a monkey ergonomic self; Fedigan's characters are mainly characterized by performance of social roles; Zihlman constructs a liberal, flexible self in the mainstream of Enlightenment doctrine; and Hrdy deploys an investing, strategic self. These primate subjects are not mutually exclusive, but each leads to a different pattern of relations among female, woman, and scientist in the texts of these writers. And each writer finds within the animals that mediate the traffic between nature and culture in their society a kind of sex and sexuality, and a kind of mind and cognition, appropriate to these variant subjects.

Zihlman, Fedigan, and Altmann have placed varying amounts of distance between their explanatory strategies and the complex of doctrines labeled sociobiology since the mid-1970s. Hrdy counts herself an unrepentant sociobiologist and insists that sociobiology must be credited with facilitating female-centered accounts of primate lives. Zihlman put maternalist themes into tension with the narrative resources provided by the liberal theory of possessive individualism. Hrdy locates herself entirely under the sign of liberalism and individualism in a story tightly ruled by the imperatives of reproductive competition under conditions of ultimate ontological scarcity. Ironically, Zihlman reproduced a modernist humanist discourse featuring a troubling universal being, woman the gatherer, who threatened to subdue the hetero-glossia of women's power-differentiated lives by means of the univocal lan-guage of sisterhood, while Hrdy delineates a map of proliferating differences written into the primate female body that might indicate directions for a postmodernist, decolonizing biopolitics. But Hrdy's map of differences, her way of narrating that females—and women—differ from one another and are therefore agents, citizens, and subjects in the great dramas of evolution and history, is perhaps more a guide to the cultural logic of late capitalism than to the prefigurative fictions and material practices of international multicultural feminisms. In contrast, Zihlman's universalizing moves might be decon-structed and rewritten as representations of ways of life necessary to postcolo-nial women's movements.

Deferring direct discussion of Hrdy's writing, let us begin with the topic that seems to pervade Hrdy's scientific stories most literally: sexual politics. The salience of sexual politics to major social controversies in the United States in the 1970s and 1980s is undeniable. Sexual politics is a polyvalent term covering a host of life-and-death issues and struggles for meanings. A list suggested by the term "sexual politics" defies termination: abortion, sterilization, birth control, population policy, high technology–mediated re-productive practices, wife beating, child abuse, family policy, definition of what counts as a family, the sexual political economy of aging, the science and politics of diet "disorders" and regimens, compulsory heterosexuality, heterodox sexual practices among lesbian feminists, sexual identity politics, lesbian and gay histories and contemporary movements, rape, pornography, transsexuality, fetal and child purchase through contract with pregnant women ("surrogacy" seems a hopelessly inadequate word), racist sexual ex-ploitation, single parenting by men and women, feminization of poverty, women's employment outside the home, unpaid labor in the home, covertly gendered norms for professional careers, restriction to populations of one sex in health research on non-sex-limited diseases, domestic divisions of labor, class and race divisions among women, high theory in the human sciences, technologies of representation, social research methodologies, the ties of masculinism to militarism and especially to nuclear politics, psychoanalytic accounts of gender and culture—and on, and on. What principle of order could reduce such a list to coherence? It is possible to argue, nonfacetiously, that every major public issue in the last two decades in the United States has been pervaded by the symbols and stakes of sexual politics. It is in this cultural and political environment that feminism and antifeminism have emerged in nearly every area of collective and personal life, contesting the constructions and representations of gender.

In her analysis of the ideological development of "second wave" feminism in the United States in the context of the postwar revolution in female (especially mothers' and married women's) labor force participation, controversies about personal and family life, and decline of the cultures of domesticity among white middle- and working-class women, Judith Stacey argued that feminism has often been credited or blamed for transformations, insecurities, and freedoms rooted in the vast rearrangements of "postindustrial" society.[8] Feminism has been a shaper of, but also deeply shaped by, fundamental historical rearrangements of daily life in late-industrial society. The ideologies and symbols associated with woman as mother, with woman constituted as object of another's desire and pleasure, and with the female body as the stakes in the contest for honor among men have all been problematized by other cultural discourses on gender and sex. Only some of these challenging moves have been feminist. But in general, the power of the image of woman as natural mother—a being consumed and fulfilled by dedication to another; a being whose meaning is the species, not the self; a being less than and more than human, but never paradigmatically man—has declined in nearly every discursive arena, from popular culture to legal doctrine to evolutionary theory. Attempts have repeatedly been made since World War II to rehabilitate the "traditional" (i.e., white, bourgeois, Western, nineteenth-century) images of the female body organized around the uterus, social motherhood, and domesticity; but they have had the feel of a blacklash, of a still-dangerous but defeated ideology.

At the same time, the languages and issues of reproductive politics have intensified in material and symbolic power. Both symbolically and practically, the fights over reproductive politics are carried out paradigmatically in and on and over the bodies of real women. But they are also carried out in the images and practices of scientific and technological research, science-fiction film, metaphoric languages among nuclear weapons researchers, and neo-liberal and neo-conservative political theory.[9] Reproductive politics provide the figure for the possibility and nature of a future in multinational capitalist and nuclear society. Production is conflated with reproduction. Reproduction has become the prime strategic question, a privileged trope for logics of investment and expansion in late capitalism, and the site of discourse about the limits and promises of the self as individual. Reproductive "strategy" has become the figure for reason itself—the logic of late-capitalist survival and expansion, of how to stay in the game in postmodern conditions. Simultaneously, reproductive biotechnology is developed and contested within the story of the final removal of making babies from women's bodies, the final appropriation of nature by culture, of woman by man. Symbolically, reproduction displaced to the laboratory and the factory becomes no longer the sign of the power of personal and organic bodies, preeminently the site of sexual politics, but the sign of the conquest of still another "last" frontier in the ideology of masculinist technology and industrial politics. Reproduction, strategic reasoning, and high technology come to inhabit the same sentences in social discourse. This is decidedly not the syntax of maternalism and domesticity.

From Western points of view, the premises of individualism and self-sufficiency break down most dramatically and inescapably in sexual reproduction by men and women. At its simplest, sexual reproduction takes two, no matter how much the theories of masculine potency in Western philosophy and medicine attempt to evade the matter.[10] Phrased in the discourse of biology, there is never any reproduction of the individual in sexually reproducing species. Short of cloning, that staple of science fiction, neither parent is continued in the child, who is a randomly reassembled genetic package projected into the next generation. To reproduce does not defeat death any more than producing other memorable deeds or words does. Maternity might be more certain than paternity, but neither secures the self into the future. In short, where there is sex, literal reproduction is a contradiction in terms. The issue from the self is always (an)other. The scandal of sexual difference for the liberal conception of the self is at the heart of the matter. Sexual difference founded on compulsory heterosexuality is itself the key technology for the production and perpetuation of Western man and for the assurance of this project as a fantastic lie. In the major Western narrative for generating self and other, one is always too few and two are always too many. In that dialectic lies the fiction made into reality of the escalation and repressive sublimation of combat as the motor of personal and collective history.

But—also at its simplest—so far, only women get pregnant. Pregnant women in Western cultures are in much more shocking relation than men to doctrines of unencumbered property in the self. In "making babies," female bodies violate Western women's liberal singularity during their lifetimes and compromise their claims to full citizenship.[11] For Western men in reproduction, setting aside the "problem" of death, the loss of self seems so tiny, the degrees of freedom so many.[12] Ontologically always potentially pregnant, women are both more limited in themselves, with a body that betrays their individuality, and limiting to men's fantastic self-reproductive projects. To achieve themselves, even if the achievement is a history-making fantasy, men must appropriate women. Women are the limiting resource, but not the actors. In the late twentieth century, this continuing narrative of the embattled and calculating mortal individual elaborates the fantasy of the breakdown of already fantastic "coherent" subjects and objects, including the Western self, for both men and women. All subjects and objects seem nothing but strategic assemblages, proximate means to some ultimate, theoretic end achieved by replicating, copying, and simulating—in short, by the means of postmodern reproduction. No wonder cloning is the imaginary figure for the survival of self-identity in cyborg culture.

In this context of the breakdown of ideologies and images of female domesticity and of the intensification of reproductive politics and cultural meanings in postmodern worlds, sociobiology's exuberant emergence and rapid claims to hegemony in evolutionary explanation in the 1970s should come as no surprise. There is a huge literature on controversies generated by sociobiology, especially applied to human beings. I am not here primarily interested in the claims and counterclaims that sociobiology is inherently racist or sexist (or the opposite) or that it is another in a long line of biological determinisms (or the best route to human self-definition and expanded choice). Such arguments have often been rather reductive, caricaturing the discourse and other practices of scientists and critics. Argument at this level reproduces the terms of representation that must be deconstructed. I am here more interested in sociobiology as a postmodern discourse in late capitalism, where problematic versions of feminism readily enter the contest for meanings, at least in retrospect and over the tired bodies of gutsy sociobiological feminists. How have sociobiological feminist arguments, like other Western feminisms, enabled deconstruction of masculinist systems of representation, while simultaneously both deepening and problematizing the unmarked yet enabling tropes of Western ethnocentrism and neo-imperialism?

Let us characterize, or perhaps caricature for emphasis, central sociobiological images in terms of this discussion. What does the famous death of the coherent, whole subject look like in neo-Darwinian evolutionary theory? The ever-granulating "unit of selection" heads the list. No bounded body seems able to resist limitless fragmentation to become at last the luminous unit-agent acting strategically to stay in the game. Who is playing? Has the evolutionary play in the ecological theater become a video game on an automated battlefield? No element of structure and function can unify all the narratives of biological meaning. Species, population, social group, organism, cell, gene: all these units atomize under the explanatory burdens they must bear.[13] No unit, least of all the individual, sexually reproducing organism, is a whole, classically reasonable, potentially rights-bearing subject in the realm of nature. The organism is in constant danger of resolving into nothing but a proximate means for the strategic ends of its own genes. The organism's offspring, its investment, is a congeries of genes that allows calculation of a coefficient of relatedness, but this genetic investment is hardly straightforward reproduction. Inclusive fitness theory demands calculations of coefficients of relatedness and produces a kind of hypothetical or hyperreal individual, put together from its fragments of scattered sameness in all those bodies of others calculating in their own terms how to get more copies of parts of themselves into play. The imperative is to identify and replicate "same" while holding "other" at bay. But otherness is everywhere, masquerading as same. Altruism must be redefined in terms of the problematic of investment in non-self: how can such a strategy yield a return on the self in the future? Which self? The Darwinian world from the start has been ruled by a reproductive natural economy, but Darwinian reproductive politics have intensified and tightened in the conditions of logical contradiction in which there is *nothing* to reproduce. How can narratives stabilize objects and produce good-enough subjects to get on with the dramas of investment? It is small wonder that female domesticity and selfless maternalism offer few useful images for such a project.

But there is a deep reservoir of universalizing images for the postmodern reproductive politics and reconceptualizations of the relations of mind and body in sociobiology: the female orgasm. Representations of female orgasm offer a map to the politics and epistemologies of sexual pleasure in a world structured by gendered antagonistic difference. In a sociobiological world, sexual difference may no longer be the figure of distinct, hierarchically arrayed, and stably complementary man and woman; but representations of male and female bodies remain ready to figure the strategic calculations of life's unequal investment battles. Neglecting the militarization of discourse implied in the ubiquitous battle-strategy-investment metaphors of modern politics and biology, ordering "life's unequal investment battles" around sexual difference has the effect of demoting or erasing other axes of subordination for women, as well as for men. Universalizing representations of the female orgasm are maps of a silent, nonetheless constitutive, racial discourse.

In particular, the racial and racist nature of sexual politics is obscured by the feminist and antifeminist discourse of the white middle class that privileges sexual difference as the definitive axis of gender inequality.[14] That is, *sex,* and especially its derivative, *sexual difference,* can be a distorting lens for seeing the asymmetries between and within *genders,* as well as other basic systems of inequality. Because of the history of sexual politics in slavery, lynching, and the contemporary coercive sexualization of nonwhite women in racist symbology and material life, this issue is particularly sharp around the politics of sexual pleasure and sexual violence in the history of U.S. feminism from the nineteenth century to the present. Ideologies of "social motherhood" and "sexual prudery" were powerful feminist tools in nineteenth-century American struggles for women's control of their bodies, but the ideologies had different resonances and subsequent histories for black and other feminist theorists of color than for white feminists.

Basic economic inequality was a principal reason that black feminists of the post-1960s "second wave" in the U.S. had a different agenda from middle-class white feminists, but it was not the only reason semiotically or materially. In this context, orgasms and female genital anatomy have vastly different racial semiotic fields.[15] Middle class, white "politics of the female orgasm" can risk privileging women's sexual pleasure in reconstructing notions of agency and property-in-the-self within liberal discourse. Black feminists of all classes confront a different history, where black women's putative sexual pleasure connoted closeness to an animal world of insatiable sensuality and black men's sexuality connoted animal aggression and the rape of white women. Hazel Carby showed that black feminists' constructions of black women's respectability were part of an antiimperialist and antiracist, as well as feminist, politics in the nineteenth century. In the late twentieth century, antiracist feminists cannot engage unproblematically in universalizing discourses about sexual pleasure as a sign of female agency without reinscribing feminism within one of the fundamental technologies for enforcing gendered racial inequality. As Carby argued, "A desire for the possibilities of the uncolonized black female body occupies a utopian space. . . . [Nineteenth-century] black feminists expanded the limits of conventional ideologies of womanhood to consider subversive relationships between women, motherhood without wifehood, wifehood as a partnership outside of an economic exchange between men, and men as partners and not patriarchal fathers."[16] If the texts that Carby foregrounds had founded the biopolitics of the primate body in the 1970s and 1980s, the discourse about female bodies in sociobiological feminism would have been different. But these texts were not part of the discursive field in which the female orgasm was rediscovered and deployed to signify universal, unmarked woman's natural body and mind within the constraints of what I will call hyper-liberalism.

A core metaphor from Thomas Laqueur's discussion of sixteenth- through nineteenth-century medical and political representations of female bodies in "Orgasm, Generation, and the Politics of Reproductive Biology" may be extended to the late twentieth century: the universalized natural body remains the gold standard of hegemonic social discourse.[17] As a gold *standard,* the natural body is inescapably figured as a convention, i.e., a construction. Neither gold nor bodies enter these equations outside convention. The natural body is a gold standard for power-differentiated social intercourse, for the unequal exchanges of "conversation." Gold is preeminently the medium of universal translation, the sign of the promise of a world of frictionless exchange, of final commodification of the body of the world in a hyper-real market ordered by a transparent language, a final common measure. Nineteenth-century Americans used the words *conversation* and *intercourse* interchangeably to signify sexual "commerce" between men and women. Illicit sex was named *criminal conversation.* "Communication" remains the central, fetishized preoccupation. Broadly, within late-twentieth-century scientific discourse the natural body is conventionally a bio-technological cyborg—an engineered communications device, an information-generating and processing system, a technology for recognizing self and nonself (paradigmatically through the immune system), and a strategic assemblage of heterogeneous biotic components held together in a reproductive politics of genetic investment. Genetic currency is golden, a sign of a world always like itself, univocal.[18]

Hrdy has been an active trader in these precious metals, products of the transmutation of representations of genitally organized pleasure into the sign of power and agency. In a process, in which Hrdy took significant part, of renegotiating the conventions that set the value of the body for political discourse, orgasmic sexual pleasure became for (unmarked, i.e., white) women what it has been for (unmarked) men before, the sign of the "same," i.e., of the capacity to be (mis)represented as the unmarked, self-identical subject— at least for a few intense seconds—in postmodern fantasy. The unmarked category is the category present to itself, the category of identity, of the "same," of gold, versus the marked category of otherness, of value defined by another, of lack of power to name, of base metal. Orgasm becomes the sign of mind, the point of consciousness, of self-presence, that holds it all together well enough to enable the subject to make moves in the game, instead of being the (marked) board on which the game is played.

Since the eighteenth century, liberal theory has required the body to be the bearer of the rational subject. If sociobiology is a form of hyper-liberalism, the organs of its hyper-bodies must be signs for the subject constituted through strategic reason. Has the *mentula muliebris,* the little mind of women, a common name for the clitoris in sixteenth-century learned texts, like the phallic *mentula,* or little mind of men, become a late twentieth-century guarantor of the status of (a desiring and investing) subject, of representability, and of agency in life's dramatic narratives? What kind of feminism could this be?

Laqueur argues that before the latter part of the eighteenth century in Europe, most medical writers assumed orgasmic female sexual pleasure was essential for conception. To simplify a complex story, it was only with the constitution of sexual difference in a (re)productionist frame that female orgasms came to seem either nonexistent or pathological from the point of view of Western medicine. Sexual difference was constituted discursively through the nineteenth-century biological reorganization of the female body around the ovaries and uterus and of the male body around a spermatic economy that linked phallus and mind through the commerce between nervous and reproductive energy. Prostitutes, nonwhite women, sick women—these might have orgasms and large clitorises, but "civiliza-tion" itself seemed to require the little mind of women to disappear. The "problem" of the clitoral *versus* vaginal orgasm would have been incomprehensible to a Renaissance doctor. But by the late nineteenth century, surgeons removed the clitoris from some of their female patients as part of reconstituting them as properly feminine, unambiguously different from the male, which seemed to be almost another species—or better, masculine and feminine connoted the odd taxonomic and linguistic inversion of two genera in a single species. Female and male structures before the late eighteenth century were almost universally regarded as homologous; the female was a kind of male turned inside herself. She even appeared to some writers to have two organs homologous to the male penis, but this apparent duplicity caused no evident trouble in the text of the body or the text of the medical writer. The female was a *lesser* human, less hot, less spirited; but she was not a *different* human.

Changing the meaning of and practices for establishing homologies, biological discourse about reproduction and sexual difference was part of a great redeployment of male and female in cultural and political space. Hierarchical homologies were abandoned for a different discursive order, comparative functional anatomy and its many biopolitical offspring. Incommensurability replaced hierarchy as the principle of relationship between the sexes. The sexes became "opposite" or "complementary," rather than more or less. And new ways of interpreting the body were new ways of representing and constituting social realities.

In particular, European-derived feminist and antifeminist debates proliferating from the late eighteenth century located themselves on the terrain of the meaning of sexual difference. The history of this modern feminism would be incomprehensible without the history of modern reproductive biology and clinical gynecology—as a moral discourse about social order and as a social technology. Evolutionary discussions were part of this larger discursive frame. In antifeminist discourse wherever the boundaries of old hierarchies were threatened by new Enlightenment liberal doctrines of universal man, biological sexual and racial difference reimposed "natural" limits.[19] The body as bearer of the rational subject in liberal theory was "neutral," sexed but not gendered, and as such could potentially be used by feminists to threaten gender hierarchy.[20] Liberal theory was a resource for feminists, but only at the price of renouncing anything specific about women's voice and position and carefully avoiding the problem of difference, for example, race, among women. The "neutral" body was always unmarked, white, and masculine. As members of the species Man, women were silenced as such. But for antifeminists, as females biologically and functionally, women were imagined to be without capacity for full citizenship. Their specificity fitted them for the home, for domestic space, not for the competitive world of business, scholarship, and politics.[21] Yet even feminists drawing on liberal theory in these debates could not and did not dispense with the contradictory resources of the emerging discourses on functional sexual difference.

Nineteenth-century American feminist doctrines of social motherhood, a major argument for the vote, drew on the discursive resources of the new reproductive biology. In these arguments, women as mothers were especially fitted for citizenship. They would heal the body politic from the wounds inflicted by militarist and competitive men. They would be mothers of the republic, acting in a public space, as they were mothers in the domestic space. The doctrine of separate spheres could be and was deployed by those opposing and those advancing (some) women's rights. From the late eighteenth to the mid twentieth century, feminists had few alternatives to maternalist discourse for claiming the right to public speech as women. The "passionless" (white) woman became a historical figure. One casualty of this map of discursive possibility was the meaning of female genital sexual pleasure. Pleasure might still occur, and the sexologists from Havelock Ellis on tried manfully to reestablish nonpathological meanings for female sexual pleasure. But what did female orgasm *mean*—and in what regions of the body did it occur—for "good" women, that is? While they *were* The Sex, they could not *have* sex—only babies, in the literal form of children or the symbolic form of an infantilized public world crying for politics as mothering. All this would change for the World War II baby-boom generation, whose members have written the texts of sociobiological feminism.

Like their human cousins, primate females seem to have been born originally into the post-eighteenth-century liberal world of primatology without orgasms and as natural altruistic mothers. This is no condition for a good strategic investor, that late-twentieth-century figure of the ideal citizen, for whom a self-possessed *mentula* is absolutely essential. How did female monkeys and apes get their orgasms back, and what does the story have to do with the white, middle-class branch of the Women's Liberation Movement and one of its daughters, sociobiological feminism?

Let us begin with the chimpanzee, Josie, living in a cage at the psychobiologist Robert Yerkes's Orange Park facility in the late 1930s. Complaining about Yerkes's confusion about sexual, nutritional, and social hungers among male and female chimpanzees, and especially about his theories of the biological origins of prostitution and female natural subordination, Josie was given speech in Ruth Hershberger's prefigurative feminist text, *Adam's Rib*, in the 1940s. Hershberger wanted to rewrite more than Josie's lines in Yerkes's papers; she was interested in a thorough scientific critique of sexist biology of the female body, most certainly including a rediscovery of the physiological and evolutionary point of having a clitoris. In 1944 Hershberger wrote Yerkes to ask him if he had seen any signs of orgasm in female chimpanzees. Yerkes expressed interest in her query and referred it to his appropriate colleague in reproductive physiology. Hershberger followed with a detailed request for specific observations about clitoral erection. Yerkes again referred her to an appropriate colleague. And there, as far as I can find, for the other primate females the matter rested until the same period that gave rise to the Women's Liberation Movement.

Twentieth-century sex-advice manuals stressed women's sexual satisfaction and even orgasm before the second wave of feminism, and Heshberger's little book is a useful guide to the terms of the discussion between the two world wars. In general, the therapeutics of marriage contained the biopolitics of women's always-on-the-verge-of-pathological sexual pleasure or sexual quiescence ("frigidity"). If before the late eighteenth century, female orgasm was assumed to be necessary to conception, before the late twentieth century, once its existence was re-admitted to polite society, its only hope for normality lay in compulsory heterosexuality, itself one of the great constructions of the last two hundred years. In the shadow of the normal has lurked the specter of the pathological—women's sexual pleasure for their own ends, as a sign of their existence as ends and not as functions, no longer as mothers, wives, or even free lovers under the reign of gender, i.e., male domination. The concept of existing as ends is incompatible with the binary division into normal and pathological; the binarism is about functions, means, not ends. In patriarchal ideology, Woman is contained by her functions, not achieved through and for her own ends.

By means of the link through orgasm of self-possession and existence as ends rather than means, in a typical universalizing discourse, women as females could be semiotically reconstructed under the sign of reason and citizenship. As long as "the family" or the "pair bond" contained the meaning of women's sexuality, women could not be social subjects, ends-in-themselves, in the hegemonic narratives of liberal theory and biopolitics. In effect, without getting their orgasms back on their own terms, late-twentieth-century Western middle-class women could not have minds. This point was implicit in the extraordinary attention that the politics of women's orgasms got in the popular media and in polemics of the Women's Liberation Movement internationally throughout the 1970s. Deep controversies about female sexual desire continue to rend the Western women's movements and "general" society in the 1980s.[22] In the early years of the Women's Liberation Movement, orgasm on one's own terms signified property in the self as no other bodily sign could. Indeed, masturbation came to promise the best kind of orgasm for women, while lesbian sadomasochism could be a utopian sign of freedom from the taxonomy of functionality and normality. In the curious logic of signs, nonreproductive, nonheterosexual, female-controlled, women's orgasmic practices could point to a possible world without gender, a science-fiction world where the rule of the normal was broken for women, and not merely (once again) for men. Sexual difference and the whole apparatus of liberal functionalism as a category of analysis were at stake in these semiotic contests. Male orgasm had signified self-containment and self-transcendence simultaneously, both property in the self and transcendence of the body through reason and desire, autonomy and ecstasy. These were the symbolic prizes sought by those who had been semiotically contained and fixed for another (i.e., men) via the notion of the normal, healthy, and functional. No longer pinned in the crack between the normal and the pathological, multiply orgasmic, unmarked, universal females might find themselves possessed of reason, desire, citizenship, and individuality. The semiotic stakes were the redefinition of white womanhood. This is quite a task to demand of the *mentula*.

It is in this historical context that I wish to read Hrdy's sociobiological feminism. Interesting contradictions leap out at once. Sociobiology is narratively both a hyper-functionalism and a hyper-liberalism. The promise of the self-contained and self-transcendent subject, which has historically been the fantastic longing embedded in liberalism, seems even more fraudulent in the postmodern landscape of disaggregating subjects and fragmented units in a vast, simulated world ruled by strategic maneuvers. Both evoked and blocked earlier within bourgeois liberalism, female individualism in the postmodern landscape threatens to be a pyrrhic victory. To escape the rule of biological sexual difference, with its patriarchal moral discourse on the normal and the pathological, only to play the board game of reproductive politics as replication of the self within sociobiological narratives, seems a parody of feminist critiques of gender. The tie between recasting females as strategic reasoners (proximate ends in themselves) and the fierce reproductive teleology of the ultimate game takes the bite out of sociobiology's deconstructions of the social functionalist dramas of maternalism. Sociobiological females/women are cast again as mothers with a vengeance, this time in the problematic guise of the rational genetic investor, a kind of genetic receptacle, holding company, or trust, not so much for the spermatic word of the male as for the contentious ultimate elements of code that assemble to make up the postmodern organism itself. There seems nothing that can elude the bottom line of genetic investment logic, no matter how much free play is allowed in the intermediate accounts. In sociobiological stories, the ideology of sexual difference seems to be called in against social functionalism only to reappear in the escalating sexual combat rooted in anisogamy—i.e., in sex cells (gametes) of unequal size. To locate a reconstruction of the biopolitics of being female in sociobiology is fraught with irony. But the irony and the contradictions cannot evict this rich contemporary discourse from the capacious and contentious house of feminism. Let us look for hints of a radical future even for hyper-liberal feminism.[23]

Hrdy recounted the history of the debate about primate female orgasms subsequent to Hershberger's 1940s queries in her popular feminist sociobiological book, *The Woman That Never Evolved*.[24] In the context of 1960s laboratory-based studies of endocrine physiology and sexual behavior, the psychiatrists Doris Zumpe and Richard Michael described a "clutch reflex" in rhesus monkey females at the time of their male partners' ejaculations. The authors suggested these spasmodic arm movements might be signs of female orgasm, or as they put it, "an external expression of consummatory sexual behavior."[25] Perhaps rhesus females not only had orgasms, but even had the most fantastic kind in the heterosexual imagination—simultaneous with a male partner. Prompted by Masters and Johnson's famous studies,[26] in an experimental design verging on a caricature of rape, the anthropologist Frances Burton "subjected three [restrained] rhesus females to five minutes of clitoral stimulation mechanically applied by the experimenter, four minutes of rest, and five more minutes of vaginal stimulation."[27] The point was to modify Masters and Johnson's recording techniques to study females who could give no verbal reports about their states of excitement. Removing vestigial doubt about the matter, Masters and Johnson had "proved" that women have orgasms by a method that did not rely on verbal report by women either.

These privileged orgasms took on the authority of natural science. They wrote, rather than spoke, their truth. Women's orgasmic bodies themselves became inscription devices, coupled to other recording instruments, tracing the trajectory of excitement and its resolution. These recordings put in writing, seemingly without the polluting intervention of an interpreting subject, graphic evidence of women's multiple peaks of sexual climax. Orgasms were recorded by a kind of automatic writing technology that could also be coupled to the body of the nonhuman primate, joining females in a sisterhood of officially recorded sexual pleasure across species and across the boundary of nature and culture. However, what the pleasure *meant* was not resolved by documentary evidence of its presence. All stages that Masters and Johnson found in women, except the anatomically obscured final stage (orgasm itself), were clearly visible in these rhesus females. Burton concluded her subjects were orgasmic under these laboratory conditions. In view of the repeated copulations reported from field observations of several species, which suggested a likely building up of sexual excitement, female orgasms in "nature" seemed a reasonable conclusion.

Beginning about the same time as Burton, during her dissertation research on the ontogeny of communication, for which she took data on communication before and after copulation, Suzanne Chevalier-Skolnikoff, Sherwood Washburn's student at UC Berkeley, reported extensive observations of likely female orgasms in captive colonies of stumptail macaques at Stanford, resulting from both heterosexual and homosexual mounting. Chevalier-Skolnikoff speculated that female orgasm was widespread among mammals and, echoing Renaissance physicians, was "an essential ingredient of fertile coitus in at least some mammalian species."[28] She argued that female orgasms likely functioned as a motivational mechanism in all female mammals. But although she gave a model for the evolution of the female orgasm, she wrote before the resources of the sociobiological narrative were available for developing this germ of a transformative story. Chevalier-Skolnikoff recalled that no one seemed to be paying much attention to homosexual behavior among nonhuman primates then. Her observations, which were incidental to her main focus on communication, bore on both homosexual and heterosexual female orgasmic sexuality in the stumptail subjects. Lucille Neuman invited her to give a talk on these matters at a symposium Neuman was organizing at the Association for the American Advancement of Science meetings in Philadelphia in 1971; Jane

Lancaster, from Chevalier-Skolnikoff's cohort at Berkeley, asked her to speak in a symposium on female sex roles at meetings of the International Primatological Society. The feminist biosocial network provided one ready audience for these observations of active female sexuality. Over a short period, Chevalier-Skolnikoff gave four different papers, publishing three of them.

Both the genesis and reactions to these papers took her by surprise. She recounted that in the original symposia where she read papers, no one said a word during the discussions, but that she would then receive 600–800 requests for copies, whereas she might have received 10–15 for a successful conference paper before.[29] She was invited to be on the editorial board of the *Archives of Sexual Behavior,* but was rebuffed by the Stanford feminist social anthropologist, Michelle Rosaldo, when she suggested putting a paper on female orgasm into what became one of the foundational U.S. texts in feminist anthropology.[30] At a 1972 presentation before a Los Angeles group supporting transsexual operations, Chevalier-Skolnikoff was cheered by an audience standing and waving banners as she walked up to the podium.

Although women's groups did not seem to receive the sex papers with the same enthusiasm, Sarah Blaffer Hrdy, a Harvard anthropology graduate student who did not yet define herself as a feminist, heard and absorbed Chevalier-Skolnikoff's 1971 presentation at the American Anthropological Association meetings in New York on the stumptail female sexual response and its implications for female mammalian sexuality. Hrdy approached Chevalier-Skolnikoff later, saying she had been impressed and amazed, but did not yet have an explanatory framework for fitting it in. Formed intellectually by Irven DeVore's undergraduate primate behavior course, for which Robert Trivers was her T.A., and then by debates in DeVore's graduate primate seminars, in which Trivers was a central presence, as well as by E. O. Wilson's ideas and personal support in graduate school, Hrdy later interpreted her dissertation research data published in *Langurs of Abu* in terms of sociobiological approaches to male and female strategies of reproduction. Active female sexuality was already part of that story; but in *The Woman That Never Evolved* and subsequent publications, the full implications of female sexual assertiveness, symbolized and facilitated by the female orgasm, emerged.[31] The orgasm was the noumenal guarantor and reward for female sexual agency. This kind of sexual agency signified the rational citizen in the natural economy of the body politic. Thus, the orgasm became the sign of the *cognito;* by the late twentieth century, the *cognito* became strategic reason in a game played by replicators.

In *The Woman That Never Evolved,* which Harvard University Press advertised in the *New York Review of Books* with a drawing of a "women's culture" stitchery that read "women's place is in the jungle," Hrdy argued against sociobiologist-anthropologist Donald Symons's view that female orgasms were a byproduct of a male adaptation. Symons put it plainly: "Orgasm may be possible for female mammals because it is adaptive for males."[32] Males have nipples because mammals are built from a bipotential plan, but nipples are adaptively meaningless except in females; ditto in reverse for the *mentula muliebris*. Milk and semen travel in different channels and to different ends. Hrdy salvaged the heterodox ideas of the feminist psychiatrist Mary Jane Sherfy who had argued that human females' recently authorized capacity for multiple orgasms showed them to be virtually sexually insatiable. Sherfy had linked this wonderful sexuality to a past matriarchal stage in human development. Hrdy had a much more respectable evolutionary narrative for restoring rationality to female genital sexual pleasure. "In strictly anatomical terms, then, the human clitoris is the core of the problem."[33] Lying in the way of an easy argument for the functional significance of the female orgasm were troubling facts. There was no way to argue that the female orgasm was essential to conception, as there once had been. Intercourse had, to say the least, been shown to be quite possible without female pleasure at all, much less orgasm. Even among orgasmic females, orgasm seemed occasional rather than entirely reliable (In contrast to males?). But still, "No function other than sexual stimulation of the female has ever been assigned to the clitoris." True to a strong biological tendency broadly, and a sociobiological imperative, an adaptive function should be found for anything as constant as that little phallus in female mammals. Hrdy struck the right tone of mild sarcasm toward dissenters: "Are we to assume, then, that this organ is irrelevant—a pudendal equivalent of the intestinal appendix?"[34] Since the proximate end was female pleasure, Hrdy had to find the ultimate explanation in the gold coin of reproductive advantage.

So how could the occasional, or the insatiable and multiple, orgasm enhance the reproductive chances of females so endowed? It wouldn't make them better mothers, but it might make them safer. Above all, orgasms enhanced females' tool kit as good genetic strategists: it made them better able to lie, to simulate, a mark of postmodern intelligence in primate studies as elsewhere. Hrdy reasoned, "If we recognize that a female's reproductive success can depend in critical ways on the tolerance of nearby males, on male willingness to assist an infant, or at least to leave it alone, the selective importance of an active, promiscuous sexuality becomes readily apparent. Female primates influence males by consorting with them, thereby manipulating the information available to males about possible paternity. To the extent that her subsequent offspring benefit, the female has benefited from her seeming nymphomania."[35] Here is no story about happily complementary heterosexuality. It is not a tale about human female sexuality taking its meaning from the origin of monogamy, enabled by constant female "receptivity" and the "loss" of estrus, called by Hrdy "situation-dependent, concealed ovulation."[36] Hrdy's is a narrative about root conflict of interest that cuts across sexual difference, in which sexual pleasure and concealed ovulation can give the added competitive edge to some females, in competition with other females, in their struggle to turn males, pursuing their own reproductive ends, into a resource, or at least into less of an enemy.

Hrdy believed that keeping males uncertain about paternity was one advantage retained by females in an evolutionary game heavily weighted toward male physical power.[37] How did this situation come about? I have read the female orgasm here as the privileged sign of female agency, where mind and body come together in female possession of the phallus. A more sober commentator would protest that orgasm is a sideshow for sociobiologists, with only a few lines in the great epic text of genetic investment strategies. What is the sociobiological first book of Genesis that recounts original hostile difference? How did it come about that nonidentity must mean competitive difference? And how did that original difference translate into cosmic limits on female power and agency?

"Part of the answer, remote in time and nonnegotiable—but not particularly satisfying—is *anisogamy,* from the Greek *aniso* (meaning unequal) plus *gametes* (eggs and sperm): gametes differing in size."[38] Whatever the merits of the tale, whose doubtfulness Hrdy signals even while invoking it in order to get her own narrative going, it is always satisfying to start an important origin story with a Greek etymology. In the primeval soup, by chance some protocells were bigger than others. These richer cells became coveted resources for any cell that could commandeer them to its own energetic replicative ends. "Competition among the small cells for access to the largest ones favored smaller, faster, and more maneuverable cells, analogous to sperm. The hostages we might as well call ova. . . . The ground rules for the evolution of two very different creatures—males and females—were laid down at this early date." One group began specializing in amassing resources into themselves, while the other specialized in "competing among themselves for access to these stockpiling organisms."[39] When these early strategists took the further fateful chance step of fully combining, inherently antagonistic sexual reproduction was born out of a prior asymmetrical, but rather innocent, economic exploitation. This mode of reproduction, with its radical legacy of excessive heterogeneity, of untamable difference across and between the generations, quickly became an inescapable necessity.

But while eggs remained necessarily vastly larger than sperm, the bearers of the gametes—males and females—took the opposite course. In very few species of primates are females bigger than males. Why? Darwin's answer was sexual selection, intra-sexual competition for access to the means of reproduction, i.e., the "opposite" sex. Since females, from large eggs, gestation, and lactation through lifelong energy-demanding social entanglements with their offspring, put more into reproduction, they become the so-called "investing sex." And the investing sex becomes the limiting resource: the sign and embodiment of what is most desired and always scarce, never really one's own, the needed and hated female as prize. The limiting resource always runs the risk of being nothing but the prize, not a player in its own right—no, not *its, her* own right. The limiting resource is *logically* gender female; this is the "syntactic" basis for the equation of nature and female in Western gendered narratives. Nature in a productionist paradigm is the limiting resource for humanist projects; Nature is female, the limiting resource for the reproduction of man, loved and hated and needed, but held in check as agent in her own right. Among primates, the intensity of male competition leads to bigger, stronger, savvier males. And in general, the greater the inequality of reproductive success among males of the species, the larger the size difference between males and females will be. Inequalities and antagonistic differences cascade synergistically in these stories. Females are not passive in all of this, but their goose was cooked in the primeval Greek alphabet soup.

Anisogamy and sexual selection converge with a third story element that knots behavioral ecology into the weave of sociobiological narrative. Given that females, not males, are the limiting resource, their ways of getting food will have the more fundamental consequences for the possibilities of social life in the species. Among primates, why do some females congregate with other females and males in large groups, while others space themselves singly or in still other social arrangements? Hrdy uses Richard Wrangham's female-centered model for the social systems of primates to advance her account.[40] If competition for scarce resources drives the whole system, competition for food will determine much else. Females will distribute themselves in space as a function of their inherited physiologies and the neighborhood's ecological opportunities and constraints for making a living. A large-bodied fruit eater will have a different range of distributive possibilities compared to a smaller-bodied leaf eater, and so on. Males will space themselves in relation to females and to their own competitive relations with one another. These competitive relations can include all kinds of coalitions and forms of cooperation, which are all proximate matters in the great ultimate game of genetic investment according to the principles of methodological individualism. Where they can, females will form social groups with related females, to take advantage of various kinds of help. In this sense, "sisterhood" is powerful; it is a question of coefficients of relatedness and the terms of economic survival. In large social groups, lineages of females will compete with one another. Ranks of females within lineages and ranks among different lineages will concern females greatly and will have large consequences for male possibilities.

Competition among assertive, dominance-oriented females is an absolutely central principle of primate social life, built into their natural status as limiting resources whose eating habits are the pivot of sexual politics.[41] Female genetic investment strategies could not have produced the mother-for-the-species of the social functionalists; complementary sexual difference in the organic liberal order gives way to the full array of sexualized agonistic strategic possibilities.

Females remain committed to reproduction, but not within a maternalist discourse. Rather, females are redeployed semiotically within a strategic investment discourse, where mind, sex, and economy collapse into a single, highly problematic figure—the hyper-real unit of selection.

This narrative of female economic agency, whose foundational female spatial "deployment" and competitive relations with each other set the constraints for shifting male "strategies," converges with the story of female sexual agency through such means as orgasmic sexual assertiveness and concealed ovulation to produce the sociobiological account of females as full citizens of the evolutionary, hyper-liberal state of nature. Here is where the story element of females as the site of internal differences is foregrounded. The bottom line of the story is that females evolve, too. That is, females, as well as males, differ among themselves in parameters that matter to differential survival and fecundity, and so are subject to natural selection. The point of this story is that females are dynamic actors of self- and species-forming dimensions. Hrdy has contributed particularly fully to elaborating these arguments. Female reproductive fitness can vary as a function of at least five categories that she has characterized: female choice of mate, female eliciting of male support or protection, competition with other females for resources, cooperation with other females, and female ergonomic efficiency. In each category, females are actors, albeit, like males, heavily constrained ones. One female is not like another. Their differences matter to the most basic of life's dramas; they are not the backdrop to someone else's action; their action is differentiated and interesting, full of conflict and ultimate risks. Females are heroes in the narrative of nature, not its plot space or its prize. This is the universal—and individualistic—account Hrdy is determined to give.

Hrdy's universalized, yet inherently differentiated and heterogeneous, females cannot be dismissed from the permanently contentious field of feminist discourse. One task of that discourse is to reconstruct what it means to be gendered in late capitalism, if not in the primeval soup. Within the discourse of primate studies, with its practices for determining "strong" and "weak" accounts, Hrdy's writing faces different standards than I have measured it by in this essay. And yet, I believe the criteria explored here can interact productively with more orthodox forms of biological criticism. I do not think deconstructive analysis of scientific narrative is hostile to biological science in its own terms, even if it is far from the same thing. Sociobiologists should be especially, indeed, professionally, sensitive to accounts of narrative strategies and models for moves in textual games. They have been among the best teachers of the analysis of narrative strategy and of how to imagine entering every high-stakes game. But, while shifting the ground from under some accounts, like functionalist maternalism, sociobiologists have been much less good at recognizing how to destabilize and defamiliarize their own ways of constraining any possible account. They have lacked a sense of *irony* about their own narrative resources. Their repertoire of tropes has excluded that corrosive, but salutary, figure for any writer entering her craft centuries after the genesis of a large cultural text on the problem of self and other. Like it or not, sociobiologists write inter-textually within the whole historically dynamic fabric of Western accounts of development, change, individualism, mind, body, liberalism, difference, race, nature, and sex. A careful dissection of the logic and history of the dialectic between same and different in evolutionary biology's stories, and of the constitutive silences that construct what can be marked and unmarked in contending models of change, might well be required in the training of a biologist.

For those who locate themselves outside the territory of primate sciences, it would be easy to argue that Hrdy's origin stories once again reify gender outside of history in another ethnophilosophical naturalizing narrative about beginnings and ends, this time in an effort to account for limits to female bonding while still foregrounding female agency within a frame of liberal individualism. But that argument fails to take seriously the craft of constrained storytelling intrinsic to biological sciences and simply assumes there is some safer place for narrative, called "inside" history, "outside" nature. There is no disinterested map for these fictional, potent boundaries. And in any case, boundary crossing and redrawing is a major feminist pleasure that might make some modest different in a struggle for differentiated meanings, material abundance, and comprehensive equality. Hrdy's naturalized postmodern females emerge full of resources for exploring many interesting topics: female complicity and collusion in male dominance, female agency of many kinds, the potency of sexual discourse in narratives of agency and of mind, the limits of functionalist principles of complementarity and difference, the power of narratives about competition, the logical errors involved in leaving the male an unmarked category in evolutionary models, ways of describing females as sites of internal difference that allow meditation on both bonding and competition, and the deep saliency of reproductive politics, semiotically and materially, in contemporary U.S. and multinational society.

The silences that structure these naturalized postmodern females also are instructive about unintended but nonetheless endemic replications of colonial or neo-imperialist discourse in white, middle-class feminism. While uncovering the logical error of the unmarked male universal, Hrdy's sociobiological construction of females as agents and sites of difference leaves intact an ethnocentric logic of sexual politics and a deep (re)productionist ethnophilosophy translated into a technostrategic language of universal investment games.[42] Female "soul-making" in natural history occurs on the ground of *constitutive* silence about other differences that make sexual narratives especially productive in Western colonizing and neo-imperialist cultures. And, in the end, Hrdy's narrative logic can only do one thing with difference. Difference is the motor of antagonism, of root, inescapable, final hostility among whatever units can provisionally stabilize themselves within sociobiology's versions of the death of the subject, no matter how many proximate causes and intermediate levels allow something else to have narrative space for a time.[43] Here is the stable, lethal, univocal inheritance from the complex history of the principles and stories of liberal possessive individualism passed onto the mutant hyper-liberal children of the late twentieth century. In sociobiological hyper-liberalism, reproductive biopolitics are finally about war. Check mate.

Notes

1. Sarah Blaffer Hrdy, *Langurs of Abu* (Cambridge: Harvard University Press, 1977), 76.

2. Sarah Blaffer Hrdy, *The Woman That Never Evolved* (Cambridge: Harvard University Press, 1981), 128.

3. Josie, the Chimpanzee, in Ruth Hershberger, *Adam's Rib* (New York: Harper and Row, 1970; originally published by Pellegrini and Cudahy, 1948), 9.

4. Thomas Laqueur, "Orgasm, Generation, and the Politics of Reproductive Biology," *Representations* 14 (1986), 1–41, 18.

5. See Fredric Jameson, *The Political Unconscious: Narrative As a Socially Symbolic Act* (Ithaca: Cornell University Press, 1981).

6. Marilyn Strathern, "An Awkward Relationship: The Case of Feminism and Anthropology," *Signs* 12 (1986):276–92.

7. Jeanne Altmann, *Baboon Mothers and Infants* (Cambridge: Harvard University Press, 1980); Linda Marie Fedigan, *Primate Paradigms: Sex Roles and Social Bonds* (Montreal: Eden Press, 1982); Adrienne Zihlman, "Women as Shapers of the Human Adaptation," in Frances Dahlberg, ed., *Woman the Gatherer* (New Haven: Yale University Press, 1981), pp. 75–120; Donna Haraway, *Primate Visions*.

8. Judith Stacey, "Sexism by a Subtler Name? Postindustrial Conditions and Postfeminist Consciousness," *Socialist Review* 17:6 (1987):7–30.

9. See Zoe Sofia, "Exterminating Fetuses: Abortion, Disarmament and the Sexo-semiotics of Extra-terrestrialism," *Diacritics* (Nuclear Criticism Issue) 14:2 (1984):47–59; Zoe Sofoulis, "Through the Lumen: Frankenstein and the Optics of Re-origination," Ph.D. thesis, University of California Santa Cruz, 1988; Carol Cohn, "Sex and Death in the Rational World of Defense Intellectuals," *Signs* 12:4 (1987):687–718; Rosalind Petchesky, "Fetal Images: The Power of Visual Culture in the Politics of Reproduction," *Feminist Studies* 13:2 (1987):263–92; Paul Edwards, "The Closed World: Computers and the Politics of Discourse," Ph.D. thesis, University of California Santa Cruz, 1988.

10. Keller shows the functions and contradictions of the peculiar language for discussing sexual reproduction "as an autonomous function of the individual organism": "I suggest that it provides crucial support for the central project of evolutionary theory—namely that of locating causal efficacy in the intrinsic properties of the individual organism." (Evelyn Fox Keller, "Problems of Radical Individualism in Evolutionary Theory," paper presented at the meetings of the American Philosophical Association, December 1986; see also Keller, "Reproduction and the Central Project of Evolutionary Theory, *Biology and Philosophy,* forthcoming.) The logical and linguistic requirements for discussing sexual reproduction should have serious consequences for the premises of methodological individualism in evolutionary theory.

11. See Val Hartouni, "Personhood, Membership and Community: Abortion Politics and the Negotiation of Public Meanings," Ph.D. dissertation, University of California at Santa Cruz, 1987.

12. See Mary O'Brien, *The Politics of Reproduction* (New York: Routledge and Kegan Paul, 1981); Simone de Beauvoir, *The Second Sex,* trans. and ed. H. M. Parshley (New York: Vintage, 1954).

13. See Richard Dawkins, *The Selfish Gene* (London: Oxford University Press, 1976); Bruno Latour and Shirley Strum, "Human Social Origins: Please Tell Us Another Story," *Journal of Social and Biological Structures* 9 (1986):167–87.

14. See Hortense Spillers, "Mama's Baby, Papa's Maybe: An American Grammar Book," *Diacritics* (Summer 1987):65–81; Chandra Talpade Mohanty, "Under Western Eyes: Feminist Scholarship and Colonial Discourse," *Boundary* 2:12 and 3:13 (1984):333–58; Paula Giddings, *When and Where I Enter: The Impact of Black Women on Race and Sex in America* (Toronto: Bantam, 1985).

15. See Sander Gilman, "Black Bodies, White Bodies: Toward an Iconography of Female Sexuality in Late-Nineteenth-Century Art, Medicine, and Literature," *Critical Inquiry* 12:1 (1985):204–42.

16. Hazel Carby, "On the Threshold of a Woman's Era": Lynching, Empire, and Sexuality in Black Feminist Theory," *Critical Inquiry* 12:1 (1985): 262–77, 276.

17. Laqueur, "Orgasm"; see also Mary Douglas, *Natural Symbols* (London: Cresset, 1970); Ludmilla Jordanova, "Natural Facts: A Historical Perspective on Science and Sexuality," in Marilyn Strathern and Carol MacCormack, eds., *Nature, Culture, Gender* (London: Cambridge University Press, 1980), 42–69.

18. A puzzle in the reporting of the multibillion-dollar project to sequence the human genome—the paradigmatic biotechnical undertaking in the late 1980s—is the absence of discussion about *whose* genome will be sequenced. Every molecular biologist knows that genes vary and that a species is made up of populations with differing gene frequencies, yet public writing about the genome project is all in the language of "the human genome," in the singular number and eternal time. The human-genome project seems to function semiotically as a promise of a gold standard and a library-bank; the complete nucleic acid linear sequence of the genetic code becomes a sign of the full library of the natural human body, the source, and the ultimate repository of information, on which all bodily conversation must rely. The genome project's transfiguration of the much older European dream of the perfect library and discovering the original tongue of man gives a nice turn to the history of philology and hermeneutics. Contemporary disputes over whether or not the human genome can be patented and whether access to the dictionary can be sold give a final twist to the trope of bodily conversation, reproductive politics, and genetic investment as commerce.

19. See Laqueur, "Orgasm," 18, and Janet Sayers, *Biological Politics: Feminist and Anti-Feminist Perspectives* (London: Tavistock, 1982).

20. See, for instance, Mary Wollstonecraft, *Vindication of the Rights of Woman* (London, 1792).

21. Antifeminist and racist positions, which were still formulated inside the discursive parameters of liberal theory, allowed powerful concepts of specific difference to be articulated cogently, but specific difference in the context of fundamental power inequality was (and remains) a ticket to continued blatant oppression and exclusion; female specificity never kept slave women out of the fields nor other working women out of factories when they were required. Liberalism has been an extremely complex inheritance for feminists, particularly since its theory of sameness and difference does not resolve the problem of inequality and power. See Wendy Brown, in her

review of Catherine MacKinnon's *Feminism Unmodified* (Cambridge, MA: Harvard University Press, 1987), for a summary of MacKinnon's analysis of the comprehensive trap of liberal theory, with its naturalization and neutralization of gender *inequality* as sex and/or gender *difference*.

22. See Frigga Haug, "The Women's Movement in West Germany," *New Left Review* 155 (1986):50–74; Frigga Haug, et al, *Female Sexualization: A Collective Work of Memory* (London: Verso, 1987); Ann Snitow, Christine Stansell, and Sharon Thompson, eds., *Powers of Desire: the Politics of Sexuality* (New York: Monthly Review Press 1983); Carole S. Vance, ed., *Pleasure and Danger: Exploring Female Sexuality* (Boston: Routledge & Keegan Paul 1984); Cherrie Moraga, *Loving in the War Years* (Boston: Southend, 1983); Carby, "On the Threshold"; MacKinnon, *Feminism Unmodified*.

23. See Zillah Eisenstein, *The Radical Future of Liberal Feminism* (New York: Longman 1981).

24. See *The Woman That Never Evolved*, 166–72. By 1985, Hrdy's book had appeared in Japanese, Italian, and French editions, and had gone through five paperback editions with Harvard University Press. The book was well received by its reviewer for the major U.S. radical feminist monthly: Alice Henry, "Sex and Society among the Primates: A Review of *The Woman That Never Evolved*," *Off Our Backs* (January 1982): 18–19. See also Elisabeth Lloyd, "On the Primate Female Orgasm," in manuscript, University of California at Berkeley.

25. Doris Zumpe and R. P. Michael, "The Clutching Reaction and Orgasm in the Female Rhesus Monkey (*Macaca mulatta*)," *Journal of Endocrinology* 40 (1968): 117–23, quoted in Hrdy, *The Woman That Never Evolved*, 169.

26. See William H. Masters and Virginia Johnson, *Human Sexual Response* (Boston: Little, Brown, 1966).

27. See Hrdy, *The Woman That Never Evolved*, 169; Frances D. Burton, "Sexual Climax in Female *Macaca mulatta*," *Proceedings of the Third International Congress of Primatology* 3 (1971): 180–91, and "Ethology and the Development of Sex and Gender Identity in Nonhuman Primates," *Acta Biotheoretica* 26 (1977): 1–18.

28. Suzanne Chevalier-Skolnikoff, "The Female Sexual Response in Stumptail Monkeys (*Macaca speciosa*), and Its Broad Implications for Female Mammalian Sexuality," paper presented at the American Anthropological Association meetings, New York City, 1971, 8; see also "Male-Female, Female-Female, and Male-Male Sexual Behavior in the Stumptail Monkey, with Special Attention to the Female Orgasm," *Archives of Sexual Behavior* 3:2 (1974): 95–116; "Heterosexual Copulatory Patterns in Stumptail Macaques, *Macaca arctoides,* and in Other Macaque Species," *Archives of Sexual Behavior* 4:2 (1975): 199–220; and "Homosexual Behavior in a Laboratory Group of Stumptail Monkeys (*Macaca arctoides*): Form, Contents and Possible Social Functions," *Archives of Sexual Behavior* 5:6 (1976): 511–27.

29. Interview, 7 February 1983.

30. Michelle Z. Rosaldo and Louise Lamphere, eds., *Woman, Culture, and Society* (Palo Alto: Stanford University Press, 1974). Rosaldo may have rejected the paper out of resistance to biological explanations of the cultural domain. In contrast, the other pivotal collection of early U.S. feminist anthropology, with its roots in Marxian narratives that permitted a careful evolutionary story, included papers by both Sally Linton Slocum and Leila Leibowitz; see Rayna Rapp Reiter, ed., *Toward an Anthropology of Women* (New York: Monthly Review Press, 1975). Neither Chevalier-Skolnikoff nor Hrdy seems to have known of Ruth Hershberger's speculations and efforts to get data in the 1930s.

31. See also Sarah Blaffer Hrdy, "The Evolution of Human Sexuality: The Latest Word and the Last. Review of Donald Symons, *The Evolution of Human Sexuality*," *The Quarterly Review of Biology* 54 (1979): 309–14; "Heat Lost," *Science 83* (October 1983) 73–78; "Empathy,

Polyandry, and the Myth of the Coy Female," in Ruth Bleier, ed., *Feminist Approaches to Science* (New York: Pergamon, 1986), 119–46; Sarah Blaffer Hrdy and George C. Williams., "Behavioral Biology and the Double Standard," in Samuel K. Wasser, ed., *Social Behavior of Female Vertebrates,* (New York: Academic Press, 1983), 3–17.

32. Donald Symons, *The Evolution of Human Sexuality* (New York: Oxford University Press, 1979), quoted in Hrdy, *The Woman That Never Evolved,* 165.

33. Hrdy, *The Woman That Never Evolved,* 166.

34. Ibid., 167.

35. Ibid., 174.

36. Ibid., 187; Hrdy, "Heat Lost."

37. Hrdy has not argued that females are naturally subordinate to males, only that they do not have the same possibilities for the same moves in the reproductive struggle; competitive females are limited only by the realities of power and resources. In her account, inherent female competition, especially among female genetically related lineages (called "kin" in sociobiological terms), blocked female bonding as a sex against male strategies, such as infanticide, that disadvantaged females as a group, while cooperation between females and males was limited by their genetic difference, and consequent non-identical reproductive interests. Hrdy regards feminist solidarity as a human achievement, fragile and precious, that could only happen in a species that could act to counter natural conditions favoring competition. In that sense, Hrdy is ironically close to important socialist feminist arguments that stressed the *achieved* quality of a feminist standpoint, rooted in an analysis of women's material conditions but not naturally part of women's consciousness. See Nancy Hartsock, *Money, Sex, and Power* (New York: Longman, 1983). For an account of Hrdy's location in debates about whether male killing of infants among nonhuman primates is adaptive or the result of pathological stress—a contest between reproductive strategy, sociobiological arguments and evolutionary structural functionalism emphasizing other narratives of adaptation—see also Donna Haraway, "The Contest for Primate Nature: Daughters of Man the Hunter in the Field, 1960–80," in Mark Kann, ed., *The Future of American Democracy: Views from the Left* (Philadelphia: Temple University Press, 1983), 175–207. For Hrdy's career and her relation to female-centred primate studies, see Meredith Small, ed., *Female Primates: Studies by Women Primatologists* (New York: Alan Liss, 1984).

38. Hrdy, *The Woman That Never Evolved,* 21.

39. Ibid., 21.

40. See Richard Wrangham, "On the Evolution of Ape Social Systems," *Social Science Information* 18:3 (1979): 335–69; and "An Ecological Model of Female-Bonded Primate Groups," *Behaviour* 75 (1980): 269–99.

41. See Hrdy, *The Woman That Never Evolved,* 122–27.

42. See Gayatri Spivak, "Three Women's Texts and a Critique of Imperialism," *Critical Inquiry* 12:1 (1985): 243–61; and "Imperialism and Sexual Difference," *Oxford Literary Review* 8:1,2 (1986): 225–40; Cohn, "Sex and Death."

43. Among feminist efforts to theorize "difference" differently, see Trinh T. Minh-ha, "Not You/Like You: Post-Colonial Women and the Interlocking Questions of Identity and Difference," *Inscriptions,* nos. 3–4 (1988): 71–77; Gloria Anzaldua, *Borderlands/La Frontera* (San Francisco: Spinsters/Aunt Lute, 1987); and Teresa de Lauretis, *Technologies of Gender: Essays on Theory, Film, and Fiction* (Bloomington: Indiana University Press, 1987). Trinh Minh-ha's critique of the Hegelian logic of appropriation and escalating domination is suggested in her typographical convention for a possible subjectivity: the inappropriate/d other.

8

Technophilia: Technology, Representation, and the Feminine

Mary Ann Doane

The concept of the "body" has traditionally denoted the finite, a material limit that is absolute—so much so that the juxtaposition of the terms "concept" and "body" seems oxymoronic. For the body is that which is situated as the precise opposite of the conceptual, the abstract. It represents the ultimate constraint on speculation or theorization, the place where the empirical finally and always makes itself felt. This notion of the body as a set of finite limitations is, perhaps, most fully in evidence in the face of technological developments associated with the Industrial Revolution. In 1858, the author of a book entitled *Paris* writes, "Science; as it were, proposes that we should enter a new world that has not been made for us. We would like to venture into it; but it does not take us long to recognize that it requires a constitution we lack and organs we do not have."[1] Science fiction, a genre specific to the era of rapid technological development, frequently envisages a new, revised body as a direct outcome of the advance of science. And when technology intersects with the body in the realm of representation, the question of sexual difference is inevitably involved.

Although it is certainly true that in the case of some contemporary science-fiction writers—particularly feminist authors—technology makes possible the destabilization of sexual identity as a category, there has also been a curious but fairly insistent history of representations of technology that work to fortify—sometimes desperately—conventional understandings of the feminine. A certain anxiety concerning the technological is often allayed by a displacement of this anxiety onto the figure of the woman or the idea of the feminine. This has certainly been the case in the cinema, particularly in the genre which most apparently privileges technophilia, science fiction. And despite the emphasis in discourses about technology upon the link between the machine and *production* (the machine as a labor-saving device, the notion of man as a complicated machine which Taylorism, as an early-twentieth-century attempt to regulate the worker's bodily movements, endeavored to exploit), it is striking to note how often it is the woman who becomes the model of the perfect machine. Ultimately, what I hope to demonstrate is that it is not so much *production* that is at stake in these representations as *reproduction*.

The literary text that is cited most frequently as the exemplary forerunner of the cinematic representation of the mechanical woman is *L'Eve future (Tomorrow's Eve)*, written by Villiers de l'Isle-Adam in 1886. In this novel, Thomas Edison, the master scientist and entrepreneur of mechanical reproduction—associated with both the phonograph and the cinema—is the inventor of the perfect mechanical woman, an android whose difference from the original human model is imperceptible. Far from investing in the type of materialism associated with scientific progress, Villiers is a metaphysician. Edison's creation embodies the Ideal (her name is Hadaly which is, so we are told, Arabic for the Ideal). The very long introductory section of the novel is constituted by Edison's musings about all the voices in history that have been lost and that could have been captured had the phonograph been invented sooner. These include, among others, "the first vibrations of the good tidings brought to Mary! The resonance of the Archangel saying Hail! a sound that has reverberated through the ages in the Angelus. The Sermon on the Mount! The 'Hail, master!' on the Mount of Olives, and the sound of the kiss of Iscariot."[2] Almost simultaneously, however, Edison realizes that the mechanical recordings of the sounds is not enough: "To hear the sound is nothing, but the inner essence, which creates these mere vibrations, these veils—that's the crucial thing."[3] This "inner essence" is what the human lover of Lord Ewald, Edison's friend, lacks. In Lord Ewald's report, although her body is magnificent, perfect in every detail, the human incarnation of the *Venus Victorious,* she lacks a *soul.* Or, more accurately, between the body and soul of Miss Alicia Clary there is an "absolute disparity." Since Lord Ewald is hopelessly in love with the soulless Alicia, Edison takes it upon himself to mold Hadaly to the form of Miss Clary.

A great deal of the novel consists of Edison's scientific explanations of the functioning of Hadaly. As he opens Hadaly up to a dissecting inspection, Lord Ewald's final doubts about the mechanical nature of what seemed to him a living woman are dispelled in a horrible recognition of the compatibility of technology and desire.

> Now he found himself face to face with a marvel the obvious possibilities of which, as they transcend even the imaginary, dazzled his understanding

and made him suddenly feel to what lengths a man who wishes can extend the courage of his desires.[4]

Hadaly's interior is a maze of electrical wizardry including coded metal discs that diffuse warmth, motion, and energy throughout the body; wires that imitate nerves, arteries, and veins; a basic electro-magnetic motor, the Cylinder, on which are recorded the "gestures, the bearing, the facial expressions, and the attitudes of the adored being"; and two golden phonographs that replay Hadaly's only discourse, words "invented by the greatest poets, the most subtle metaphysicians, the most profound novelists of this century."[5] Hadaly has no past, no memories except those embodied in the words of "great men." As Annette Michelson remarks, in a provocative analysis of the novel,

> Hadaly's scenes, so to speak, are set in place. Hadaly becomes that palimpsest of inscription, that unreasoning and reasonable facsimile, generated by reason, whose interlocutor, Lord Ewald, has only to submit to the range and nuance of mise-en-scene possible in what Edison calls the "great kaleidoscope" of human speech and gesture in which signifiers will infinitely float.[6]

As Edison points out to Lord Ewald, the number of gestures or expressions in the human repertoire is extremely limited, clearly quantifiable, and hence reproducible. Yet, precisely because Villiers is a metaphysician, something more is needed to animate the machine—a spark, a touch of spirit.

This spark is provided, strangely enough, by an abandoned mother, Mrs. Anny Anderson (who, in the hypnotic state Edison maintains her in, takes on the name Miss Anny Sowana). Her husband, Howard, another of Edison's friends, had been seduced and ruined by a beautiful temptress, Miss Evelyn Habal, ultimately committing suicide. Miss Evelyn Habal was in a way the inspiration for the *outer* form of Hadaly, for through his investigations, Edison discovered that her alleged beauty was completely *artificial*. He displays for Lord Ewald's sake a drawer containing her implements: a wig corroded by time, a makeup kit of greasepaint and patches, dentures, lotions, powders, creams, girdles, and falsies, etc. Edison's cinema reveals that, without any of these aids, Evelyn Habal was a macabre figure. The display demonstrates to Ewald that mechanical reproduction suffices in the construction of the forms of femininity. But its spirit, at least, is not scientifically accessible. The abandoned Mrs. Anderson, mother of two children, suffers a breakdown after the suicide of her husband. Only Edison is able to communicate with her and eventually her spirit establishes a link with his android Hadaly, animating it, humanizing it. The mother infuses the machine. Perhaps this is why, for

Edison, science's most important contribution here is the validation of the dichotomy between woman as mother and woman as mistress:

> Far from being hostile to the love of men for their wives—who are so necessary to perpetuate the race (at least till a new order of things comes in), I propose to reinforce, ensure, and guarantee that love. I will do so with the aid of thousands and thousands of marvelous and completely innocent facsimiles, who will render wholly superfluous all those beautiful but deceptive mistresses, ineffective henceforth forever.[7]

Reproduction is that which is, at least initially, unthinkable in the face of the woman-machine. Herself the product of a desire to reproduce, she blocks the very possibility of a future through her sterility. Motherhood acts as a limit to the conceptualization of femininity as a scientific construction of mechanical and electrical parts. And yet it is also that which infuses the machine with the breath of a human spirit. The maternal and the mechanical/synthetic coexist in a relation that is a curious imbrication of dependence and antagonism.

L'Eve future is significant as an early signpost of the persistence of the maternal as a sub-theme accompanying these fantasies of artificial femininity. It is also, insofar as Edison (a figure closely associated with the prehistory of cinema) is the mastermind of Hadaly's invention, a text that points to a convergence of the articulation of this obsession and the cinema as a privileged site for its exploration. In Michelson's argument, Hadaly's existence demonstrates the way in which a compulsive movement between analysis and synthesis takes the female body as its support in a process of fetishization fully consistent with that of the cinema:

> We will want once more to note that assiduous, relentless impulse which claims the female body as the site of an analytic, mapping upon its landscape a poetics and an epistemology with all the perverse detail and somber ceremony of fetishism. And may we not then begin to think of that body in its cinematic relations somewhat differently? Not as the mere object of a cinematic *iconography* of repression and desire—as catalogued by now in the extensive literature on dominant narrative in its major genres of melodrama, *film noir,* and so on—but rather as the fantasmatic ground of cinema itself.[8]

Indeed, cinema has frequently been thought of as a prosthetic device, as a technological extension of the human body, particularly the senses of perception. Christian Metz, for instance, refers to the play "of that *other mirror,* the cinema screen, in this respect a veritable psychical substitute, a prosthesis for our primally dislocated limbs."[9] From this point of view it is not surprising that the articulation of the three terms—"woman," "machine," "cinema"—

and the corresponding fantasy of the artificial woman recur as the privileged content of a wide variety of cinematic narratives.

An early instance of this tendency in the science-fiction mode is Fritz Lang's 1926 film, *Metropolis*, in which the patriarch of the future city surveys his workers through a complex audio-visual apparatus resembling television. In *Metropolis*, the bodies of the male workers become mechanized; their movements are rigid, mechanical, and fully in sync with the machines they operate. The slightest divergence between bodily movement and the operation of the machine is disastrous, as evidenced when the patriarch's son, Freder, descends to the realm of the workers and witnesses the explosion of a machine not sufficiently controlled by a worker. Freder's resulting hallucination transforms the machine into a Moloch-figure to whom the unfortunate workers are systematically sacrificed. When Freder relieves an overtired worker, the machine he must operate resembles a giant clock whose hands must be moved periodically—a movement that corresponds to no apparent logic. In a production routine reorganized by the demands of the machine, the human body's relation to temporality becomes inflexible, programmed. The body is tied to a time clock, a schedule, a routine, an assembly line. Time becomes oppression and mechanization—the clock, a machine itself, is used to regulate bodies as machines. *Metropolis* represents a dystopic vision of a city run by underground machines whose instability and apparent capacity for vengeance are marked.

But where the men's bodies are analogous to machines, the woman's body literally becomes a machine. In order to forestall a threatened rebellion on the part of the workers, the patriarch Fredersen has a robot made in the likeness of Maria, the woman who leads and instigates them. Rotwang, who is a curious mixture of modern scientist and alchemist, has already fashioned a robot in the form of a woman when Fredersen makes the request. The fact that the robot is manifestly female is quite striking particularly in light of Rotwang's explanation of the purpose of the machine: "I have created a machine in the image of man, that never tires or makes a mistake. Now we have no further use for living workers." A robot which is apparently designed as the ultimate producer is transformed into a woman of excessive and even explosive sexuality (as manifested in the scene in which Rotwang demonstrates her seductive traits to an audience of men who mistake her for a "real woman"). In Andreas Huyssen's analysis of *Metropolis*, the robot Maria is symptomatic of the fears associated with a technology perceived as threatening and demonic: "The fears and perceptual anxieties emanating from ever more powerful machines are recast and reconstructed in terms of the male fear of female sexuality, reflecting, in the Freudian account, the male's castration anxiety."[10]

Yet, the construction of the robot Maria is also, in Huyssen's account, the result of a desire to appropriate the maternal function, a kind of womb envy on the part of the male. This phenomenon is clearly not limited to *Metropolis* and has been extensively explored in relation to Mary Shelley's *Frankenstein*, in which the hero, immediately before awakening to perceive his frightful creation, the monster, standing next to his bed, dreams that he holds the corpse of his dead mother in his arms. The "ultimate technological fantasy," according to Huyssen, is "creation without the mother."[11] Nevertheless, in *Metropolis,* the robot Maria is violently opposed to a real Maria who is characterized, first and foremost, as a mother. In the first shot of Maria, she is surrounded by a flock of children, and her entrance interrupts a kiss between Freder and another woman so that the maternal effectively disrupts the sexual. Toward the end of the film, Maria and Freder save the children from a flood unwittingly caused by the angry workers' disruption of the machinery. The film manages to salvage both the technological and the maternal (precisely by destroying the figure of the machine-woman) and to return the generations to their proper ordering (reconciling Freder and his father). The tension in these texts which holds in balance a desire on the part of the male to appropriate the maternal function and the conflicting desire to safeguard and honor the figure of the mother is resolved here in favor of the latter. The machine is returned to its rightful place in production, the woman hers in reproduction.

The maternal is understandably much more marginal in a more recent film, *The Stepford Wives* (1975), in which the machine-woman is not burned at the stake, as in *Metropolis,* but comfortably installed in the supermarket and the suburban home. In this film, a group of women are lured to the suburbs by their husbands who then systematically replace them with robots, indistinguishable from their originals. The robots have no desires beyond those of cooking, cleaning, caring for the children, and fulfilling their husbands' sexual needs. Even the main character, Joanna, who claims, "I messed a little with Women's Lib in New York," finds that she cannot escape the process. As in *L'Eve future,* the husbands record the voices of their wives to perfect the illusion, but unlike that of Hadaly, the Ideal, the discourse of these robot-housewives consists of hackneyed commercial slogans about the advantages of products such as Easy On Spray Starch. Here the address is to women and the social context is that of a strong and successful feminist movement, which the film seems to suggest is unnecessary outside of the science-fiction nightmare in which husbands turn wives into robots. *The Stepford Wives* indicates a loss of the obsessive force of the signifying matrix of the machine-woman—as though its very banalization could convince that there is no real threat involved, no reason for anxiety.

The contemporary films that strike me as much more interesting with respect to the machine-woman problematic are those in which questions of the maternal and technology are more deeply imbricated—films such as *Alien* (1979) and its sequel, *Aliens* (1986), and *Blade Runner* (1982). As technologies of reproduction seem to become a more immediate possibility (and are certainly the focus of media attention), the impact of the associative link between technology and the feminine on narrative representation becomes less localized—that is, it is no longer embodied solely in the figure of the female robot. *Alien* and *Aliens* contain no such machine-woman, yet the technological is insistently linked to the maternal. While *Blade Runner* does represent a number of female androids (the result of a sophisticated biogenetic engineering, they are called "replicants" in the film), it also represents male replicants. Nevertheless, its narrative structure provocatively juxtaposes the question of biological reproduction and that of mechanical reproduction. Most importantly, perhaps, both *Alien* and *Blade Runner* contemplate the impact of drastic changes in reproductive processes on ideas of origins, narratives, and histories.

Alien, together with its sequel, *Aliens,* and *Blade Runner* elaborate symbolic systems that correspond to a contemporary crisis in the realm of reproduction—the revolution in the development of technologies of reproduction (birth control, artificial insemination, *in vitro* fertilization, surrogate mothering, etc.). These technologies threaten to put into crisis the very possibility of the question of origins, the Oedipal dilemma and the relation between subjectivity and knowledge that it supports. In the beginning of *Alien,* Dallas types into the keyboard of the ship's computer (significantly nicknamed "Mother" by the crew) the question: "What's the story, Mother?" The story is no longer one of transgression and conflict with the father but of the struggle with and against what seems to become an overwhelming extension of the category of the maternal, now assuming monstrous proportions. Furthermore, this concept of the maternal neglects or confuses the traditional attributes of sexual difference. The ship itself, *The Nostromo,* seems to mimic in the construction of its internal spaces the interior of the maternal body. In the first shots of the film, the camera explores in lingering fashion corridors and womblike spaces which exemplify a fusion of the organic and the technological.[12] The female merges with the environment and the mother-machine becomes mise-en-scene, the space within which the story plays itself out. The wrecked alien spaceship which the crew investigates is also characterized by its cavernous, womblike spaces; one of the crew even descends through a narrow tubelike structure to the "tropical" underground of the ship where a field of large rubbery eggs are in the process of incubation. The maternal is not only the subject of the representation here, but also its ground.

The alien itself, in its horrifying otherness, also evokes the maternal. In the sequel, *Aliens,* the interpretation of the alien as a monstrous mother-machine, incessantly manufacturing eggs in an awesome excess of reproduction, confirms this view. Yet, in the first film the situation is somewhat more complex, for the narrative operates by confusing the tropes of femininity and masculinity in its delineation of the process of reproduction. The creature first emerges from an egg, attaches itself to a crew member's face, penetrating his throat and gastrointestinal system to deposit its seed. The alien gestates within the stomach of the *male* crew member who later "gives birth" to it in a grotesque scene in which the alien literally gnaws its way through his stomach to emerge as what one critic has labeled a *phallus dentatus*.[13] The confusion of the semes of sexual difference indicates the fears attendant upon the development of technologies of reproduction that debiologize the maternal. In *Alien*, men have babies but it is a horrifying and deadly experience. When the alien or other invades the most private space—the inside of the body—the foundations of subjectivity are shaken. The horror here is that of a collapse between inside and outside or of what Julia Kristeva refers to, in *Powers of Horror*, as the abject. Kristeva associates the maternal with the abject—i.e., that which is the focus of a combined horror and fascination, hence subject to a range of taboos designed to control the culturally marginal.[14] In this analysis, the function of nostalgia for the mother-origin is that of a veil which conceals the terror attached to nondifferentiation. The threat of the maternal space is that of the collapse of any distinction whatsoever between subject and object.

Kristeva elsewhere emphasizes a particularly interesting corollary of this aspect of motherhood: The maternal space is "a place both double and foreign."[15] In its internalization of heterogeneity, an otherness within the self, motherhood deconstructs certain conceptual boundaries. Kristeva delineates the maternal through the assertion, "In a body there is grafted, unmasterable, an other."[16] The confusion of identities threatens to collapse a signifying system based on the paternal law of differentiation. It would seem that the concept of motherhood automatically throws into question ideas concerning the self, boundaries between self and other, and hence identity.

According to Jean Baudrillard, "Reproduction is diabolical in its very essence; it makes something fundamental vacillate."[17] Technology promises more strictly to control, supervise, regulate the maternal—to put *limits* upon it. But somehow the fear lingers—perhaps the maternal will contaminate the technological. For aren't we now witnessing a displacement of the excessiveness and overproliferation previously associated with the maternal to the realm of technologies of representation, in the guise of the all-pervasive images and sounds of television, film, radio, the Walkman? One response to such anxiety is the recent spate of films that delineate the horror of the maternal—of that which harbors an otherness within, where the fear is always that of giving birth to the monstrous; films such as *It's Alive, The Brood, The Fly*, or the ecology horror film, *Prophecy. Alien*, in merging the genres of the horror film and science fiction, explicitly connects that horror to a technological scenario.

In *Blade Runner*, the signifying trajectory is more complex, and the relevant semes are more subtly inscribed. Here the terror of the motherless reproduction associated with technology is clearly located as an anxiety about the ensuing loss of history. One scene in *Blade Runner* acts as a condensation of a number of these critical terms: "representation," "the woman," "the artificial," "the technological," "history," and "memory." It is initiated by the camera's pan over Deckard's apartment to the piano upon which a number of photos are arranged, most of them apparently belonging to Deckard, signifiers of a past (though not necessarily his own), marked as antique—pictures of someone's mother, perhaps a sister or grandmother. One of the photographs, however—a rather nondescript one of a room, an open door, a mirror—belongs to the replicant Leon, recovered by Deckard in a search of his hotel room. Deckard inserts this photograph in a piece of equipment that is ultimately revealed as a machine for analyzing images. Uncannily responding to Deckard's voiced commands, the machine enlarges the image, isolates various sections, and enlarges them further. The resultant play of colors and grain, focus and its loss, is aesthetically provocative beyond the demonstration of technical prowess and control over the image. Deckard's motivation, the desire for knowledge that is fully consistent with his positioning in the film as the detective figure of *film noir*, is overwhelmed by the special effects which are the byproducts of this technology of vision—a scintillation of the technological image which exceeds his epistemophilia. Only gradually does the image resolve into a readable text. And in the measure to which the image becomes readable, it loses its allure. The sequence demonstrates how technology, the instrument of a certain knowledge-effect, becomes spectacle, fetish. But one gains ascendancy at the price of the other—pleasure pitted against knowledge.

Historically, this dilemma has been resolved in the cinema by conflating the two—making pleasure and knowledge compatible by projecting them onto the figure of the woman. The same resolution occurs here: as the image gradually stabilizes, what emerges is the recognizable body of a woman (neglecting for a moment that this is not a "real" woman), reclining on a couch, reflected in the mirror which Deckard systematically isolates. The mirror makes visible what is outside the confines of the photograph strictly speaking—the absent woman, object of the detective's quest. To know in *Blade Runner* is to be able to detect difference—not sexual difference, but the difference between human and replicant (the replicant here taking the place of the woman as marginal, as Other). Knowledge in psychoanalysis, on the other hand, is linked to the mother's body (knowledge of castration and hence of sexual difference, knowledge of where babies come from)—so many tantalizing secrets revolving around the idea of an origin and the figure of the mother. There are no literal—no embodied—mothers in *Blade Runner* (in fact, there are no "real" women in the film beyond a few marginal characters—the old Chinese woman who identifies the snake scale, the women in the bar). Yet this does not mean that the concept of the maternal—its relation to knowledge of origins and subjective history—is inoperative in the text. As a story of replicants who look just like "the real thing," *Blade Runner* has an affinity with Barthes's analysis of photography, *Camera Lucida*.[18] Barthes's essay is crucially organized around a photograph of his mother which is never shown, almost as though making it present would banalize his desire, or reduce it. Both film and essay are stories of reproduction—mechanical reproduction, reproduction as the application of biogenetic engineering. In the film, however, our capability of representing human life begins to pose a threat when the slight divergence that would betray mimetic activity disappears.

In *Blade Runner,* as in *Camera Lucida,* there are insistent references to the mother, but they are fleeting, tangential to the major axis of the narrative. In the opening scene, the replicant Leon is asked a question by the examiner whose task it is to ascertain whether Leon is human or inhuman: "Describe in single words only the good things that come into your mind about—your mother." Leon answers, "Let me tell you about my mother" and proceeds violently to blow away the examiner with a twenty-first-century gun. The replicants collect photographs (already an archaic mode of representation in this future time) in order to reassure themselves of their own past, their own subjective history. At one point Leon is asked by Roy whether he managed to retrieve his "precious photographs." Later Rachel, still refusing to believe that she is a replicant, tries to prove to Deckard that she is as human as he is by thrusting forward a photograph and claiming, "Look, it's me with my mother." After Rachel leaves, having been told that these are "not your memories" but "somebody else's," Deckard looks down at the photo, his voice-over murmuring "a mother she never had, a daughter she never was." At this moment, the photograph briefly becomes "live," animated, as sun and shadow play over the faces of the little girl and her mother. At the same moment at which the photograph loses its historical authenticity vis-à-vis Rachel, it also loses its status as a photograph, as dead time. In becoming "present," it makes Rachel less "real." Deckard animates the photograph with his gaze, his desire, and it is ultimately his desire that constitutes Rachel's only subjectivity, in the present tense. In this sense Rachel, like Villiers's *L'Eve future,* becomes the perfect woman, born all at once, deprived of a past or authentic memories.

Reproduction is the guarantee of a history—both human biological reproduction (through the succession of generations) and mechanical reproduction (through the succession of memories). Knowledge is anchored to both. Something goes awry with respect to each in *Blade Runner,* for the replicants do not have mothers and their desperate invocation of the figure of the mother is symptomatic of their desire to place themselves within a history. Neither do they have fathers. In the scene in which Roy kills Tyrell he, in effect, *simulates* the Oedipal complex,[19] but gets it wrong. The father, rather than the son, is blinded. Psychoanalysis can only be invoked as a misunderstood, misplayed scenario. Similarly, the instances of mechanical reproduction which should ensure the preservation of a remembered history are delegitimized; Leon's photograph is broken down into its constituent units to become a clue in the detective's investigation, and Rachel's photograph is deprived of its photographic status. The replicants are objects of fear because they present the humans with the specter of a motherless reproduction, and *Blade Runner* is at one level about the anxiety surrounding the loss of history. Deckard keeps old photos as well, and while they may not represent his own relatives, they nevertheless act as a guarantee of temporal continuity—of a coherent history which compensates for the pure presence of the replicants. This compensatory gesture is located at the level of the film's own discourse also insofar as it reinscribes an older cinematic mode—that of *film noir*—thus ensuring its own insertion within a tradition, a cinematic continuity.

Yet, science fiction strikes one as the cinematic genre that ought to be least concerned with origins since its "proper" obsession is with the projection of a future rather than the reconstruction of a past. Nevertheless, a great deal of its projection of that future is bound up with issues of reproduction—whether in its constant emphasis upon the robot, android, automaton, and anthropomorphically conceived computer or its insistent return to the elaboration of high-tech, sophisticated audio-visual systems. When Deckard utilizes the video analyzer in *Blade Runner*, it is a demonstration of the power of future systems of imaging. Furthermore, the Voight-Kampf empathy test designed to differentiate between the replicant and the human being is heavily dependent upon a large video image of the eye. In both *Alien* and its sequel, *Aliens,* video mechanisms ensure that those in the stationary ship can see through the eyes of the investigating astronauts/soldiers outside. Danger is signaled by a difficulty in transmission or a loss of the image. Garrett Stewart remarks on the overabundance of viewing screens and viewing machines in science fiction in general—of "banks of monitors, outsized video intercoms, x-ray display panels, hologram tubes, backlit photoscopes, aerial scanners, telescopic mirrors, illuminated computer consoles, overhead projectors, slide screens, radar scopes, whole curved walls of transmitted imagery, the retinal registers of unseen electronic eyes."[20] And in his view, "cinema becomes a synecdoche for the entire technics of an imagined society."[21]

Since the guarantee of the real in the classical narrative cinema is generally the visible, the advanced visual devices here would seem, at least in part, to ensure the credibility of the "hyperreal" of science fiction. And cetainly insofar as it is necessary to imagine that the inhabitants of the future will need some means of representing to themselves their world (and other worlds), these visual devices serve the purpose, as Stewart points out, of a kind of documentary authentication.[22] Yet, the gesture of marking the real does not exhaust their function. Technology in cinema is the object of a quite precise form of fetishism, and science fiction would logically be a privileged genre for the technophile. Christian Metz describes the way in which this fetishism of technique works to conceal a lack:

A fetish, the cinema as a technical performance, as prowess, as an *exploit,* an exploit that underlines and denounces the lack on which the whole arrangement is based (the absence of the object, replaced by its reflection), an exploit which consists at the same time of making this absence forgotten. The cinema fetishist is the person who is enchanted at what the machine is capable of, at the *theatre of shadows* as such. For the establishment of his full potency for cinematic enjoyment [*jouissance*] he must think at every moment (and above all *simultaneously*) of the force of presence the film has and of the absence on which this force is constructed. He must constantly compare the result with the means deployed (and hence pay attention to the technique), for his pleasure lodges in the gap between the two.[23]

Metz here finds it necessary to desexualize a scenario which in Freud's theory of fetishism is linked explicitly to the woman and the question of her "lack" (more specifically to the question of whether or not the mother is phallic). Technological fetishism, through its alliance of technology with a process of concealing and revealing lack, is theoretically returned to the body of the mother. Claude Bailblé, from a somewhat different perspective, links the fascination with technology to its status as a kind of transitional object: "For the technology plays the role of transitional object, loved with a regressive love still trying to exhaust the pain of foreclosure from the Other, endlessly trying to repair that initial separation, and as such it is very likely to be the target of displacements."[24] In both cases, the theory understands the obsession with technology as a tension of movement toward and away from the mother.

It is not surprising, then, that the genre that highlights technological fetishism—science fiction—should be obsessed with the issues of the maternal, reproduction, representation, and history. From *L'Eve future* to *Blade Runner*, the conjunction of technology and the feminine is the object of fascination and desire but also of anxiety—a combination of affects that makes it the perfect field of play for the science fiction/horror genre. If Hadaly is the first embodiment of the cinematic woman (this time outside of the cinema)—a machine that synchronizes the image and sound of a "real" woman, Rachel is in a sense her double in the contemporary cinema, the ideal woman who flies off with Deckard at the end of the film through a pastoral setting. Yet, Rachel can be conceived only as a figure drawn from an earlier cinematic scene— 1940s film noir—the dark and mysterious femme fatale with padded shoulders and 1940s hairdo, as though the reinscription of a historically dated genre could reconfirm the sense of history that is lost with technologies of representation. What is reproduced as ideal here is an earlier reproduction.

Again, according to Baudrillard: "Reproduction . . . makes something fundamental vacillate." What it makes vacillate are the very concepts of identity, origin, and the original, as Benjamin has demonstrated so provocatively in

"The Work of Art in the Age of Mechanical Reproduction."[25] There is always something uncanny about a photograph; in the freezing of the moment the real is lost through its doubling. The unique identity of a time and a place is rendered obsolete. This is undoubtedly why photographic reproduction is culturally coded and regulated by associating it closely with the construction of a family history, a stockpile of memories, forcing it to buttress that very notion of history that it threatens to annihilate along with the idea of the origin. In a somewhat different manner, but with crucial links to the whole problematic of the origin, technologies of reproduction work to regulate the excesses of the maternal. But in doing so these technologies also threaten to undermine what have been coded as its more positive and nostalgic aspects. For the idea of the maternal is not only terrifying—it also offers a certain amount of epistemological comfort. The mother's biological role in reproduction has been aligned with the social function of knowledge. For the mother is coded as certain, immediately knowable, while the father's role in reproduction is subject to doubt, not verifiable through the evidence of the senses (hence the necessity of the legal sanctioning of the paternal name). The mother is thus the figure who guarantees, at one level, the possibility of certitude in historical knowledge. Without her, the story of origins vacillates, narrative vacillates. It is as though the association with a body were the only way to stabilize reproduction. Hence the persistence of contradictions in these texts that manifest both a nostalgia for and a terror of the maternal function, both linking it to and divorcing it from the idea of the machine woman. Clinging to the realm of narrative, these films strive to rework the connections between the maternal, history, and representation in ways that will allow a taming of technologies of reproduction. The extent to which the affect of horror is attached to such filmic narratives, however, indicates the traumatic impact of these technologies—their potential to disrupt given symbolic systems that construct the maternal and the paternal as stable positions. It is a trauma around which the films obsessively circulate and which they simultaneously disavow.

Notes

1. G. Claudin, *Paris* (Paris, 1867), 71–72, quoted in Wolfgang Schivelbusch, *The Railway Journey: The Industrialization of Time and Space in the 19th Century* (Berkeley: The University of California Press, 1986), 159.

2. Villiers de l'Isle-Adam, *Tomorrow's Eve,* trans. Robert Martin Adams (Urbana, Chicago, and London: University of Illinois Press, 1982), 13.

3. Ibid., 14.

4. Ibid., 125.

5. Ibid., 131.

6. Annette Michelson, "On the Eve of the Future: The Reasonable Facsimile and the Philosophical Toy," in *October: The First Decade, 1976–1986,* eds. Annette Michelson, et al. (Cam-

bridge: The MIT Press, 1987), 432. See also Raymond Bellour, "Ideal Hadaly: on Villier's *The Future Eve*," *Camera Obscura* 15 (Fall 1986): 111–35.

7. Villiers de l'Isle-Adam, 164.

8. Michelson, 433.

9. Christian Metz, "The Imaginary Signifier," *Screen* 16:2 (Summer 1975), 15.

10. Andreas Huyssen, *After the Great Divide: Modernism, Mass Culture, Postmodernism* (Bloomington: Indiana University Press, 1986), 70.

11. Ibid.

12. See Barbara Creed, "Horror and the Monstrous-Feminine—An Imaginary Abjection," *Screen* 27:1 (January–February 1986): 44–71; and James H. Kavanagh, " 'Son of a Bitch': Feminism, Humanism and Science in *Alien*," *October* 13 (1980), 91–100.

13. Kavanagh, 94.

14. Julia Kristeva, *Powers of Horror* (New York: Columbia University Press, 1983).

15. Julia Kristeva, "Maternité selon Giovanni Bellini," *Polylogue* (Paris: Édition du Seuil, 1977), 409; my translation.

16. Ibid.

17. Jean Baudrillard, *Simulations*, trans. Paul Foss, Paul Patton, and Philip Beitchman (New York City: Semiotext(e), 1983), 153.

18. Roland Barthes, *Camera Lucida: Reflections on Photography*, trans. Richard Howard (New York: Hill and Wang, 1981). For a remarkably similar analysis of *Blade Runner*, although differently inflected, see Giuliana Bruno, "Ramble City: Postmodernism and *Blade Runner*," *October* 41 (Summer 1987), 61–74. Bruno also invokes Barthes's *Camera Lucida* in her analysis of the role of photography in the film.

19. See Glenn Hendler, "Simulation and Replication: The Question of *Blade Runner*," honors thesis, Brown University, Spring 1984.

20. Garrett Stewart, "The 'Videology' of Science Fiction," in *Shadows of the Magic Lamp: Fantasy and Science Fiction in Film*, eds. George Slusser and Eric S. Rabkin (Carbondale and Edwardsville: Southern Illinois University Press, 1985), 161.

21. Ibid., 161.

22. Ibid., 167.

23. Metz, 72.

24. Claude Bailblé, "Programming the Look," *Screen Education* 32/33, 100.

25. Walter Benjamin, "The Work of Art in the Age of Mechanical Reproduction," *Illuminations*, trans. Harry Zohn (New York: Schocken Books, 1969), 217–52.

9

From Secrets of Life to Secrets of Death

Evelyn Fox Keller

> It is not in giving life but in risking life that man is raised above
> the animal. . . . Superiority has been accorded in humanity not to
> the sex which brings forth but to that which kills.[1]—Simone de
> Beauvoir

> The living blind and seeing Dead together lie
> As if in love . . . There was no more hating then,
> And no more love: Gone is the heart of Man.
> —Edith Sitwell, "Dirge for the New Sunrise"
>   (Fifteen minutes past 8:00, on the morning of
>   Monday the 6th of August, 1945)

In reminding us of the somatic substratum of our mental products, one
of Freud's greatest contributions was to restore for us the connection
between body and mind that Descartes had severed. In much the same
spirit—in the spirit of what might be called the old psychoanalysis—I want
to examine some of the corporeal springs of what is generally regarded as
the most purely mental endeavor to which modern culture has given rise.
I am referring, of course, to the scientific impulse. In particular, I want to
explore a perennial motif that underlies much of scientific creativity—
namely, the urge to fathom the secrets of nature, and the collateral hope
that, in fathoming the secrets of nature, we will fathom the ultimate secrets
(and hence gain control) of our own mortality. This motif, like mortality
itself, has two sides (or perhaps I might say, this campaign proceeds on
two fronts), both of which are evident throughout the history of science:
They are, the search for the wellspring of life, and, simultaneously, for ever
more effective instruments of death. Yet more concretely (or corporeally), I
want to suggest a relationship between these two subthemes and the even
more intimate (and at least equally secretive) bodily counterparts of fetal
and fecal productivity.

In an earlier paper, I attempted a preliminary exploration of these two
motifs in the language of modern science—the one concerned with the secrets
of life and the other with secrets of death—in the context of two specific
historical episodes: the discovery of the structure of DNA and the making of
the atomic bomb.[2] My concern was to explore the meaning of secrecy in
these two episodes, focusing in particular on the important distinction made
manifest by asking, whose secrets? And secrets from whom? As background

to this sequel, I would like to summarize the principal points of that earlier paper.

Well-kept secrets, I argued, pose a predictable challenge to those who are not privy to them. Secrets function to articulate a boundary: an interior not visible to outsiders, the demarcation of a separate domain, a sphere of autonomous power. And if we ask whose secret life has historically been, and from whom has it been secret, the answer is clear: Life has traditionally been seen as the secret *of* women, a secret *from* men. By virtue of their ability to bear children, it is women who have been perceived as holding the secret of life. With the further identification of women with nature, it is a short step from the secrets of women to the secrets of nature. Indeed, throughout most cultural traditions, the secrets of women, like the secrets of nature, are and have traditionally been seen by men as potentially either threatening—or alluring—simply by virtue of the fact that they articulate a boundary that excludes them. Secrets of men, equally, exclude women, of course, and no doubt may be experienced by women as equally threatening and alluring. But in most cultures, strong taboos prevent open expression of such responses, effectively protecting the boundary of secrecy. With the granting of cultural permission, however, such a boundary can come to serve less as a taboo and more as an invitation to exposure—even, under some conditions, as a demand to be found out. Nobel laureate Richard Feynman once said, perhaps by way of explaining the extraordinary facility for lock picking that had won him so much fame as a young physicist at Los Alamos: "One of my diseases, one of my things in life, is that anything that is secret, I try to undo."[3]

In Western culture, the threat or the allure presented by nature's secrets has met with a definitive response. Modern science has invented a strategy for dealing with this threat, for asserting power over nature's potentially autonomous sphere. That strategy is, of course, precisely the scientific method—a *method* for undoing nature's secrets: for the rendering of what was previously invisible, visible—visible to the mind's eye if not to the physical eye.

The ferreting out of nature's secrets, understood as the illumination of a female interior, or the tearing of nature's veil, may be seen as expressing one of the most unembarrassedly stereotypic impulses of the scientific project. In this interpretation, the task of scientific enlightenment—the illumination of the reality behind appearances—is an inversion of surface and interior, an interchange between visible and invisible, that effectively routs the last vestiges of archaic, subterranean female power. Like the deceptive solidity of Eddington's table, the visible surface dissolves into transparent unreality. Scientific enlightenment is in this sense a drama between visibility and invisibility, between light and dark, and also, between female procreativity and male productivity—a drama in need of constant reenactment at ever-receding recesses of nature's secrets.

The story of the rise of molecular biology can be read as a particularly vivid reenactment of this drama—a drama that in the initial phases of this reenactment was in fact quite explicitly cast in the language of light and life, its goal, equally explicitly, as the quest for the secret of life. The drama ended, once that secret was claimed to have been found, in the effective banishment of the very language of secrets, mystery, and darkness from biological discourse. With the triumph of molecular genetics, it was said that biology at long last achieved a truly scientific status.

In its classical format, the story of the rise of molecular biology is usually told as a drama taking place between science and nature. It begins with the claim of a few physicists—most notably Erwin Schroedinger, Max Delbruck, and Leo Szilard—that the time was ripe to extend the promise of physics for clear and precise knowledge to the last frontier: the problem of life. Emboldened by the example of these physicists, two especially brave young scientific adventurers, James Watson and Francis Crick, took up the challenge and did in fact succeed in a feat that could be described as vanquishing nature's ultimate and definitive stronghold. Just twenty years earlier, Niels Bohr had argued that one of the principal lessons taught by quantum mechanics was that "the minimal freedom we must allow the organism will be just large enough to permit it, so to say, to hide its ultimate secrets from us."[4] Now, as if in direct refutation of Bohr's more circumspect suggestion, Watson and Crick showed, with the discovery of the structure of DNA, and accordingly, of the mechanism of genetic replication, "that areas apparently too mysterious to be explained by physics and chemistry could in fact be so explained."[5]

There is another story here, however: one that takes place in the realm of science itself—a drama not between science and nature, but between competing motifs in science, indeed among competing visions of what a biological science should look like. When Watson and Crick embarked on a quest that they themselves described as a "calculated assault on the secret of life," they were employing a language that was, at the time, not only grandiose and provocatively unfashionable, but also, as Donald Fleming has pointed out, "in total defiance of contemporary standards of good taste in biological discourse."[6] To historians of science, the story of real interest might be said to lie in the redefinition of what a scientific biology meant: in the story of the transformation of biology from a science in which the language of mystery had a place not only legitimate but highly functional, to a different kind of science—a science more like physics, predicated on the conviction that the mysteries of life were there to be unraveled, a science that tolerated no secrets. In this retelling, the historian's focus inevitably shifts from the accomplishments of molecular biology to the representation of those accomplishments.

The subplot is in effect a story of cognitive politics. It is a story of the growing authority of physics, and physicists: an authority that drew both from the momentous achievements of quantum mechanics early in the century, and from the very fresh acclaim accruing to physicists for their role in winning World War II. Told in this way, we can begin to make sense of the puzzle that has long plagued historians of contemporary biology. Despite initial claims and hopes, molecular biology gave no new laws of physics and revealed no paradoxes. What then did the physicists, described as having led the revolution of molecular biology, actually provide?

Leo Szilard said it quite clearly: It was "not any skills acquired in physics, but rather an attitude: the conviction which few biologists had at the time, that mysteries can be solved." He went on to say, "If secrets exist, they must be explainable. You see, this is something which the classical biologists did not have . . . They lacked the faith that things are explainable—and it is this faith . . . which leads to major advances in biology."[7]

And indeed, he was right. This attitude, this conviction that life's secret could be found, this view of themselves (especially Watson and Crick) as *conquistadores* who could and would find it—a stance that drew directly and vigorously on the authority of physicists for its license—proved to be extraordinarily productive. It permitted the conviction, and just a few years later, the sharing of that conviction, that in the decoding of the mechanism of genetic replication, life's secret *had* been found. As Max Delbruck said in his Nobel address in 1970,

> Molecular genetics has taught us to spell out the connectivity of life in such palpable detail that we may say in plain words, "the riddle of life has been solved."[8]

Their success was the culmination of a long tradition—now, with the representation of life as the molecular mechanics of DNA, even the darkest recesses of nature's interior seemed to have been illuminated.

For both historical and psychological reasons, it is useful to juxtapose this story with another story of secrets—a story that might be seen as the polar opposite of this one. Among the events that historically served to bolster the authority of physics, just at the time when molecular biology was coming into existence, surely one of the foremost was the development of the atomic bomb.

The making of the bomb was perhaps the biggest and best-kept secret that science ever harbored. It was a secret kept from the Germans and the Japanese, from the American public, and indeed from the wives of the very men who produced the bomb.[9] Several of the Los Alamos wives have remarked that Alamogordo was the first they knew of what their husbands had been doing, and indeed of what their entire community—a community fully dependent on intimacy and mutual dependency for its survival—had been working toward.

The Manhattan Project was a project in which the most privileged secret belonged not to the women, but to the men. It was a scientific venture predicated not on openness, but on its opposite, on absolute secrecy. Hardly an open book that anyone could read, Los Alamos had an interior. And what was produced out of this interiority was (shall we say, with pregnant irony?) "Oppenheimer's baby"—a baby with a father, but no mother. As Brian Easlea has amply documented, the metaphor of pregnancy and birth became the prevailing metaphor surrounding the production and the testing, first, of the atomic bomb, and, later, of the hydrogen bomb. If the A-bomb was Oppenheimer's baby, the H-bomb was "Teller's baby." The metaphor of birth was used not only as a precautionary code but also as a mode of description that was fully embraced by the physicists at Los Alamos, by the government, and ultimately by the public at large.

As early as December 1942, physicists at Chicago received acknowledgment for their work on plutonium with a telegram from Ernest Lawrence that read, "Congratulations to the parents. Can hardly wait to see the new arrival."[10] In point of fact, they had to wait another two and a half years. Finally, in July 1945, Richard Feynman was summoned back to Los Alamos with a wire announcing the day on which the birth of the "baby" was expected. Robert Oppenheimer may have been the father of the A-bomb, but Kistiakowsky tells us that "the bomb, after all, was the baby of the Laboratory, and there was little the Security Office could do to dampen parental interests."[11]

Two days after the Alamogordo test, Secretary of War Henry Stimson received a cable in Potsdam which read:

> Doctor has just returned most enthusiastic and confident that the little boy is as husky as his big brother. The light in his eyes discernible from here to Highhold and I could have heard his screams from here to my farm.[12]

And, as the whole world was to learn just three weeks later, the "little boy" was indeed as husky as his brother.

In this inversion of the traditional metaphor, this veritable backfiring, nature's veil is rent, maternal procreativity is effectively coopted, but the secret of life has become the secret of death. When the bomb exploded, Oppenheimer was reminded of the lines from the Bhagavad-Gita:

> If the radiance of a thousand suns
> were to burst into the sky,
> that would be like
> the splendor of the Mighty One.[13]

As the cloud rose up in the distance, he also recalled,

I am become Death, the shatterer of worlds.

Such a historical juxtaposition reveals the story of the making of the bomb as an antithesis of the successes of molecular biology—the two stories connected only by a metaphor that works to set the stories apart by its own inversion. Here, I want to return to these two themes, focusing less on the contrasts between them, and more on their connection; less on the question of whose secrets, and the important difference that question marks between the two stories, and more on the meanings of creativity that both stories share in common. To this end, my focus is here less on their place in the history of science, and more on their affective content. That is, I want to focus on a certain interweaving of fantasies of birth and death that, at least on a psychological level, can be seen to connect the project of uncovering the secret of life with that of producing instruments of death rather than distinguishing them. To assist in this effort, I want to add to the two polar stories I began with—Watson and Crick's "calculated assault on the secret of life" and the Manhattan Project's equally calculated assault on the secret of death—three other generic stories of a pre- (or proto-) scientific genre; on the surface, these stories may seem unrelated, but, I suggest, they can be read as filling in the spectrum between the two poles, perhaps even constituting their effective closure into a circle.

The first such story requires the biggest conceptual as well as cultural leap on our part (I relate it first just because it is the one that is most conspicuously remote from the culture of modern science). I am thinking of the story of the "bullroarer"—to Europeans, just an innocent children's toy that is swung rapidly through the air to produce a whirring, humming sound, but seen by some anthropologists at least as "perhaps the most ancient, widely spread, and sacred religious symbol in the world."[14] Building on the earlier work of Bruno Bettelheim,[15] Alan Dundes offers an interpretative account of this symbol that brings it into surprising proximity to our concerns here. I therefore want to summarize (in some detail) the major points of his interpretation and description.

One of the first features of this curious object that was early remarked upon by anthropologists is that, in many instances, it "is kept secret and hidden from light by the head chief, and is considered to possess some mysterious and supernatural power or influence. The women and children are not permitted to see it; if seen by a woman or shown by a man to a woman, the punishment to both is *death*."[16] In other words, the bullroarer is a secret belonging to men, protected both from the light of day and the knowledge of women. Upon close examination, however, it appears that, though its secrecy from women is obligatory, a number of myths suggest that "the bullroarer is something which is produced initially by a woman and is stolen by, and for, men." In one such myth, originally reported by Jan Van Baal,

> a man kills his wife. From her dead body, all the vegetables sprouted. However, the man collects them all and swallows them. Undigested, they pass through his body into his genital organ. With a new wife, he engages in sexual intercourse, but he withdraws his organ, allowing all the vegetables to scatter over the field.

Dundes continues:

> This symbolic process is paralleled in many initiation rites where a male spirit or deity is said to swallow initiates. Later he disgorges them, thereby making the boys into men.

In another myth, also originally reported by Van Baal, the origin of the bullroarer is more explicit:

> The wife of Tiv-r . . . is pregnant of the bullroarer. Tiv-r hears a soft whining in his wife's abdomen and is highly intrigued. One bird after another is sent out by him to extract the mysterious something. At last, while the woman is stooping down with legs wide apart, brooming the place, a bird manages to get hold of the protruding thing and extract it. It is the first bull-roarer.

The conclusion Dundes draws seems hard to dispute: The bullroarer "represents the male equivalent of female procreativity."[17] As such, it is like other symbols used in male initiation rites—rites that assume, as Margaret Mead has written, "that men become men only by . . . taking over—as a collective group—the functions that women perform naturally." In this way, Mead continues, "Man has hit upon a method of compensating himself for his basic inferiority . . . Women, it is true, make human beings, but only men can make men."[18]

But why, Dundes goes on to ask, "does the [bullroarer] function in symbolic form—through the making of noise, wind, thunder, etc.?" This question he answers with an equally obvious interpretation: The bullroarer represents the particular, but nonetheless quite common, attempt of males "to supplant female procreativity through the symbolic creativity of the anus." Its frequent use in male initiation rites, often in conjunction with such other fetal and fecal signifiers as blood, mud, and excrement, suggests to Dundes that the bullroarer is the symbolic representation of a widespread belief that "boys became [or are reborn as] men by means of male anal power."[19]

To account for the equally prominent phallic features of the bullroarer symbolism, Dundes proposes the frequently concomitant practice of homosexual intercourse as a natural link (sic) between the phallic and anal. "It may now be more clear," he concludes,

> why the initiation rites must be kept secret from women. Whether it is males attempting to emulate female procreativity by means of anal power, or homosexual intercourse in lieu of heterosexual intercourse, or ritual masturbation, the consistent element is that men seek to live without recourse to women . . . [But] engaging in acts normally carried out by women must at all cost be kept from women. The would-be superiority of males would be revealed as a sham if women were allowed to observe.[20]

This explanation of the importance of secrecy—an explanation echoed by Gilbert Herdt in his own, rather different, account of male initiation rites among the Sambia—seems to me somewhat weak. The need for secrecy, I would suggest, is fueled by more than the desire to protect a sham—even if we add the notion that such a sham can serve to evoke a counter-envy among women[21] and hence provide a new basis for male power. I suggest also that secrecy here serves to contain the aggressive potential of this redistribution and redefinition of procreative power. Not only is maternal procreativity symbolically replaced; it is also countered by the assertion of an opposing principle. Let us ask, in particular: What is produced by anal birth that is not produced by normal birth? That is, what is it about the transformation of boys into men in the cultures that employ this symbolism that is particularly dependent on their anal rebirth? Surely one important difference that marks the emergence of the adult male in many cultures, and that might be particularly pertinent to our concerns here, is precisely his ability to assume responsibility as an effective hunter and/or warrior, i.e., as a competent master of death. In this ritualized script, the boy undergoes a symbolic death in order to be reborn with a new kind of power—a form of protection against the vicissitudes of life and death that is radically different from the protection promised by maternal power. It is the power to arbitrate over life and death not through the generation (or sustenance) of life, but through the capacity to legislate death. Fertility is countered by virility, measured now by its death-dealing prowess. Finally, secrecy functions here not simply to protect an autonomous domain. Rather, I suggest, it functions additionally as a necessary mechanism of containment; it serves to circumscribe the domain of the destructive powers unleashed.

My second story is a little closer to home, and because it is more familiar, I can be much briefer. It is the story of the mad scientist (or alchemist) pursuing the secrets of life—not in the broad light of day, as did Watson and Crick, but in the dark recesses of a secret laboratory (usually below ground, in a basement or cellar), often producing vile-smelling vapors in the process, until finally, he succeeds (and it is always a "he")—not merely in finding the secret of life, but in using that secret to produce life itself. Inevitably, however, that life form is monstrous—itself unable to procreate, only to kill, a life form that becomes an agent of death. The most famous story of this genre is of course *Frankenstein*—written, as it happened, not by a man, but by a woman. As a result of a number of increasingly sophisticated literary analyses in the last few years, Mary Shelley's plot has come to be seen as considerably more complex than we had earlier thought; the major point, however, remains quite simple. *Frankenstein* is a story first and foremost about the consequences of male ambitions to coopt the procreative function, an "implicit critique" simultaneously of a plot and a birth conceived without women. But Shelley's narrative is finally not so much a feminist critique as a remarkably compelling—compelling, ironically, because written by a woman—rendering of a familiar tale of male fears. In popular fiction, the ambition of male scientists to produce life almost inevitably results in the unleashing of destruction, i.e., in death.

The third story (or image) is even nearer to home. It is drawn not from science fiction, but from the real lives of those contemporary scientists who got their start as boy scientists, producing explosives in their kitchens, bathrooms, or, if they were lucky, in a hand-fashioned basement laboratory. (A generation ago, a common sideline of these basement laboratories used to be the production of "stink bombs"—ready to be set off by the young scientist whenever crossed by an uncooperative or angry mother.) We are all familiar with the preoccupation many boys have with explosives, and with the great affective investment some of them show in producing bigger and more spectacular explosions—often, indeed, continuing beyond boyhood into student days—but perhaps those of us who have spent time around places like MIT and Cal Tech are especially familiar with such behavioral/developmental patterns.[22] We would probably even agree that these patterns are more common in the early-life histories of scientists and engineers than they are in the population at large. Certainly, it is the case that for the great majority of the scientists and engineers who started out life as play-bomb experts, the energy invested in such primitive attempts at the resolution of early conflicts has been displaced onto mature creative endeavors that leave no trace of their precursors. But in some cases, the traces are evident, even conspicuous. As the result of a fortuitous convergence between personal, affective interests and public, political and economic interests, a significant number of these young men actually end up working in weapons labs (just how many would be interesting to document)—employing their creative talents to build bigger and better (real rather than play) bombs. In other cases, traces of earlier preoccupations may be evoked only by particular circumstances, such as, for instance, by the collective endeavor of a Manhattan project. The differences between these adult activities and their childhood precursors are of course enormous, both for the researchers themselves and for the world at large. The adult activities are public and communal, while their childhood precursors are private and individual; the consequences of real bombs are themselves both real and lethal, while the implications of play explosives are usually merely symbolic. Yet it seems to me that the affective and symbolic continuity between the two also warrants attention.

Not unlike the initiation rites of the bullroarer, modern-day weapons research is generally conducted in labs that are overwhelmingly (if not exclusively) male, and highly secretive; also like the bullroarer, the bombs that are produced are likely to be associated with a provocative mix of phallic and birth imagery. The phallic imagery is keyed not only by Helen Caldicott's infamous phrase "missile envy," but more directly by talk of "penetration aids," "big bangs," and "orgasmic whumps"—talk that has by now become routine in the rhetoric of nuclear weapons. And almost equally familiar is the joining of phallic to birth imagery—as illustrated by the example already cited, where a bomb with "thrust" is identified as a boy baby, while a girl baby is clearly understood as a dud.

I reiterate that the stories I cite vary dramatically in both the real and symbolic lethalness of their outcomes; they also vary in their particular mixes of phallic, anal, and birth imagery. But when we focus on the themes that tie these stories together, what we cannot fail to notice is the extent to which they all share one or more elements of the familiar motif of male appropriation of female procreativity. We might attempt to characterize the commonality in these stories under the general rubric "womb envy"—a concept that some feminists have argued properly belongs at the center of psychoanalytic theory, alongside that of "penis envy."[23] But if we do, I suggest that we should place the emphasis quite centrally on the term "envy." Melanie Klein defines envy as "the angry feeling that another person possesses and enjoys something desirable—the envious impulse being to take it away or to spoil it."[24] "Envy" thus can serve to capture simultaneously the stories' similarities and their differences. Whether supplanted by fantasies of anal production or by a light/life generating activity of the mind, the real life-giving power of the woman—often indeed women themselves—is effectively absented from all five of these stories. In some cases it is simply denied, in others, actively "spoiled."

A text that provides a particularly interesting view of the former (the more benign form of the absenting of female procreativity, and of women) is given to us in *The Double Helix*, James Watson's classic account of his and Crick's important discovery of the mechanism of genetic replication. In Mary Jacobus's elegant paper, "Is There a Woman in This Text?"[25] the author finds *The Double Helix* notable not for a simple but for a complex elision of both the real and the symbolic woman, repeated simultaneously (or perhaps serially) on every level of Watson's own description of his endeavor. To Jacobus's own examples of such symbolic displacements—e.g., the displacement of reality by a model, of real women by "popsies," of Rosalind Franklin by "Rosy"—

I would add two more: The story of the double helix is first and foremost the story of the displacement and replacement of the secret of life by a molecule. Ironically enough, DNA is popularly called "the mother-molecule of life." Gone in this representation of life are all the complex undeciphered cellular dynamics that maintain the cell as a living entity: "Life Itself"[26] has finally dissolved into the simple mechanics of a self-replicating molecule. Indeed, living organisms themselves are no longer the proper subject of biology—all but absent from the most up-to-date biology textbooks.[27] The second example I would add to Jacobus's list is perhaps more trivial, but still, I think, worth noting: with the single exception of Rosy's hypothesized "unsatisfied mother," there are, in fact, no mothers present anywhere in the story of *The Double Helix*. Mothers and life are equally absented, discounted, and by implication at least, devalued, though not, to be sure, "spoiled" or actually hurt.

The Watson-Crick discovery was unquestionably a great discovery—if not of the secret of life, certainly of an extremely important facet of the continuity of life. It gave rise (if not birth) to an enormously productive era in biology. But my purpose here is not to review the all-too-familiar successes of that story, but rather to point elsewhere—to a rather more subtle (and negative) dimension of that same story. The net result of their discovery was in no sense an agent of death, but it did give rise to a world that has been effectively devivified. The base pairing of the double helix (perhaps, as the critic John Limon suggests, like the quasi-eroticism of Watson's own relation with Crick[28]) is not life threatening, but it *is* life-less.

When we look at the displacement of flesh-and-blood reference—of life itself—that is symbolically effected in this story, we can begin to see another level of connection between Watson and Crick's apparently successful appropriation of the secret of life and the polar-opposite story of the production of atomic bombs. It is with the move away from "life itself" that the enormous gap between the production of lifeless, devivified forms and the production of life-destroying, devivifying forms—perhaps paralleling the differences between fantasies of mental and anal production—achieves a curious kind of closure.

To see this closure, I would like to return to the metaphor of bombs as babies—a metaphor in one sense familiar and in another sense, shocking, almost horrifying, on the face of it, indeed, impossible. This is a metaphor that sits comfortably with us only to the extent that we see it as a dead metaphor, i.e., one in which the original reference has been lost from view. Much as the wooden supports of a piano are legs, bombs *are* babies in some circles, but only if they are no longer evocative of the flesh-and-blood referents that the words *legs* and *babies* originally denoted. I want to argue, though, for a significance—in the latter case at least—in the very deadness of the metaphor, i.e., in the distancing from the flesh-and-blood referent that its familiarity invites.

In an important paper on the language of "defense intellectuals," Carol

Cohn makes an interesting argument about the use of metaphors in weapons rhetoric that are blatantly inappropriate to outsiders, focusing less on their psychodynamic sources and rather more on their function. Describing a tour of a nuclear-powered submarine, she writes,

> A few at a time, we descended into the long, dark, sleek tube in which men and a nuclear reactor are encased underwater for months at a time. We squeezed through hatches, along neon-lit passages so narrow that we had to turn and press our backs to the walls for anyone to get by. We passed the cramped "racks" where men sleep, and the red and white signs warning of radioactive materials. When we finally reached the part of the sub where the missiles are housed, the officer accompanying us turned with a grin, and asked if we wanted to stick our hands through a hole to "pat the missile."[29]

"Pat the missile"? In an attempt to make sense of what turns out to be a frequently recurring image, Cohn suggests:

> Patting is an assertion of intimacy, sexual possession, affectionate domination. The thrill and pleasure of "patting the missile" is the proximity of all that phallic power, the possibility of vicariously appropriating it as one's own.
>
> But if the predilection for patting phallic objects indicates something of the homoerotic excitement held by the language, it also has another side. For patting is not just an act of sexual intimacy. It is also what one does to babies, small children, the pet dog. One pats that which is small, cute, harmless—not terrifyingly destructive. Pat it, and its lethality disappears.[30]

The same effect, she argues, is induced by a host of other "domestic" metaphors that are endemic in this language. Missiles, ready for launching, are lined up on "Christmas tree farms"; their landing patterns are called "footprints"; warheads are referred to as "RV's"; and they are "delivered" in a "bus." Acronyms for electronic missile systems include PAL and BAMBI. Cohn writes:

> In the ever-friendly, even romantic world of nuclear weaponry, enemies "exchange" warheads; one missile "takes out" another; weapons systems can "marry up"; "coupling" refers to the wiring between mechanisms of warning and response.[31]

Replacement of the flesh-and-blood referents by their macabre substitutes becomes total when the world thus created includes death itself—i.e., when it is bombs and missiles rather than people that are "killed"; where "fratricide" refers to the destruction of one warhead by another; where "vulnerability" and "survival" refer to weapons systems, not living beings; where strategic advantage is measured by the number of "surviving" warheads, independent of whether or not there are any human survivors.

In this surrogate world—a world that may have originated (in fantasy as well as in reality) as a world with only one sex—there is, finally, no sex. Once this world has become split off from its human origins, taking on a "life" of its own, disassociated from its capability for destroying actual living bodies, one doesn't need to be a Frankenstein or a Dr. Strangelove to participate. One can be an ordinary, decent, caring man—or woman. Once the metaphor is dead, missiles can be patted with equal comfort by both men and women (though perhaps not so easily by mothers).

In this world, there are no longer "men's secrets" and "women's secrets." Modern biology has revealed the secret of life to everyone, and nuclear discourse permits the sharing of secrets of death by men and women alike. Only the deadly danger we all live in remains a secret—a secret we collectively learn to keep from ourselves—split off from our everyday consciousness as we learn to talk not of the threat of actual annihilation, but of surgical strikes and collateral damage. (Even the word *bomb* is gone: in its place we have "nuclear devices.")

But secrets that we keep from ourselves work rather differently from those we keep from one another. The latter, everyone actually knows; the former, nobody knows. And as Freud taught us, secrets we keep from ourselves serve very different psychological functions from those we at least pretend to keep from one another. Most crucially, they serve to contain not the forces of death, but the forces of life. In this process, they work by foreclosing the normal processes of integration and reparation. Split off, unopposed by guilt or love, or even by the impulse for self-preservation, our destructive impulses can take on, as it were, a life of *their* own.[32] The language of techno-strategic analysis may indeed represent a kind of ultimate success of rational discourse; but surely it also bespeaks a kind of ultimate psychosis.

The question I end with is this: Granting the urgency of our situation, and even its psychotic aspects, in what way might we hope such an analysis as this could be helpful? Surely, the fantasies I describe can neither be seen as causal (in any primary sense) nor as inconsequential. Where then, between causal and inconsequential, are we to place the role of such fantasies?—fantasies that are in one sense private, but at the same time collectively reinforced, even exploited, by collateral interests. What is their role in the dynamics of the overtly (and primarily) public and political crisis we find ourselves in? And finally, is such an analysis as this itself an attempt to fend off an unacceptable reality?—a quasi-magical attempt to gain control over what may have already gotten away from us? My hope, of course, is that it can provide some help in a cause not yet entirely lost.

Notes

1. Simone de Beauvoir, *The Second Sex* (New York: Alfred A. Knopf, 1970), 58.

2. See Evelyn Fox Keller, "Making Gender Visible," in *Feminist Studies/Critical Studies*, ed. Teresa de Lauretis (Bloomington: Indiana University Press, 1986), 67–77.

3. Richard Feynman, "Los Alamos from Below," *Engineering and Science* 39:2 (1976): 19.

4. Nils Bohr, "Light and Life," in *Atomic Physics and Human Knowledge* (New York: John Wiley and Sons, 1958), 9.

5. Robert Olby, "Francis Crick, DNA, and the Central Dogma," *Daedalus* 99:4 (1970): 938–87.

6. Donald Fleming, "Emigré Physicists and the Biological Revolution," in vol. 2 of *Perspectives in American History* (Cambridge, MA: Harvard University Press, 1968), 155.

7. Quoted in Fleming, 161.

8. Max Delbruck, "A Physicist's Renewed Look at Biology: Twenty Years Later," *Science* 168 (1970): 1312.

9. It was also a secret that separated the men from the boys; as Jeremy Bernstein recollects, "Although all of us at Los Alamos had our Q Clearance, we were divided in two classes . . . The adults knew the 'secret' . . . the rest of us were not going to know it until we became adults, i.e., actually began working on weapons;" quoted in Paul Forman, "Behind Quantum Electronics," *Historical Studies in the Physical and Biological Sciences* 18:1 (1987): 221–22.

10. See Brian Easlea, *Fathering the Unthinkable: Masculinity, Scientists, and the Nuclear Arms Race* (London: Pluto Press, 1983), 107.

11. Ibid., 203.

12. Ibid., 90.

13. Quoted in Robert Jungk, *Brighter Than a Thousand Suns* (New York: Grove Press, 1958), 201.

14. Alan Dundes, "A Psychoanalytic Study of the Bullroarer," *Man* 11 (1976): 220.

15. See Bruno Bettelheim, *Symbolic Wounds, Puberty Rites and the Envious Male* (New York: Collier Books, 1955).

16. Quoted in Dundes, 221.

17. Ibid., 224–25.

18. Margaret Mead, *Male and Female* (New York: William Morrow and Co., 1949), 98, 102–3.

19. Dundes, 228. Note the following account of a New Guinea myth reported by Van Baal: "Finally Sosom [the name of a deity as well as a term for bullroarer] devours all the neophytes and adolescents . . . each time he swallows one, disgorging another through his posterior parts." (Dundes, 230).

20. Ibid., 234–35.

21. See Eva Kittay, "Womb Envy: An Explanatory Concept," in *Mothering*, ed. Joyce Trebilcot (Totowa, NJ: Rowman and Allanheld, 1984), 94–128.

22. To my knowledge, it is almost always young men rather than young women who exhibit these preoccupations.

23. See, e.g., Kittay, *Mothering*, 94–128.

24. Melanie Klein, *Envy and Gratitude* (London: Tavistock Publications, 1957), 187.

25. Mary Jacobus, "Is There a Woman in This Text?", *New Literary History* 14 (Autumn, 1982): 117–41; reprinted in Mary Jacobus, *Reading Woman: Essays in Feminist Criticism* (New York: Columbia University Press, 1986), 83–109.

26. The title of a more recent book by Francis Crick, *Life Itself* (New York: Simon and Schuster, 1981).

27. This signals yet another level of displacement, in which the meaning of biology shifts from its traditionally wide-ranging subject to that of molecular biology.

28. See John Limon, "The Double Helix as *Literature*," *Raritan* 5:3 (1986): 26–47.

29. Carol Cohn, "Sex and Death in the Rational World of Defense Intellectuals," *Signs* 12:4 (1987): 687–718.

30. Ibid. 12:4, 695–96.

31. Ibid. 12:4, 698.

32. See, e.g., Hanna Segal, "Silence Is the Real Crime," *International Review of Psycho-Analysis* 14:1 (1987): 3–12.

Index

Contributors

Susan Bordo is Associate Professor of Philosophy at LeMoyne College, specializing in the philosophy of culture, feminist theory, and philosophy of the body. Her publications include *The Flight to Objectivity: Essays on Cartesianism and Culture* (1987) and, co-edited with Alison Jaggar, *Gender/Body/Knowledge: Feminist Reconstructions of Being and Knowing* (1989). She is currently working on a cultural study of eating disorders.

Mary Ann Doane is Associate Professor of Film and Semiotic Theory at Brown University. She is the author of *The Desire to Desire: The Woman's Film of the 1940s* (1987) and co-editor of *Re-vision: Essays in Feminist Film Criticism* (1984), as well as articles on feminism, psychoanalysis, and film theory. She is currently writing a book on technology and representation.

Donna Haraway is Professor of Feminist Theory and Science Studies in the History of Consciousness program at the University of California at Santa Cruz. She is the author of *Crystals, Fabrics, and Fields: Metaphors of Organicism in 20th Century Developmental Biology* (1976), *Primate Visions: Gender, Race, and Nature in the World of Modern Science* (1989), and *Simians, Cyborgs, and Women: The Reinvention of Nature* (forthcoming, 1990). She is currently writing on feminist theory, science fictions, and fictions of science, and on the material and semiotic productions of the immune system in late capitalism.

Mary Jacobus is John Wendell Anderson Professor of English at Cornell University. She is the author of *Reading Woman: Essays in Feminist Criticism*

(1986), the editor of *Women Writing and Writing about Women* (1979), and the author of two books on Wordsworth—*Tradition and Experiment in Wordsworth's Lyrical Ballads, 1798* (1976) and *Romanticism, Writing, and Sexual Difference: Essays on The Prelude* (1989). She is currently working on a book about psychoanalysis, feminism, and the maternal body.

Evelyn Fox Keller is Professor of Rhetoric and Women's Studies at the University of California at Berkeley. She has worked in mathematical biology; theoretical physics; molecular biology; and the history, philosophy, and sociology of science. Her books include *A Feeling for the Organism: The Life and Work of Barbara McLintock* (1983) and *Reflections on Gender and Science* (1985). Among her current projects are two books: *Keywords in Evolutionary Biology* (with Elisabeth Lloyd) and *Conflicts in Feminism* (with Marianne Hirsch).

Emily Martin is Mary Garrett Professor of Anthropology at Johns Hopkins University. She is the author of two books on Chinese rituals and politics, *The Cult of the Dead in a Chinese Village* (1973) and *Chinese Ritual and Politics* (1981); and of *The Woman in the Body: A Cultural Analysis of Reproduction* (1987). She is currently working on a revision of the 1986 Lewis Henry Morgan lectures on the meaning of money in China and the U.S.

Mary Poovey is Professor of English at Johns Hopkins University. She is the author of *The Proper Lady and the Woman Writer: Ideology as Style in the Works of Mary Wollstonecraft, Mary Shelley, and Jane Austen* (1984) and *Uneven Developments: The Ideological Work of Gender in Mid-Victorian Britain* (1989). She is currently working on a study of the politics of the public health movement in Victorian England.

Sally Shuttleworth is Lecturer in the School of English, University of Leeds. She is the author of *George Eliot and Nineteenth-Century Science: The Make-Believe of a Beginning* (1984) and co-editor, with John Christie, of *Nature Transfigured: Essays on Science and Literature, 1700–1900* (1989). She is currently working on a study of Charlotte Brontë's fiction in the light of nineteenth-century medical and psychological discourse.

Paula A. Treichler is Associate Professor at the University of Illinois at Urbana-Champaign with joint appointments in the College of Medicine, the Institute of Communications Research, and Women's Studies. She is the co-author of *A Feminist Dictionary* (1985) and *Language, Gender, and Profes-*

sional Writing: Theoretical Approaches and Guidelines for Nonsexist Usage (1989) and co-editor of *For Alma Mater: Theory and Practice in Feminist Scholarship* (1985). She is currently working on a cultural analysis of AIDS and on a book-length study, *Authority, Feminism, and Medical Discourse: Current Contests for Meaning.*